Yesterday's Children

THE ANTIQUES AND HISTORY OF CHILDCARE

A charming portrait in oils by Edwin Landseer, R.A., of Allen and Selina Bathurst with their Pet Rabbits, c.1838-40.

Private Collection

Yesterday's Children

THE ANTIQUES AND HISTORY OF CHILDCARE

Sally Kevill-Davies

Antique Collectors' Club

For Harriette, Thomas and Edmund, who were the inspiration for this book.

'There is nothing, Sir, too little for so little a creature as man. It is by studying little things that we attain the great art of having as little misery and as much happiness as possible.'

Dr Samuel Johnson (1709-1784).

© 1991 Sally Kevill-Davies
World copyright reserved
First published 1991

Published for the Antique Collectors' Club
by the Antique Collectors' Club Ltd.

British Library CIP Data
Kevill-Davies, Sally
    Yesterday's children: the antiques and history of childcare
    I. Title
941.081

ISBN 1 85149 135X

Endpapers: A lithographed pictorial sheet coloured by hand, mounted on wood and cut to form a dissected puzzle. Published by J.W. Barfoot and dated 1859. Sotheby's.

Printed in England by
the Antique Collectors' Club Ltd.
Woodbridge, Suffolk

CONTENTS

FOREWORD

This is not a book about toys and dolls, which already have enough literature of their own, but rather a book about the everyday objects which were used in the day-to-day care and upbringing of a child. They are the objects which anybody who has ever been involved with small children will instantly recognize, together, perhaps, with some surprises. Some are costly and beautiful, but many more are humble and without aesthetic merit. But through them we can re-create the lives of long-dead children and, in part, re-live their experiences.

Because the subject is so vast, boundaries have had to be set, and some readers may be disappointed. The age of five to six seemed to be a good cutting-off point, since maturity was reached so much earlier by our ancestors. Therefore samplers, which were worked by older children, are not described here, and nor is the equipment for games and sports such as cricket or archery, nor indeed indoor educational games such as board games and jigsaws. Children's books are a huge subject and already have their reference books and histories. I have tried to cover merely the learning of letters and numbers rather than the further implications of literacy. Costume, too, is a far-ranging field, and so I have restricted myself to baby or christening clothes, which are highly collectable for the fine needlework which they contain, and to fashions which reflect a change in society's attitude towards children, such as the skeleton suit, or which are still worn today, such as the smock, sailor suit, or kilt.

It is impossible to try to please everyone, and I would therefore like to take this opportunity of apologising to any readers who feel cheated or downright disappointed because their pet subject has been left out or dealt with in what they feel is too cursory a way.

Because there are still parents grieving over desperately ill children today, twenty per cent of the royalties from the sale of this book are to be donated to the Great Ormond Street Hospital for Sick Children, with admiration and respect for the doctors and nurses who care for them.

Sally Kevill-Davies

This eminently readable account of the changing attitudes to childcare in Britain and America through the centuries must be of particular interest to all parents and to all those who have a love of children. It is fitting therefore that Sally Kevill-Davies should so kindly have decided to benefit Great Ormond Street from the sales of the book, and all at the Hospitals for Sick Children are very grateful to her for this support. The Hospitals have pressing needs for funds for equipment, research, comforts for the children and support for their parents who have to stay in the Hospitals. The money which is raised will be of great benefit in the care of our sick children.

We wish her all success with the book which we warmly commend.

Paddy Vincent.

Paddy Vincent CBE
Director of Fundraising and Public Affairs
Great Ormond Street Children's Hospital Fund

ACKNOWLEDGEMENTS

My thanks are due to very many people who have helped me with the writing of this book, and some who gave particular help are listed below:

The staff of Sotheby's, in particular Jennifer Cox, Sîan Andrews, Janet Green, Michael Heseltine, Lizzie Tait, Dr Christopher de Hamel and Claire Morris Eyton; the staff of Christie's, including Anton Gabsccwicz. At Christie's South Kensington Olivia Bristol has been especially generous, and thanks are also due to Stephen Halliwell and Victoria Walcough. Other people and organizations whom I must single out for thanks include the Rt Hon the Lord Croft; Edward Gelles; Messrs Cow & Gate; Paul van Biene, Mappin & Webb; Elisabeth Bennion; Diana Dick; Pauline Flick; Patricia Carter; John Tomkinson; David Knight; Pcnnc Smith; Marjolein Amphlet; Lanto Synge; Richard Dennis; Mrs Carmen Turbett; Chris Gatiss, Courtauld Institute; Mrs Noreen Marshall, Bethnal Green Museum of Childhood; Penelope Byrd, Museum of Costume, Bath; Isabel Glennie, Bonham's; Robert Brown, Museum of Childhood, Anglesey; Lynne Miller, Wedgwood Museum; Anne-Marie Benson, Phillips; Messrs Bonham's; John Austin, Colonial Williamsburg Foundation; Charles Noble, Victoria Colfox and Claire Hunter-Craig at the Royal Collection; John Heyes, Museum of Childhood, Edinburgh; Dianne Whinney and Diana McMillan at the Antique Collectors' Club; and last but not least Tom Doig, former Curator of the Cambridge and County Folk Museum, who has been a tower of strength with his encyclopaedic knowledge and who kindly and gently pushed my manuscript in the right directions. Most important of all my thanks are due to my long-suffering and deliciously one-track-minded husband, Christopher, who has presented me, during the writing of this book, with three nipple shields, a breast pump and a bubby pot, and has kept me going with his love and support.

INTRODUCTION

'The want of affection in the English is strongly manifested towards their children.'   Venetian envoy to the Court of Henry VII in 1497.

'Over half the children received by the Parish Officers in the past seven years have disappeared; 109 were either lost or dead, or never were.'
Reports of the Middlesex Justices, 1686.

'Childish actions and gaiety of carriage, which whilst he is very young is as necessary to him as meat or sleep.'
John Locke, *Some Thoughts Concerning Education,* 1693.

'If children are reasonably and affectionately educated, scarcely any punishment will be requisite.'
Maria and Richard Edgeworth, *Essays on Practical Education,* 1789.

'One cannot love lumps of flesh, and little infants are nothing more.'
Lord Byron (1788-1824).

'A mere little red lump was all I saw; and I fear the 7th grand-daughter and 14th grandchild becomes a very uninteresting thing — for it seems to me to go on like the rabbits in Windsor Park.'
Queen Victoria after the birth of her grand-daughter, Victoria Alexandra Olga Marie, daughter of Edward VII and Queen Alexandra, born in 1868.

'What you say of the pride of giving life to an immortal soul is very fine, dear, but I own I cannot enter into that, I think much more of our being like a cow or a dog at such moments; when our poor nature becomes so very animal and unecstatic.'   Queen Victoria to her daughter, Princess Vicky, 1858.

'Where did you come from, baby dear?
Out of the everywhere into here.

Where did you get your eyes so blue?
Out of the sky I came through.'
George MacDonald,
At the Back of the North Wind, 1871.

'When the first baby laughed for the first time his laugh broke into a million pieces and they all went skipping about. That was the beginning of fairies.'
J.M. Barrie, *Peter Pan and Wendy,* 1911.

8

'The old, bad days when every woman was supposed to know by instinct how to nurse, feed and teach children, have gone forever; the art of looking after children is *recognized* as an art — if not a science.'

The Nursery World, First Issue, 1925.

Amid the nostalgia for 'things past' which pervades our modern and sometimes sterile world, we should be grateful that we are bearing and raising our children in the last part of the twentieth century. The portraits of children which line the walls of the great houses of England portray vivacious rosy-cheeked brothers and sisters, immaculate in satin or ethereal in muslin, clutching a favourite toy while a pet spaniel yaps playfully at their feet, the idyllic scene set against some undulating pastoral landscape which recalls a vanished and better world.

It was not so. Until our own century was well advanced the whole business of childbirth and infant care was fraught with pain, danger, terror, loss, grief, exhaustion, fever and fret. It is a tribute to our ancestors that their spirits were not quenched by almost continual pregnancy, and that the real horrors of childbirth were confronted with so much courage and goodwill. For the children whom they brought unplanned into the world, childhood was often a nightmare, cold, half-starved and beaten into submission, Mary Coleridge was not alone when she described herself as 'a dumb unliving child', scarcely able to 'recall anything except the sharp sensations of fear that broke the dull dream of my days', and childish *joie de vivre* was too often dampened down by adult disapproval.

Innocence is a virtue which we commonly associate with children, and yet it was not always so. It is hard for us to imagine a time when the teachings of the Church and an all-pervasive network of superstition and ritual influenced almost every aspect of daily life. This was never more true than in the sensitive area of childbirth and baptism. The doctrine of original sin claimed that every child born into the world carried with him the weight of the first sin committed by his ancestors, Adam and Eve, in the Garden of Eden, when they chose to disobey God and eat the fruit of the Tree of the Knowledge of Good and Evil. Too young to repent for himself, the symbolic pouring of the water at baptism represented a cleansing from sin, a wiping clean of the spiritual slate, thus allowing the child to be re-born into the Church, and ultimately received into Heaven. As the Catechism in the Book of Common Prayer says, baptism bestowed 'a death unto sin, and a new birth unto righteousness; for being by nature born in sin, and the children of wrath, we are hereby made the children of grace'.

The concept of original sin led parents to believe fervently and deeply that their children were, in the words of Hannah More, 'beings who bring into the world a corrupt nature and evil disposition which it should be the great aim of education to rectify'. This belief was reinforced vigorously and terrifyingly by Puritanical teachers and theologians, who urged parents to practise

Draconian discipline in a misguided effort to save their children's souls from Hell, 'a terrible place... worse than a thousand time whipping'. Fearful beatings were inflicted on small children who were barely able to walk, in the firm belief that it would ensure for them a place in Heaven, and in the days when barely one child in two reached his fifth birthday, the fear of Hell was a very real one. (The London Bills of Mortality for 1765 revealed that sixty per cent of baptised children died before they were two years old). John Locke, an influential and enlightened writer on children's upbringing, whose *Some Thoughts Concerning Education* was first published in 1693, thoroughly approved of a mother who 'was forced to whip her little daughter on her first coming home from nurse, eight times successively the same morning, before she could master her stubbornness and obtain her compliance in a very easy and indifferent matter'. The emotional implications of a virtual stranger wrenching a child away from her wet-nurse, who had been in effect her only mother for months, if not years, would not have worried a parent in those pre-Freudian days. The mother of three year-old Susan Murray complained at the end of the seventeenth century 'I have got a little pain in my back with whipping Susan today, who struggled so that I have got a wrench'. Nowadays all our sympathies go out to the child, and we care little for the mother and her wretched wrenched back.

Published in 1762, Jean-Jacques Rousseau's revolutionary novel, *Emile,* pleaded the cause of the 'noble savage' and advocated an upbringing for children based on the laws of Nature. In an outburst of calculated exasperation he condemned contemporary mothers. 'From birth you are always checking them, your first gifts are fetters, your first treatment torture'.

Indeed, the maternal instinct, that invisible commodity which we nowadays assume that all mothers automatically possess, appears to have been in remarkably short supply two or three hundred years ago. One of the most ironic and depressing facts about childcare in the past is the way in which ignorance, superstition and imperfectly applied reasoning appear to have triumphed over instinct. Mothers seemed to be forever doing all the wrong things for most of the right reasons. Babies were trussed up into parcels at birth, so that their limbs would be forced to grow straight, yet the process of swaddling almost guaranteed that their hips would dislocate and that they would contract rickets by being starved, through molly-coddling, of sunlight and fresh air. Scurvy and other vitamin deficiency diseases, were promoted by depriving children of the vitamin C in fruit and vegetables which were thought to spread the plague and, because they seethed with caterpillars and maggots in the days before pesticides, to give the children worms. Fear of malnutrition and 'the watery gripes' caused nurses to bombard the stomachs of babies with papboats full of solid food before their immature digestive systems could cope, in the mistaken belief that liquids would run straight through, but that solids would in some way help to 'set' the life-threatening diarrhoea. High fevers, a frequent occurrence in the days before antibiotics, painkillers and antiseptics, were treated not by cooling the child down, but by wrapping him up by a fire in a hermetically-sealed room. Febrile convulsions were, not unnaturally, a common cause of death, and appear to have killed John Evelyn's son in 1658, when he was 'suffocated by ye women and maids that tended him and cover'd him too hot with blankets as he lay in a cradle near an excessive hot fire in a close room'.

Perhaps the strangest of all maternal aberrations, unthinkable to us today, was the practice of 'both high and low ladies, of farming out their babies to women in the country', Robert Pennell, 1653. This 'baby-farming' was practised at least until the 1880s, and sometimes the baby stayed 'at nurse' for up to two or three years, or until it was fully weaned, sometimes with only infrequent and irregular visits from its parents.

The catalogue of such blunders is endless, and against this background of maternal floundering, a cacophony of conflicting (mostly male) voices issued from the childcare manuals of the day, the pundits of each new generation contradicting the views of the one before. During the sixteenth, seventeenth and eighteenth centuries, children were to be treated more or less as miniature, though defective, adults, with virtually no concessions made to their youth and immaturity. Adult realities had to be faced young. Required reading for many children in 1672 included the Puritan James Janeway's *A Token for Children, or an Account of the Conversion, Holy and Exemplary Lives and Joyful Deaths of Several Young Children.* At the other end of the social spectrum, Daniel Defoe noted in the account of his *Tour of Great Britain,* written in 1724, that in some districts there was not a child of five that could not earn its own bread. Play was considered unnecessary, toys were few, a doll, a wooden horse or a drum to bang perhaps, and such books as existed for children were concerned in lurid terms with matters of religion and morality. Dress aped that of grown-ups, with uncomfortable stays and corsets worn from the earliest age, and nurseries scarcely existed as we know them today. Cradles and high chairs were made in the same styles as adult furniture and childish actions, such as crawling, were frowned upon as 'animal-like'. Babies of less than a year old were forced onto their feet, and baby-walkers both restrained and supported the drunken stumblings of the weak-kneed little dolls. Imperfect bodies, ravaged by rickets and malnutrition, were agonisingly straightened with the aid of stays, corsets, backboards and correction chairs, and in some cases small bones were broken and re-set, without anaesthetic, to achieve a straight gait and upright posture. John Evelyn's niece was crushed to death at the age of two by an iron bodice.

Kisses and cuddles were discouraged since they were thought likely to breed infection, children were left standing in the presence of their parents as a mark of respect, and young tongues were literally held to prevent the repetition of foolish and 'sinful' phrases.

The teachings of John Locke, Jean-Jacques Rousseau and other enlightened writers such as Richard and Maria Edgeworth, gradually bore fruit and people began to become aware of an increased interest in freedom, liberalism and the forces of Nature. Children were seen to have rights alongside adults. During the eighteenth century terrible cruelities had been inflicted on children. Unwanted and illegitimate infants were 'left to die on dung-hills' in their hundreds, a fact which moved Captain Thomas Coram to set up his Foundling Hospital in London in 1739. Other poor children were maimed before being sent out into the streets, the more effectively to beg, and in 1761 Anne Martin was sentenced to two years' imprisonment for deliberately blinding children that she intended to use for begging. 'Excellent killing nurses' was how some wet-nurses were described who were employed by parishes to foster orphans. Wet-nurses in the country parishes often took poor children from London parishes. Paid by the Churchwardens from the Poor Rate, often in a lump sum, they pocketed the money and allowed the children in their care to starve to death. Jonas Hanway in his *Earnest Appeal for Mercy to the Children of the Poor,* 1766, estimated that only one child in seventy survived while in their care, and admitted that the facts and figures contained in his report after a fact-finding tour of London work-houses were 'so melancholy that they were generally disbelieved'.

During the nineteenth century, reformers such as Lord Shaftesbury, and later, Thomas Barnardo, awakened the awareness of society to the widespread abuse of children, and writers such as Charles Dickens, Charles Kingsley and Charlotte Brontë, set alight the public imagination with novels in which oppressed children assumed the roles of morally irreproachable heroes. Charles Darwin's theories of evolution helped to give the lie to the idea of original sin, and *The Ladies' Magazine,* June 1833, echoed the sentiments of many in describing childhood 'as a state which speaks to us of Heaven, which tells us of those pure angelic beings which surround the throne of God, untouched by sin, untainted by the breath of curruption'. Even the hellfire of earlier centuries was converted by contemporary hymn-writers into 'All Things Bright and Beautiful'.

Four years later, in 1837, England acquired a new young Queen who, in time, produced nine children and was seen by her subjects to have a happy and successful home life, far removed from the rollicking and often disastrous indiscretions of her ancestors. She came to be portrayed as an icon of motherhood, the matriarch of an Empire abroad, and at home the virtuous mother of a growing brood. Paintings of the royal parents and children depicted them in the guise of an almost-Holy Family, and motherhood was elevated to a semi-sanctified state.

As wealth rapidly increased and Society became more concentrated in towns and cities, so husbands left home each day to work in the manufacturing industries or the professions. Left at home to their own devices, with servants to take care of all the chores, women were desperate to find a role to play. Motherhood became a *cause-célèbre.* 'If the rearing and training of childhood be an art (and who can deny that it is so?), it must be learned, practised and perfected like any other art', cooed the impressive-sounding Baroness B.M.

Von Marenholtz-Buelow persuasively, in 1855. Vast amounts of money, not to mention yards of organdie and lace, were lavished on extravagant dresses for babies and children, who rapidly became the focus of maternal ambition. They were smothered in frills and kisses, perhaps in a sub-conscious effort to shut out the more unpleasant aspects of their 'biology', though Queen Victoria remained refreshingly unpersuaded, in private at least. Her forthright remark 'An ugly baby is a very nasty object, and the prettiest is frightful when undressed' was a stout antidote to an almost overwhelming whimsicality. Nannies, a by-product of the increases in population and wealth, compared their small charges in the park, and metaphorical points were given for finery, show and social position.

By 1895, Mrs Douglas, *The Gentlewoman's Book of Dress,* warbled excitedly, 'Almost more interesting to a woman than her own clothes are those of her children, and perhaps nothing has more encouraged extravagance in the department than the recent furore for child-pictures, child-stories, child-heroes and child-actors. Some of our best litterateurs write fairy tales and collect poems for children; some of our best-known artists paint them, and the most serious minds are very solemnly concerning their wise nurture and education'. The wheel had come full circle. The cult of the child was complete, and 'Baby-worship' as Queen Victoria witheringly called it, had become big business. However, it was not until the first decades of the twentieth century that Freud's psychological revelations were given any credence, while the later writings of Dr Spock caused parents to agonise over the development of infant egos.

The slave labour of children up the chimneys and down the mines, where Lord Shaftesbury described their stunted bodies as like 'a mass of crooked alphabets', the precocious prostitutes and child opium addicts, and the murdered infants (192 infant homicides were recorded in London alone in 1864, and in 1870 the bodies of 276 newborn babies were found in the streets of the capital), were beginning to be a thing of the past, and nothing, it seemed, would ever be quite as bad again, although Society was always to find itself curiously ambivalent in its attitudes towards children whose vulnerability seemed, like war, to bring out the worst and the best in people.

However, in spite of the horrors recounted in this book, it must not be forgotten that the human spirit is indomitable, and that there were very many families who did love each other and children who *were* happy against all odds. Through the objects described in the following pages, the brief lives of the mothers and children who used them can be, for a moment, relived, and we can share in their sorrows and their joys, and show greater appreciation for the lives of our own happy children, raised in such different circumstances.

Chapter 1

CHILDBIRTH

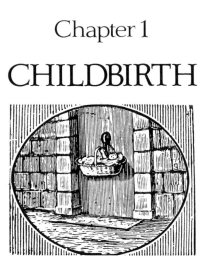

Family Planning

'The Great Blessing of many Children'
(Extract from the *Private Diarie of Elizabeth, Viscountess Mordaunt*, 1650s.)

'The rich get rich, and the poor get children'
(From *Ain't We Got Fun*, hit song, 1920s, by Kahn, Egan and Whiting.)

To our ancestors contraception was a subject rarely written about, and which remains shrouded in a mist of prejudice and obscurity. The desire for big families was virtually universal, for the rich to produce male heirs to ensure the family succession, and for the poor to provide future bread-winners for the family. Children were regarded as 'the nurseries of families, the church and the nation', and both Protestant and Roman Catholic theologians alike repeated the need for constant child-bearing. The Protestants were anxious to ensure the increase of Christian souls in a wicked world, and the Catholics could not countenance the idea of sex in marriage being for any purpose other than procreation. Women were trapped between these twin doctrines in a state of almost constant pregnancy.

To bear a child a year during the seventeenth century was the norm, and indeed the size of families was limited by infant deaths rather than by any effective method of birth control. The only means of contraception available were highly unlikely to have averted a pregnancy in any normal woman, and consisted of a series of lurid old wives' tales and vague herbal remedies. These included the use of marjoram, thyme, parsley, lavender and 'brake', or bracken. Honeysuckle was also thought to be efficacious, particularly if the juice was drunk continuously for thirty-seven days. A man following such an expedient would 'never beget any more children'. Daniel Defoe (1661-1731), in a pamphlet on 'Conjugal Lewdeness', spoke darkly of powders drunk 'in Warm Ale' for putting women 'out of danger', and rue was widely used in pessaries and vaginal douches, or 'clysters'.

Many of the recipes recommended for contraception were also considered to be effective for inducing miscarriage, and the distinction between the two was left to the discretion, or otherwise, of the user. For the man who took the initiative in such matters, the penis could be bathed in cold water, vinegar, or the juice of hen-bane and nightshade, a practice likely to douse the flames of passion, and thus, by a circuitous route, prevent conception.

Coitus interruptus was almost certainly practised, and it was also widely acknowledged that the process of breast-feeding suppressed ovulation and rendered a woman less fertile. Hugh Downman observed sagely in 1788 that 'the nursing time was meant by wisest Nature, as a stay', and thus encouraged more mothers to breast-feed their children. Less healthy was the fact that many wet-nurses were drawn from the ranks of prostitutes and 'loose women', because of the contraceptive effects of breast-feeding.

It was not until the introduction from France in the eighteenth century of the condom, or French letter, made of leather or of pigs' bladders, that birth control became a less hit or miss affair.

There were always women who failed to conceive, for various reasons, and there were many 'cures' for infertility. One was for the infertile woman to sit over a bath in which skeins of raw yarn had been boiled and steeped and mingled with ash, while another advised the woman to bathe in water in which 'Ale-hoof, oaten and pease straw have been boiled together — then let her dry herself, and presently let her Husband do his best endeavour'. The long-suffering and barren Mrs. Pepys (whose husband's 'best endeavours' on behalf of other women must have tried her so sorely), was advised, without success, to wear 'cool Holland drawers' and at night to prop up the marriage bed or 'lie with our heads where our heels do'. The hot-blooded Samuel was to drink quantities of sage juice, but alas, all to no avail.

Delivery

'The smart and the punishment which thou (Lord) laidst upon me being in the loins of my Grandmother Eve, for my disobedience towards thee; Thou hast greatly increased the sorrows of our sex and our bearing of children is full of pain'.
(Prayer to be said by a woman in labour, written by Samuel Hieron, 1613.)

'Though child-bearing since Eve's sin is ordained to be painful as a punishment thereof, yet sometimes it is more painful than ordinary'.
(Nicholas Culpeper, A Directory for Midwives, 1651.)

'These are doubtless the greatest of all pains that Women naturally undergo upon Earth'.
(Jane Sharpe, The Midwives' Book, 1671.)

'If... the Waters break away too long before the Birth... there are many things... Physicians affirm are good... among which a Piece of red coral hung near the Privities.'
(Aristotle's Midwife, c.1740.)

'The ONLY thing I dread'.
(Queen Victoria, December 1839.)

The joy and euphoria of a newly-married woman, in love with her husband, was often quickly tempered by the realisation that she was pregnant, and that after nine months or so she would have to bow to an inexorable fate — 'the pain and the peril' of childbirth. This *schattenseite,* or shadow-side, of marriage, as Queen Victoria described it, filled even rich and well-born women with dread. For the poor, of course, it was always much worse.

The image of Eve as the primeval temptress, lurking seductively in the garden in wait for poor, easily-led Adam, allowed the male-dominated society of the time to perpetuate conveniently the link between the pain of childbirth and the idea of eternal female atonement for Eve's sins. Moreover, there was clear Biblical evidence to support these views. In the book of Genesis God said, 'Unto the woman, "I will greatly multiply thy sorrow and thy conception; in sorrow thou shalt bring forth children" ', and later in St Paul's Second Epistle to Timothy, 'Adam was not deceived, but the woman being deceived was in the transgression. Notwithstanding she shall be saved in childbearing'. The memorial in Barkway Church, Hertfordshire, to Mrs Susanna Castell, who died in 1633 and was buried four days after the baptism of her baby, records with chilling clarity: 'She now hath found it true that Childbirth paines By faith through Death, life and salvation gaines'.

In spite of the suspicion and ambivalence with which many men, and indeed the Church, viewed pregnancy and childbirth, not all were insensitive to the sufferings of women. The diarist, John Evelyn, reassured Margaret Godolphin in her terror of childbirth, 'Little women, I told her, had little pain'. (Perhaps

Plate 1. An Augsburg Woodcut, 1540, showing a midwife delivering a baby, while the mother, who sits upright on a chair, is supported by two attendants. A wooden tub and a ewer of water stand ready on the floor.   Mary Evans Picture Library.

it was the same forced optimism bred by panic which led Anne Boleyn to rejoice in her 'little neck' before she walked to her execution on the block.) Evelyn's reassurances were in vain, and Margaret developed puerperal fever after the birth, which was treated with bloodletting and with the curious expedient of applying live pigeons to her feet. In spite of all this, she was dead within one week of her delivery. She was twenty-five.

Although things had improved somewhat by the nineteenth century, childbirth was still viewed with trepidation which sometimes verged on hysteria or revulsion. Queen Victoria was thoroughly depressed by the whole business, as a letter written to her daughter Vicky, soon after her marriage in 1858, shows. 'If you have hereafter (as I had constantly for the first two years of my marriage) — aches — and sufferings and miseries and plagues — which you must struggle against — and enjoyments etc. to give up — constant precautions to take, you will feel the yoke of a married woman!... I had nine times for eight months to bear with those above-named enemies and real misery... and I own it tried me sorely; one feels so pinned down — one's wings clipped... only half oneself... and therefore, I think our sex a most unenviable one'.

The old Queen felt that Princess Alexandra, Princess of Wales, had been 'utterly disgusted' by her experience of childbirth in 1864, and Princess May of Teck, later Queen Mary, echoed the secret thoughts of many women when she wrote in 1902 after the birth of her fourth child, 'I think I have done my duty and may now stop, as having babies is highly distasteful to me, tho' once they are there they are very nice!'

She was more fortunate than her ancestors in being able to stop, as early forms of birth control were of the most rudimentary nature. The size of families was, in fact, limited by death rather than contraception. Sir William Brownlow and his wife, Elizabeth, had nineteen children in the twenty-two years between 1626 and 1648, of which only six survived, and Mrs Elizabeth Walker gave birth to eleven children, plus other undetailed 'untimely' births, which miscarried. Of the total of three daughters who survived, Mary died at six years, Elizabeth at sixteen years, and the third died in childbirth herself. No wonder then that many women felt that God was personally visiting his wrath upon them, or that so much superstition and folklore surrounded the process of childbearing.

Up to the eighteenth century, the midwives who assisted at the birth of a child were invariably women, since it was considered indecent for a man to attend a birth. Often they were housewives who had raised a large family themselves and had a reputation for sound good sense in the local community, or the Lady of the Manor, who had spent time and effort in teaching herself the art of distilling and mixing herbal remedies. However, this was not always the case, many 'red-nosed' midwives being no better than drunken village crones, often with an unsavoury reputation for practising witchcraft or undercover abortions. Even the best relied heavily on superstition and 'farmyard' obstetrics, and as many of the midwives doubled-up as layers-out of corpses, disease was rampant. In 1726, when Joseph Gibson was appointed Professor of Midwifery in Edinburgh, the Town Council recorded 'many fatal consequences have happened to women in childbirth and to their children through the ignorance and unskilfulness of midwives... who enter upon that difficult sphere at their own hand without the least trial taken of their knowledge'.

During the eighteenth century, the male-midwife, or accoucheur, gradually became more acceptable, since Madame de Montespan, mistress of Louis XIV had been attended by a man, and lying-in hospitals for women were established, notably in Dublin in 1745 and twenty years later at the Westminster Lying-In Hospital in London. However, most women continued to be delivered at home, often under doubtful conditions, and it was not until 1902 that the Midwives Act was passed, ensuring that only certified, State-registered midwives could attend a birth.

The first book on childbirth was published in Germany in 1513, *A Rose Garden for Pregnant Women and Midwives,* and from the end of the sixteenth century a number of textbooks on the subject were published to offer advice to midwives. Among these were Thomas Delaney's *The Gentle Craft,* 1597, Jacques Guillemeau's *Childbirth, or the Happie Deliverie of Women,* 1612, Paré's *De Generatione,* 1651, and Nicholas Culpeper's *A Directory for Midwives,* 1651. The celebrated herbalist wrote his treatise from a personal standpoint. 'Myself having buried many of my children young, caused me to fix my thoughts intently on this business'. Although most were written by male 'authorities', a few female voices were heard, notably in Jane Sharpe's *The Midwives' Book,* 1671 and Elizabeth Clinton's account of *The Countesse of Lincolne's Nurserie,* 1622.

When the onset of labour was suspected, the midwife was called for, along with any female attendants whose company the mother had requested. Swaddling bands were unrolled and hung up to air near the fire, and the low stool or 'cricket' to be used by the midwife, set out. A plentiful supply of candles was also ensured, lest darkness engulf the proceedings, and hot water was carried in to wash the mother and baby. The cradle and its coverings were prepared and, in the case of high-born women, the mother's bed was hung with special hangings. All her clothes were loosened, with pins sent flying and seams hastily unpicked, so as to ease the way of the baby into the world, and windows and doors were symbolically flung open and all locks in the house unfastened, for the same reason.

Into a room heavy with anxiety and trepidation arrived the midwife, possibly lugging a birthing chair with her. These wooden chairs, which could be taken apart and folded flat so that the midwife could carry them from one confinement to another, were used if the woman preferred to give birth to her child in a sitting position. The midwife knelt before the woman, ready to grasp the child and pull him out, while a neck-rest supported the mother's head. Some elaborate examples, particularly from Germany, had hand-grips, reclining backs and ascending seats. Other wicker chairs with hoods were also

Plate 2. An oak parturition chair, c.1750. The mother sat on the seat, with her head leaning back against the neck-rest, while the midwife knelt in front of her in the space provided, ready to grasp the child as it emerged. Such chairs were sometimes hinged for folding-up, and were carried about by the midwife from one confinement to another.
Royal College of Surgeons of Scotland. (Reproduced from *Antique Medical Instruments* by Elisabeth Bennion.)

used by mothers and are described in Randle Holme's *Academie of Armory*, 1649. 'Twiggen chaires because they are made of Owsiers, and withen twigs having round covers over the heads of them like unto a canapy. These are principally used by sick and infirm people, and such women as have bine lately brought to bed; from whence they are generally termed Growneing chaires or Child-bed chaires'.

Very often it was many hours before the child's first cry was heard. Bad diet lead women to be small and stunted, and very many suffered from deformities of the pelvis which resulted from the effects of the dreaded rickets contracted in childhood. Repeated and unsupervised pregnancies weakened mothers and increased the danger of the baby lying in an abnormal position in the womb. Labours were inevitably often obstructed, and could last for as much as five days. Midwives, watching helplessly, were faced with the agonising expedient of groping for a small limb with a metal hook in order to yank out the child, or of crushing the skull and dismembering the baby in order to deliver it piecemeal, thus hopefully saving the life of the mother. Many practitioners resorted to any blunt instruments which were available, to aid them in their grisly task, and in the seventeenth century Dr Percival Willughby, in *The Country Midwive's Opusculum,* condemned outright the use of 'pothooks, pack-needles, silver spoons, thatching hooks and knives'. Not surprisingly, many women who avoided death by mutilation went on to die of septicaemia.

Dr Peter Chamberlen, an obstetrician and member of a Huguenot family who had settled in England, was present at the birth of Charles II. His experience of childbirth urged him to propose setting up a body for training midwives, but this was turned down because of dark rumours that he used 'instruments of iron' to assist him in his deliveries. Fears of surgical intervention were no doubt compounded by the superstitious belief, based on the legend of St Dunstan, that iron could repel the Devil. The secret of these 'instruments of iron' was guarded paranoically by the family, and the Chamberlens carried them to confinements concealed in large bags, with the metallic clanking muffled by cloths. Peter Chamberlen's son, Hugh, was a doctor who had treated victims of the Plague in London in the 1660s, and he made various surreptitious attempts to sell the 'Family Secret'. In 1699 he fled

Plate 4. An engraving from Elementarwerke Fur die Jugend und ihre Freunde (Fundamentals for Young People and their Friends), by J.B. Basedow, published in Germany, 1774. This shows an expectant mother being attended by her accoucheur. The cradle stands in readiness, while swaddling bands hang airing in front of the stove. A group of instruments including what may be a clamp for the umbilical cord, or obstetrical forceps, are set out on the table, and a pan of water with a sponge is ready to mop the mother's brow, and then wash her and her baby after the delivery.
Colonial Williamsburg
Foundation.

to Amsterdam, where he accepted a successful offer of 10,000 crowns. Knowledge of the Chamberlen's forceps, as the 'instruments of iron' turned out to be, gradually leaked out, but it was not until 1813 that the original instruments eventually reappeared, hidden jealously by Peter Chamberlen beneath the floorboards of a house at Woodham Mortimer in Essex, before he died there.

The first known publication on the forceps, which was to save the lives of so many mothers and children hopelessly bound together in obstructed labours, came from Amsterdam in 1747, by which time William Smellie (1697-1763) was teaching midwifery in London. This humane and kindly Scot, who, with his large hands and coarse manner, taught his students on 'machines' and live patients, delivered countless poor women for nothing, and came to be known as 'The Father of English Obstetrics'. His *Treatise on Midwifery,* published in 1752, strenuously advocated the use of forceps in an obstructed labour, and he developed his own special instruments. At first these were made of wood, and then of steel covered with leather, which was replaced after every delivery. This made the cold steel more comfortable for the mother, and disguised the ominous clinking noise which so terrified women. 'Smellie's lock' made a major contribution to obstetrics, and his forceps were made for him by Best of Lombard Street. According to the attitudes of the time, he delivered all the women in his care with a sheet tied around both their necks, so that, for decency's sake, he was unable to see what was happening beneath the sheet.

Because of their previous experiences with male-midwives, many pregnant women were terrified of men with their bags of clanking metal, and Smellie often introduced the forceps without telling the mother lest she be too alarmed, carrying one of the blades in each of his breeches' pockets and assembling them beneath the sheet. Some obstetricians preferred never to use them, but to let·

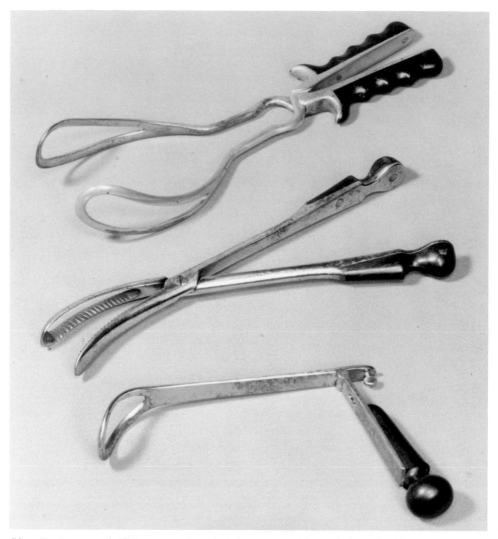

Plate 5. A group of 19th century obstetrical instruments. Top: *Anderson's Obstetrical Forceps, c.1850, by Thistlewaite.* Centre: *Dr Murphy's Craniotomy Forceps, c.1850.* Bottom: *Lowder's Vectis, c.1820, by Evans.*

Lowder's Vectis was used for hooking a limb through in order to pull it out. Poor nutrition and rickets lead to small stature and pelvic deformity in women. Repeated pregnancies lead to a greater risk of the baby growing in an abnormal position, and very often in a hopelessly obstructed labour the baby had to be destroyed or literally torn limb from limb in order to be delivered at all.

I. Freeman & Son, Simon Kaye Ltd.
(Reproduced from *Antique Medical Instruments* by Elisabeth Bennion.)

'Dame Nature' take Her course. Sir Richard Croft bitterly regretted just such a decision when, in 1817, Princess Charlotte, the only daughter of the Prince Regent, was left in labour unaided for fifty-two hours. As a result, the wildly popular twenty-one year-old mother died along with her baby, and three months later Sir Richard shot himself in a surge of uncontrollable remorse.

Forceps were further developed during the nineteenth century, and many women and their babies were saved by the use of these and other instruments. Craniotomy was the act of breaking down the skull of the child in an obstructed labour so that it could be delivered, and for this a perforator was needed to pierce the soft spot in the skull in order to collapse and empty it. A cranioclast was used in conjunction with a cephalotribe to break down and grip the baby's head before pulling it out.

In more normal births a wicked-looking crotchet, or sharp hook, was used to grip hold of the head, and a lever or vectis helped to ease the baby out. A pelvimeter measured the pelvis, and a vaginal speculum was used to explore and dilate the vagina. Although some such instrument had been in use since Roman times, Marion Sims of Louisville, Kentucky, pioneered his own variety, which he developed after an experiment with a dessert spoon. The bowl of the spoon was bent at right angles to the handle and inserted into the mother's vagina. With the aid of a lighted candle, the interior of the vagina mirrored in the bowl of the spoon was reflected on to the handle outside the woman's body. In the male-dominated world of nineteenth century midwifery, modesty often mattered more than the well-being of the mother. *Hints to Husbands,* 1857, described in blustering terms its opinion of the speculum. 'Its employment plunges its wretched victim, woman, into the lowest depths of infamy and degradation. We will not pollute these pages by describing its methods of action'.

Delivery by Caesarian section, which could have denied the need for many of these horrors, was not performed successfully until 1793, when only the mother survived, and was not widespread until very much later.

It is unlikely that most modern women could withstand, either physically or emotionally, the rigours of childbirth which our ancestors endured as their common lot, and in a normal labour, pain relief was not given automatically until the middle of this century.

In 1847 Sir James Young Simpson (1811-1870), Professor of Midwifery at Edinburgh, began to use ether and then chloroform as an anaesthetic during labour. Because so many men, particularly in the baby business, maintained that pain in childbirth was necessary for the well-being of a woman's soul, as well as her body, there was much opposition to the use of drugs. One doctor claimed that they 'exerted a most powerful and salutary influence upon their (women's) religious and moral character, and upon all their future relations to life'. Queen Victoria, however, remained steadfastly unamused by such male prejudices, and in 1853 chloroform was administered during the birth of her eighth child, Prince Leopold. She referred to it later as 'the inestimable blessing of chloroform', which she described as 'soothing, quieting and delightful'. One mother was so overcome with gratitude and relief after a labour dulled by chloroform that she named her daughter, not unattractively, Anaesthesia. Queen Victoria had the liquid dropped onto a handkerchief held over her face, but by the 1860s an Ellis Inhaler, or some similar device, was being used.

After the traumas of the birth, the mother would lie back on her pillows exhausted, ready to enjoy the next four to six weeks of her 'lying-in', with a sense of success achieved and danger averted. Until the next time...

Cauls

Occasionally it happened that a baby was born with a piece of the afterbirth membrane covering his face. This thin membrane, through which the infant could breathe, was known as a caul, coif, sillie how (hood) or hallihoo (holy hood), and was thought to presage great good fortune in many areas of life. Such a circumstance was often recorded after a birth, although clearly James, the baby son of Mary Queen of Scots, did not attract outstanding luck in spite of having been born with a caul stretched over his face. After the birth the caul was removed and laid on a piece of paper to dry. Some can be found enclosed in silver cases engraved with suitable commemorative inscriptions, and the health of the original owner could be determined by the state of the caul. If it was crisp and dry he was well, if damp and flabby, he was in poor health or sickening.

In particular, the presence of a caul was thought to confer the gift of the gab, or oratory, and midwives with an eye to the main chance were known to sell them to gullible lawyers and advocates. They were also thought to preserve the life of the owner, and to protect him from drowning. No doubt a sea voyage one hundred and fifty years ago was regarded with considerable anxiety, and as a result cauls were highly prized. They were advertised for sale at high prices

Plate 6. A rare silver caul case, with its contents intact, engraved:

> Robert Williams
> Born 13 March
> 1842

The engine-turned silver case bears the initials 'R.W.' on the outside, and is dated 1843, the year after the child's birth. It comes complete in a silk-lined red morocco case.

I. Freeman & Son, Simon Kaye Ltd. (Reproduced from *Antique Medical Instruments* by Elisabeth Bennion.)

to sailors, and an insertion in *The Morning Post,* 21 August 1779 reads 'To the Gentlemen of the Navy, and others going long voyages to sea. To be disposed of, a CHILD'S CAUL. Enquire at the Bartlet Buildings Coffee-house in Holborn. NB to avoid unnecessary trouble the price is Twenty Guineas'. In 1813 *The Times* carried a similar advertisement 'To Persons going to sea. A child's caul in a perfect state, to be sold cheap. Apply 5 Duke Street, Manchester Square, where it may be seen'. Some commentators deplored the superstition attached to such things, and *John Bull Magazine,* January 1822, complained bitterly that bills advertising cauls were widely posted on the walls of the Royal Exchange. However, cauls were still carried by servicemen during the early part of this century, and indeed the price for cauls was pushed up by the advent of the First World War and its attendant dangers.

Swaddling

'He must be swaddled to give his little body a straight figure, which is most decent and convenient for a man and to accustom him to keep upon his feet, for else he would go upon all fours as most other animals do'.
(François Mauriceau, *The Accomplish't Midwife,* 1673.)

'Away with swaddling clothes, give the child large and flowing robes that leave all his limbs free'.
(Jean-Jacques Rousseau, *Emile,* 1762.)

As soon as the new-born baby had been given a wash in salt and warm water, or wine, or had been rubbed over with salt as a protection against evil, he was then taken by the midwife or other female attendant, and wrapped up in a cocoon-like parcel, before being laid in his cradle to sleep off the after-effects of birth. His first garments included an open-fronted shirt, a 'tail-clout' or nappy, a 'bed' or broad cloth which wrapped him tightly and enclosed his feet for warmth, a roller, or long swaddling band, a waistcoat which pinioned the arms and over all a long linen strip known as a swaddling band. His head was similarly encased in a 'cross-cloth', or head-piece and one or two 'biggins' or caps.

It was thought essential to keep the baby really warm and well-protected from the Arctic draughts which ravaged every English house. It was also considered important to straighten the infant's limbs after birth, and hold them in as rigid a position as possible for the first two or three months, so as to ensure untwisted and straight growth, and protect the fragile limbs from being broken during natural episodes of kicking or stretching. Rickets, also known as the 'London disease' was prevalent and resulted in terrible crippling deformities in later life. The real causes of rickets, which included lack of vitamin D through insufficient exposure to fresh air and sunlight, and a lack of dairy products and fish-liver oils, were not understood, and the disease was thought to be transmitted by parents kissing their children. Tight swaddling

Plate 7. A portrait of Cornelia Burch, aged two months, dated 1581, by an unknown artist of the Dutch School. Cocooned like a chrysalis in her swaddling bands, Cornelia is nevertheless dressed up to the nines for her portrait, with an elaborate and very grown-up looking arched hood head-dress over her baby cap. Having reached the age of two months, her arms have already been released from her swaddling bands, with expensive velvet sleeves pinned on for the occasion. With her hands free, she can grasp her new coral gum-stick hung with bells, although her feet are still encased in their woollen 'bed'. Collection of Viscountess Kemsley.

was, tragically, more likely to encourage than ward off the onset of the dread disease, and indeed, to cause dislocation of the hip joints as well. In 1773 there were in London alone 'nearly twenty thousand children ill... of the Hectic Fever, attended with tun-bellies, swelled wrists and ankles or crooked limbs', in reality suffering from rickets.

The practice of swaddling had been carried on since Roman times, and 'swaddle' or 'swatheing bands' were part of most midwive's equipment. Made of linen, they usually measured ten or twelve feet in length, and were sometimes edged with a simple lace border. In 1667 the Duchess of Hamilton paid £1 2s. for '1 child's swaddling band'. A more lowly example was recorded in an account of 1729 in the Essex County Records, 'Bought of Thomas Heckford... a swaddling ban. 7d.'

The discomfort of the swaddled baby must have been extreme, resulting in long bouts of crying and wakefulness, which only constant rocking in his cradle, or in the arms of his nurse, could alleviate. Heat, itching, rawness, stiffness and long hours of boredom with his body encrusted or soaked in his own mess, was the normal lot of most babies until the last part of the eighteenth century.

Efforts were made to ease the boredom by strapping the little howling bundle onto a board and hanging it on the wall so that the baby could see what was going on around him. This was often an easy option for a lazy nurse, and Dr William Cadogan, *Essay on the Nursing and Management of Children,* 1748, describes how the swaddled baby 'at the least annoyance... is hung from a

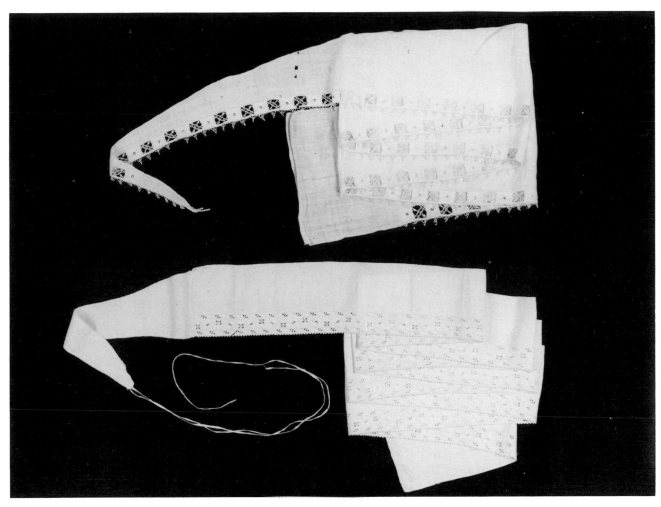

Plate 8. Two linen swaddling bands, the one above of late 16th century date, with a band of alternate whitework and reticella panels, and with 'punto-in-aria' border. The lower band is early 17th century with a cut and whitework border, the tapering ends still with the original ties. When the child was swaddled, the decorative borders would form a zig-zag pattern around his body.

David Knight, Esq.

nail like a bundle of old clothes, and while without hurrying the nurse attends to her business, the unfortunate one remains crucified'. Such 'crucifixion' was only slightly less horrifying than the form of 'exercise' sometimes meted out to swaddled babies. During the seventeenth century Elizabeth, daughter of Mary Rich, Countess of Warwick, was killed by two careless nursemaids who 'tossed her between them'.

Opinions varied as to the benefits of swaddling. Pamela, the virtuous maid in Richardson's novel of the same name (1740), laments 'how has my heart ached many and many a time when I have seen poor babies rolled and swathed, ten or a dozen times round, then blanket upon blanket, mantle upon that; its little neck pinned down to one posture... its legs and arms as if to prevent that kindly stretching which we rather ought to promote... the former bundled up, the latter pinned down; and how the poor thing lies on the nurse's lap, a miserable little pinioned captive'. *Pamela* was influenced by John Locke's liberalising book, *Thoughts Concerning Education,* 1693, and the same thoughts were echoed in Rousseau's revolutionary novel, *Emile,* 1762. However,

Theresa Parker, a new mother in the second half of the eighteenth century, still complained bitterly that 'a child is no sooner born than it is bound up as firmly as an Egyptian mummy in folds of linen'. As late as 1813 the Reverend Weedon Butler, Jnr., described the conflict between nature and nurture in the treatment of his fifth child.

'Enslav'd to female power,
Lapp'd, fondl'd, sooth'd, kiss'd, patted and carest,
Then — all within the compas of an hour,
Pinion'd and truss'd, swath'd, manacled and drest.'

William Blake's poem, *Infant Sorrow*, graphically describes the plight of most new-born babies as they exchanged the warm security of the womb for the rigours of the outside world.

'My mother groan'd, my father wept,
Into the dangerous world I leapt;
Helpless, naked, piping loud;
Like a fiend hid in a cloud.

Struggling in my father's hands,
Striving against my swaddling bands,
Bound and weary I thought best
To sulk upon my mother's breast.'

However, by the middle of the nineteenth century swaddling had all but died out, due to the teachings of Rousseau and others, although babies were still trussed-up for their own 'good' in an amazing array of arcane-sounding rollers, body-belts, binders, corsets and stays, which served to keep the dressing of the umbilical cord in place and prevent hernias thought to be caused by sneezing or crying.

Chapter 2

BREAST FEEDING

'Let the twin hills be white as mountain snow,
Their swelling veins with circling juices flow;
Each in a well-projecting nipple end,
And milk in copious streams from these descend'.
(Sainte-Marthe, *Paedotrophia*, translated 1797.)

'The thrilling sensations that accompany the act of giving suck can be conceived
only by those who have felt them, while the mental raptures of a fond mother at-
such moments are far beyond the powers of description or fancy.'
(Dr. William Buchan, *Advice to Mothers*, 1803.)

Breastfeeding has always been a subject of controversy. Nicholas Culpeper
wrote in his *Directory For Midwives,* 1651 'Oh! what a raket do authors make
about this, what thwarting and contradicting'.

Since Roman times semen was thought to turn milk sour, and so women
attempted to keep themselves chaste while nursing their children. Under-
standably enough, their husbands became cantankerous and impatient,
especially as weaning might not be completed until the child was two or three
years old. Sir William Knollys, writing to Anne Fitton in 1598, agreed to stand
godfather to her new baby, but commented, on her plans to suckle her baby,
'I should like it nothing that you play the nurse if you were my wife... it
breedeth much trouble'.

Many women found the process too 'biological' to contemplate. Anthony
Trollope noted sarcastically in *Dr Thorne,* 1858, 'Of course Lady Arabella could
not suckle the young heir herself. Ladies Arabella never can. They are gifted
with the powers of being mothers, but not nursing mothers. Nature gives them
bosoms for show but not for use'. Although the Duchess of Kent had suckled
the infant Queen Victoria, a process which the bemused Duke found 'most
interesting in its nature', her maternal feelings were not passed on to her
daughter. Queen Victoria was revolted by the idea of 'making a cow of oneself', and refused to breast-feed her own children.

Added to the feelings of delicacy experienced by Queen Victoria were the
problems of ruined figures, broken nights, a severely interrupted social life and

a bad-tempered husband who was persistently denied his frolics and fun. It was small wonder that large numbers of women from the aristocracy, professional and merchant classes turned to other women whom they paid to feed their children. Wet-nurses flourished during the seventeenth and eighteenth centuries and William Cobbett reported in his *Rural Rides,* 1830, that 'nothing is so common as the rent breasts for children to suck'. They were still going strong well into the nineteenth century, as can be seen by Mrs Isabella

Plate 9. A detail of a painting showing a childbirth scene in the life of Sir Henry Unton, by an unknown artist of the English School, c.1596. His mother, Anne, sits in a chair holding her new baby, while a wet-nurse with bare breasts approaches to suckle him. On the table are various pewter utensils, including spoons, bowls and a spouted vessel, possibly a baby feeder. The wicker cradle on rockers stands on the floor, and a small stool, for the midwife, is seen in the foreground. Thomas Delaney's treatise on childbirth, The Gentle Craft, *1597, recommended that a stool or 'cricket' be made ready for the midwife, along with soap and candles.*　　National Portrait Gallery.

Plate 10. A Chelsea porcelain figure of a wet-nurse, known as 'La Nourrice', 7½ in. (19.1cm), c.1755. This clearly shows a swaddled baby clutching at the breast of his nurse. William Cobbett noted in 1829 that 'nothing is so common as the rent breasts for children to suck', and places for wet-nurses were still being advertised in The Times *in the 1880s, since many women found breast-feeding distasteful.*　　Sotheby's.

Beeton's advice on choosing such a woman in her *Book of Household Management*. *The Times* was advertising places for wet-nurses in the 1880s, and Sir Winston Churchill, born in 1874, was raised by one.

Since the character of the wet-nurse was thought to be transmitted to the baby through her milk, great care had to be taken to find a morally irreproachable woman — 'Who draws the flaggy breasts of wanton Dames, Shall base Desires imbibe, and burn with guilty Flames'. The wives of clergymen were sometimes approached, but prostitutes and unmarried mothers also thronged to take up wet-nursing since breast-feeding was thought to act as a contraceptive by suppressing ovulation. They were also eager to earn money, a fact which gained the profession the sub-title of 'Vice Rewarded'. The milk of red-headed women was thought to be 'sour, stinking and vicious', and was thus to be avoided. Otherwise a 'pleasing countenance' with clear bright eyes, well-formed nose, red mouth and white teeth, together with a cheerful and sociable disposition, were all considered amiable qualities. They must 'keep a good diet and abstain from hard wine, and copulation and passions', but most important of all were the ever-flowing 'twin hills... white as mountain snow'. Wet-nurses were traditionally supplied with soap and candles, in order to maintain good personal hygiene, and see what they were doing, and were well paid (six shillings a month was the going rate during Queen Elizabeth I's reign, and a wet-nurse in the 1730s could expect 100 guineas a year). Anne, Duchess of Hamilton, paid £2 18s on 14 June 1690 'To the woman who gave suck to Lady Mary'.

Frightful fates awaited those babies consigned to the wrong woman. In the 1650s, the second child of Alice Thornton was almost crushed by its wet-nurse who fell asleep while feeding it, only to be saved in the nick of time by its mother who heard it 'groaning troublesomely'. Dr Johnson was supposed to have received his bad eyesight and scrofula from his unwashed wet-nurse, and the woman who suckled the Prince of Wales in 1841 later became morose and 'stupid', and murdered her own six children. It was common for wet-nurses to be drunk, or to drug their small charges to make them sleep by rubbing opium on their nipples. Some even soaked the baby's bedding with water to convince parents that the child was so well-fed that it was constantly wetting itself, when in reality the woman's milk had dried up and the baby was starving to death. Probably the most bizarre danger of all was that the nurse would exchange her own baby for her little charge, thus ensuring that her child grew up under the best conditions that money and status could afford, and the changeling was a theme which haunted drama and literature since the sixteenth century.

It is also perhaps a little-known and surprising fact, that adult invalids and the frail and elderly, were urged to take human milk as a restorative. Dr Caius, founder of Caius College, Cambridge, existed during the last years of his life on human milk supplied by a variety of wet-nurses, and John Wesley recommended 'sucking a healthy woman daily', to consumptives, as this had cured his own father.

Nipple Shields

Plate 11. A 19th century wood and ivory nipple shield.
Sotheby's.

Some childcare experts were so vociferous in their claims that mothers should feed their own babies, particularly after the publication of Jean-Jacques Rousseau's influential novel, *Emile*, in 1762, that many mothers did decide to breast-feed. They had to be careful of their diet, avoiding fried or spiced meat, and vegetables such as onions or garlic, but most important of all, they were urged to cultivate 'good nipples so that the child will take to them with pleasure'.

The stays and corsets which seventeenth and eighteenth century fashion decreed forced the breasts upwards into the bulging cleavages so typical of Restoration comedy, but devastated the nipples by flattening them to the point of inversion. As late as 1857 Dr John Walsh, in his *Manual of Domestic Economy,* bemoaned the fact that 'in the present state of society, from the pressure of stays carried through several generations, the nipples are so shortened and injured in their development that, if left to itself, many a child would actually starve'.

To remedy this, nipple shields were worn by the nursing mother both night and day, and either removed or left in place when the child sucked. They were

Plate 12 (Clockwise, from left). A group of nipple shields, in various materials. Silver, by Phipps & Robinson, 1809; Silver, by Phipps & Robinson, 1801; a rare wooden example, c.1800; a glass example with folded rim, c.1840.
I. Freeman & Son, Simon Kaye Ltd. (Reproduced from *Antique Medical Instruments,* by Elisabeth Bennion.)

32

made in a variety of materials which included pewter, horn, bone, ivory, wood, leather, glass and silver. Writing in 1674, Scultetus, *The Chyrurgeon's Storehouse,* described a contemporary nipple shield as 'a silver cap and full of holes which is applied. . . to the breasts that nurses may suckle the infants without trouble'.

Among the silversmiths known to have made nipple shields are Samuel Pemberton, Birmingham; James Jackson, London; T.J. Phipps, London; Phipps, Robinson and Phipps, London; and Anne Robertson, Newcastle.

'Leaden nipples' were described in *The Workes* by Ambroise Paré, translated in 1634, and must have been used with disastrous consequences. More prosaic, but safer, were the India rubber examples advertised by Maw's in their 1868 *Catalogue.* Poor women simply had to make do with a hollowed-out nutmeg or walnut shell.

Plate 13. Some nipple shields depicted in The Workes *by Ambroise Paré, 1634, described as 'leaden Nipples to be put upon the Nipple or Teat of the Nurfe when it is ulcerated'. Painful nipples, distended breasts and breast abscesses were major problems in the days before antibiotics, and contemporary textbooks abounded with useless, if colourful, remedies.*

If the nipples were ulcerated or infected with an abscess, the nipple shield could be left in place and the baby could suck the milk through the small holes in the shield. Before the days of antibiotics, such infections were rife, and Fanny Burney, writing in March 1795 of her new baby, gave a graphic acount of what women had to endure. 'In a fortnight the poor thing had the Thrush — communicated it to my Breast — and in short — after torment upon torment a milk fever ensued — an abscess in the Breast followed — and till that broke I suffered so as to make life — even my happy life — scarce my wish to preserve'.

Because the weaning of children was completed so late, nipple shields were also necessary as protection against rodent offspring. In 1688 Lady Katherine Murray's sister, Susan, breastfed her son on a visit to Hamilton Palace, where her mother remarked 'he had 8 teeth and is a fine lusty child'. *The Englishwoman's Domestic Magazine,* 1859, was firm on the matter. 'Nature never ordained a child to live on suction after having endowed it with teeth to bite and to grind, and nothing is more out of place and unseemly than to hear a child with a set of twenty teeth ask for the breast'. However, many mothers weakened, with painful results.

Breast Pumps and Breast Warmers

For mothers who had handed their babies over to a wet-nurse, the problem of what to do with their unwanted milk was a trying one. When the breasts became sore and distended a 'sucking glass' could be placed over the breast and the mother could, herself, draw off the surplus milk through a curved tube. Such a glass is shown in W.H. Reiff's *Schwangerer Frauen Rosengarten,* 1545 (Plate 14). A more primitive method was for attendant women or young puppies to draw off the excess.

The Victorians developed the 'breast pump', 'breast Exhauster' or 'breast Reliever' into something of an art form. Some, in brass with fitted mahogany cases or satin-lined morocco, appear to resemble instruments from a brass band, while others have tubes for 'self use'. Maw's romantic-sounding

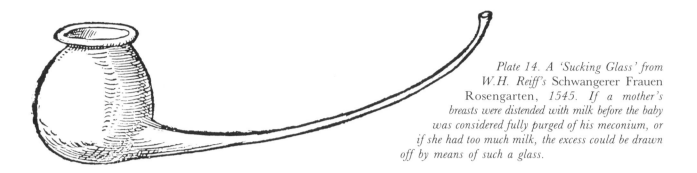

Plate 14. A 'Sucking Glass' from W.H. Reiff's Schwangerer Frauen Rosengarten, 1545. If a mother's breasts were distended with milk before the baby was considered fully purged of his meconium, or if she had too much milk, the excess could be drawn off by means of such a glass.

'Arabesque, for Hot Climates' no doubt offered blessed relief to Memsahibs in the Punjab, and helped to lighten the 'White Woman's Burden'. In 1859 'A Surgeon's Advice to Mothers' appeared in *The Gentlewoman's Domestic Magazine,* urging that 'Every mother who can should certainly be provided with a breast pump or glass tube so as to draw off the superabundance which has been accumulating in her absence from the child', and many such pumps appear in Maw's 1868 *Catalogue.*

Breast warmers appear in Doulton & Watts *Lambeth Pottery Catalogue* for 1883, at 2s. 6d. each. Insulated from the cold in our modern centrally-heated houses, we are oblivious to the rigours which Victorian mothers and wet-nurses must have endured, rising in the middle of the night to feed crying babies when the house was silent and all the fires had gone out.

Glass dress protectors were made towards the end of the nineteenth century, and were used 'for overflowing breasts to protect the dress' in the days before plastic shields and paper tissues.

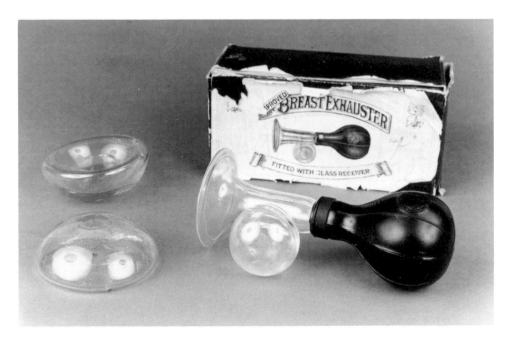

Plate 15. An 'Improved Breast Exhauster', fitted with Glass Receiver, complete with its original box, priced at 4/-. These were also known as Breast Relievers and, more frequently, Breast Pumps. They feature in Maw's 1868 Catalogue at 3/6d and were still there in 1911 at 33/6d per dozen; and a Pair of glass Dress Protectors, c.1880. These were 'worn for overflowing breasts to protect the dress'.
Private Collection.

S. MAW & SON, 11, ALDERSGATE STREET, LONDON. 29

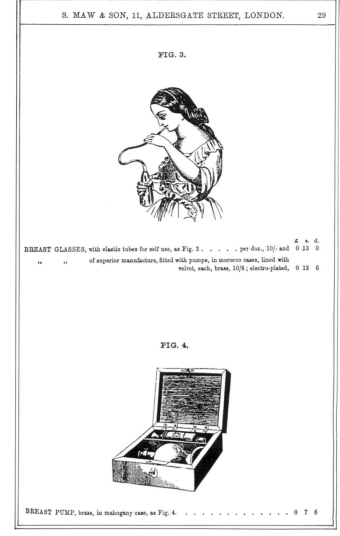

FIG. 3.

	£	s.	d.
BREAST GLASSES, with elastic tubes for self use, as Fig. 3 . . . . . per doz., 10/- and	0	13	0
" " of superior manufacture, fitted with pumps, in morocco cases, lined with velvet, each, brass, 10/6 ; electro-plated,	0	12	6

FIG. 4.

BREAST PUMP, brass, in mahogany case, as Fig. 4.	0	7	6

Plate 16. A page from Maw's 1868 Catalogue, *showing a young mother using a 'Breast Glass with elastic tube for self use', which cost 13s. 0d. A superior example 'fitted with pumps, in morocco case, lined with velvet' cost 10/6 for brass, 12/6 for electro-plate. Below is shown a brass breast pump in its mahogany case at 7/6.*
Maw's.

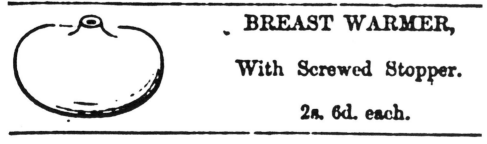

BREAST WARMER,

With Screwed Stopper.

2s. 6d. each.

Plate 17. Extract of a page from a Doulton & Watts, Lambeth Pottery Catalogue *dated 1883, showing a Breast Warmer with Screwed Stopper at 2s. 6d. each.* Royal Doulton Ltd.

Chapter 3

'RAISING BY HAND'

Feeding Cups and Bubby Pots

*'Disease and death are the usual consequences of the present erroneous method of
bringing children up by hand. Scarcely one out of four of these little innocents live
to get over the cutting of their teeth'.*
(The Female Instructor, *or* Young Woman's Companion, 1815.)

*'For the next 8 or 10 months, Oliver was the victim of a coarse treachery and
deception — he was brought up by hand'.*
(Charles Dickens, *Oliver Twist,* 1838.)

From early times, spouted pewter vessels were used to feed newborn babies
with liquids such as milk, broth, or watered-down wine. These are shown
clearly in childbirth scenes in manuscripts dating from the late fifteenth
century.

Since the thin, watery colostrum which issues from a mother's breasts before
her milk 'comes in ' on the second or third day after the birth, was thought
to be harmful, the new-born baby was fed straight away on a purgative to
sustain him and purge his system of the dark green contents of his bowels,
known as meconium. Although entirely natural, meconium, too, was thought
to be harmful. A typical purgative, which would have been administered from
one of these spouted vessels, consisted of butter and honey or sugar, oil of sweet
almonds and sugar or syrup, and sugared wine. The Old Pretender, Prince
James Francis Edward Stuart, was apparently dosed with thirty different
medicines and given a panada of barley flour, sugar, currants and canary
wine, before being 'rescued' to suckle at his wet-nurse's breasts. As late as
1748, Dr William Cadogan, medical adviser to Captain Thomas Coram's
Foundling Hospital in London, complained in his *Essay on the Nursing and
Management of Children* that 'the general Practice is, as soon as a child is born,
to ram a Dab of Butter and Sugar down its Throat, a little Oil, Panada, Caudel
or some such unwholesome mess'.

Caudle, or posset, made with milk and eggs to form a kind of custard, and
flavoured with sugar and wine, would have been given during the seventeenth
and early eighteenth century from a spouted delftware vessel known as a posset
pot, and miniature examples made for children exist. Possets and caudles were

Plate 18. A collection of pewter baby feeders spanning the 18th century. They are not dissimilar to the early 16th century example shown in the Nativity of St John from the Arunberg Missal (see Colour Plate 1).

I. Freeman & Son, Simon Kaye Ltd.

soothing at times of illness, and in January 1699 Sir John Clerk's little son, Jamie, was treated with a 'marigold posset' when he caught smallpox. Adults, too, enjoyed warming possets for ill-health and in October 1663 Samuel Pepys skulked guiltily off to bed with a posset to ease the symptoms of his cold, caught while 'lewdly sporting with Mrs Lane by a broken window'.

During the second half of the eighteenth century feeding cups were made in silver and in porcelain, particularly by the Lowestoft factory, who appeared to make an unusual speciality of children's requisites. Blue and white painted Lowestoft examples are rare, and were superseded by printed examples around 1770. Some bear names and dates. They were also made at the Wedgwood factory in cream-coloured earthenware. If the flow of liquid was too free for a baby or small child to manage without choking, a piece of sponge wrapped in a small cotton rag could be tied over the spout to help stem the flow and form a kind of teat. Yet another example of the kind of practice which, through ignorance, must have carried many children to an early grave.

During the first half of the nineteenth century a similar type of vessel made in glass with a globular body and curved spout, was also in use. The glass, being transparent, allowed the vessel to be more thoroughly cleaned.

However, the most sensationally successful infant feeding vessel of the eighteenth century was Dr Hugh Smith's amusingly named Bubby Pot which, after experiments in his own nursery, he developed for his infant brood and launched in 1777. He graphically describes this vessel, which was to be the *sine qua non* of all up-to-date nurseries of the late eighteenth century, in his own words in his *Letters to Married Women on the Nursing and Management of Children*. 'Since this book made its first appearance (in 1772), I have contrived a milk pot for my own nursery. It appears to my family and to many of my patients preferable to those now in use, and may probably be still further improved. This pot is somewhat in form like an urn; it contains little more than a quarter

Plate 19. A rare survivor, from the end of the 17th century, is this small English delftware posset pot, only 5ins. (12.7cm) high, and almost certainly made for use by a child, who would have sucked the posset directly from the spout. Made in London, it is decorated in blue, in the manner of late Ming porcelain. Possets and caudles were often given in times of sickness, and must have had something of the soothing properties of a cup of alcoholic Ovaltine.
Sotheby's.

Plates 20 and 21. A Lowestoft porcelain feeding cup, painted in underglaze-blue with sprays of flowers and inscribed with the name Ann Smith Norwich, and the date 1772, 3 ¼ in. (8.3cm) high. Printed examples are more common than painted. Very similar feeding cups were made in English delftware at the same date.
Sotheby's.

of a pint, its handle and neck or spout are not unlike those of a coffee pot, except that the neck of this arises from the very bottom of the pot, and is very small; In short, it is upon the same principle as those gravy pots which separate the gravy from the oily fat.' (These were known as 'Argylls', and said to have been invented by the third Duke). 'The end of the spout is a little raised, and forms a roundish knob, somewhat in appearance like a small heart; this is perforated by 3 or 4 small holes, a piece of fine rag is tied loosely over it, which serves the child to play with instead of the nipple, and through which, by the infant's sucking, the milk is constantly strained and the infant is obliged to labour for every drop he receives'. He adds with philanthropic good humour, not untinged by a touch of entrepreneurial pride, that 'the milk-pots are now also in Queensware (Wedgwood's cream-coloured earthenware) in order that the poor may be accomodated'. The pots were also made in blue-printed Wedgwood earthenware, and variations were made in silver for the nurseries of the rich. Dr Smith's undoubted confidence in his product, which he proudly claimed 'the nurses confess. . . is more convenient than a boat' (pap-boat), was confirmed by Michael Underwood in his *Treatise on the Diseases of Children,* 1789. The bubby pot 'is nearly as acceptable to many children as the breast, as I have often been a witness'.

Plate 22. A creamware Bubby Pot, as introduced by Dr Hugh Smith in 1777 after successful experiments in his own nursery at home. It was made on the same principle as contemporary gravy pots, or Argylls. I. Freeman & Son, Simon Kaye Ltd.

Plate 23. A George III silver feeding cup by Rebecca Emes and Edward Barnard, London, 1812, 6½in. (16.5cm). The partnership of Emes and Barnard was also noted for its fine quality christening mugs. Silver was often used for feeding vessels because of its anti-bacterial qualities, and silver rims were often fitted onto stoneware tankards to guard against infection if the cup were to be shared. The poor would have had to do with earthenware or pewter.

Christie's South Kensington.

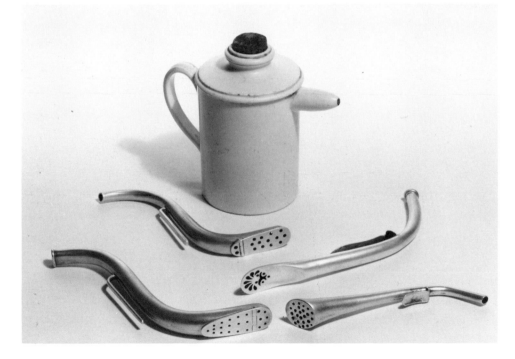

Plate 24. An early cream-ware Baby Feeder, c.1780, and a group of silver sick syphons, used by babies, invalids and children, 1800-30. The clip at the side fitted over the edge of the cup, and the liquid was sucked up through the mouthpiece, with the small holes straining any unmanageable lumps.

I. Freeman & Son, Simon Kaye Ltd. (Reproduced from *Antique Medical Instruments* by Elisabeth Bennion.)

Yet another device made for the use of children and the elderly or invalid, was known as the 'sick syphon'. Generally made of silver, and dating from the beginning of the nineteenth century, these S-shaped objects had a clip to hold them on to the rim of the cup. The liquid, such as thin gruel or beef tea, was sucked up, as through a straw, with unmanageable lumps being strained through the holes.

Early Bottles and Feeding Horns

'March 6, 1700. This morning the child received almost a miraculous deliverance from choking, by a pin, which he suck'd out of the silver nipple of his bottel, tho' wee knew not how it came there.'
(Cotton Mather, *Diary.*)

'The invention of horns, sucking bottles, and many other contrivances for artificial nipples, are too lame and imperfect imitations of nature to be useful . . . as these machines cannot be kept perfectly clean.'
(Thomas Mantell, *Short Directions for The Management of Infants*, 1787.)

To describe an infant during the eighteenth or nineteenth century as 'hand-raised' was not to liken him to a pork pie, but to indicate that he had been fed from the bottle rather than the breast.

There were numerous reasons why a baby might be bottle-fed, including the curious, and temporary, custom that mother's milk should not be given during a thunderstorm, as it was thought to turn sour, but the main reason was when the mother had died, or was too ill to suckle her child, and no suitable wet-nurse could be found or, in the case of the poor, afforded. Benjamin Haydon, the Romantic painter (1786-1846), recounts the harrowing story of his daughter, Fanny, who died aged two years, nine months and twelve days. 'She was weaned at three months from her mother's weakness, and attempted to be brought up by hand. This failed, and she was reduced to a perfect skeleton . . . I got a wet-nurse instantly, and she seized the bosom like a tigress'. In spite of this, she later died, as did the child of the wet-nurse, who was forced to be weaned too early as a result. It was considered, by many paediatricians, to be tantamount to a death sentence to bottle-feed a baby. The Dublin Foundling Hospital which hand-raised over ten thousand babies between the years of 1775 and 1796, had only forty-five successes, representing a staggeringly high 99.6 percent mortality rate. Things were no better in the nineteenth century when only one in eight bottle-fed babies was calculated to survive, and in Dickens' *Great Expectations* Pip explained that his older sister, Mrs Joe Gargery, 'had established a great reputation with herself and her neighbours because she had brought me up "by hand" '. Even the 1907 edition of Mrs Beeton's *Household Management* underlined that bottle-feeding 'is the most difficult kind of bringing up to accomplish satisfactorily, and many more hand-fed children die than those brought up at the breast'.

It was only the effects of Pasteurisation on cow's milk, and the successful analysis of breast milk, together with the development of suitable substitutes from the 1930s onwards, that made the process safe. Before that it was a minefield. Cow's milk was too full of protein and mineral salts for the immature systems of babies to digest, and yet it lacked sufficient sugar and vitamin C to be really nourishing and ward off infection. The cows themselves were often diseased and kept in sorely insanitary conditions, particularly in towns and cities. If the milk was brought in from the country it would already

Plate 25. A late 16th century portrait of a small child holding its wooden feeding bottle. The painting is dated 1593, and unbelievably gives the sitter's age as only fifteen weeks. Similar bottles were also made of leather, and were thought to have originated in Italy and the Low Countries.

Sotheby's.

be too old, after perhaps half a day's journey on a bumpy cart, for vulnerable infant stomachs. The almost total lack of refrigeration, save for ice-houses during the eighteenth century and primitive ice-boxes from the second half of the nineteenth century, meant that bacteria multiplied at an alarming rate. (Pasteurisation was initially introduced in 1890 for commercial reasons, but hygienically bottled milk was not generally available until the 1920s.) Far from providing the precious antibodies, so vital in building up the baby's immune system, which mother's milk contained, cow's milk was literally alive with life-threatening germs. Added to this, milk was often polluted with water and chalk by unscrupulous dairymen to make it go further.

Goat's and asses' milk were considered the best substitute for human milk, by some experts, and Mrs Gladstone sensibly took an ass on holiday with her when her baby was tiny. In 1857 the British Pharmacopoeia suggested the interesting substitute of vineyard snails boiled up with pearl barley if no fresh milk was to be found.

Quite apart from the multitude of dangers inherent in the cow's milk, the feeding bottles themselves were incubators of germs *par excellence,* and Milton's, a pioneer in the field, did not begin to produce their sterilising fluid until 1916. It was sold and used mainly for babies' bottles from 1947, and prior to that boiling was the only way of sterilising. The first definite awareness of the

Plate 26. An English 18th century pewter feeding bottle, 5⅝in. (14.3cm) high. Although some two hundred years later, it is very similar in shape to that shown in the 16th century portrait in Plate 25.

Colonial Williamsburg Foundation.

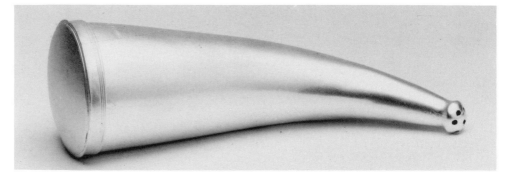

Plate 27. An unusual Georgian silver baby feeder in the shape of a cow's horn, 1805. Thousands of children died each year from the bacteria which flourished unseen in the traces of stale, unpasteurised milk which lurked in the recesses of these bottles.
I. Freeman & Son, Simon Kaye Ltd. (Reproduced from *Antique Medical Instruments* by Elisabeth Bennion.)

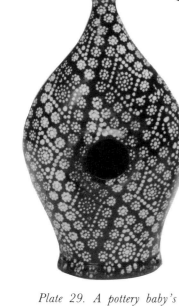

Plate 28. A silver feeding bottle, c.1810, probably Indian Colonial. I. Freeman & Son, Simon Kaye Ltd.

Plate 29. A pottery baby's feeder, in brown and cream glazed earthenware, c.1820. These were filled through the central hole, which was covered by the nurse's thumb in order to regulate the flow of milk during a feed. Later examples had screw-tops made of boxwood for the same purpose.
I. Freeman & Son, Simon Kaye Ltd. (Reproduced from *Antique Medical Instruments* by Elisabeth Bennion.)

importance of cleanliness in babies' feeding bottles came from Thomas Mantell in 1787. They 'cannot be kept perfectly clean, the victuals that hangs about them will be liable to become in a few hours very unfit for a nice taste to swallow, or a delicate stomach to digest'.

Feeding bottles for babies had been known from earliest times. Terracotta examples were used by the Greeks and the Romans, and a Roman glass example is in the Castle Museum, Colchester.

The simplest form of feeding bottle, in use in England from the Middle Ages until the early eighteenth century, was an inverted hollowed-out cow's horn, with an opening in the top over which a rudimentary teat could be fitted. Although basic, the cow's horn had one great advantage. It could not be set down while half-full of milk, and picked up again later. Unfinished feeds had to be thrown away, thus preventing the health hazard of stale milk. George Armstrong, who treated thirty-five thousand children at his Dispensary for the Infant Poor, recommended in 1767 that an ideal feeding horn should contain four to five fluid ounces, and that a finger stall of parchment or soft leather be tied over the end to act as a teat, and filled with cotton wool, so that the milk would seep through the gaps between the stitching as the baby sucked. Other experts recommended the unappetising expedient of an actual calf or heifer's teat which had been pickled in spirit. Yet another alternative, no more palatable than the other two, was a small piece of sponge tied up in a piece of cotton rag.

Sixteenth century portraits show globular baby feeders of pressed leather or wood, with removable tapering teat-like tops, which were thought to have been developed in Italy or the Low Countries, and by the eighteenth century globular pewter bottles were widely used, as well as cylindrical creamware examples with short high spouts.

Glass Feeding Bottles

Around 1800 the flat boat-shaped feeding bottle appeared. A central hole on the upper side of the bottle allowed the milk to be poured in, and was then covered with the thumb during a feed, to control the flow of liquid. Later examples had a screw-in stopper made of boxwood, which could be adjusted for the same purpose. Generally the spouts were short and straight, ready for a teat to be attached to the end, but others were longer and curved upwards. This type of boat-shaped bottle was made in large numbers in earthenware, sometimes with blue-printed decoration, and examples exist from most of the major Staffordshire factories, including Spode, Davenport and Wedgwood. Such bottles still appear in Maw's 1868 *Catalogue,* where they are affectionately described as 'old-fashioned'. A few are also known in pewter and silver, but by the 1840s had been supplanted by other materials, notably glass.

Hand-blown glass boat-shaped feeders made their appearance around 1825 or 1830, and proved to be very popular. Being transparent they were easier to keep clean, and did not cause quite so much of a risk to health as the pottery examples. They were widely distributed by Maw's, a firm which was founded in 1807 and started selling feeders in 1832. In their 1868 *Catalogue,* glass feeders were sold in three qualities from 3/6 to 10/- a dozen, with 'boxwood-topped corks' or 'vegetable-ivory topped corks' at a small extra price.

Later examples of feeding bottles in pressed and moulded glass became more and more elaborate, of globular, pear or double-ended boat shape, and some were made more decorative by pouring the moulten glass onto wire netting. A French bottle called 'The Biberon', was shown at the Great Exhibition in 1851. The normally staid medical journal, *The Lancet,* was clearly seduced by this sophisticated Gallic mass of tubes and ivory pins, which helped to regulate the flow, and pronounced euphorically that it had 'never seen anything so beautiful'.

In 1864 (ironically the very year in which Pasteur had declared with

Plate 30. Hand-blown glass 'Sucking Bottle' with boxwood stopper, c.1840.   Cow & Gate.

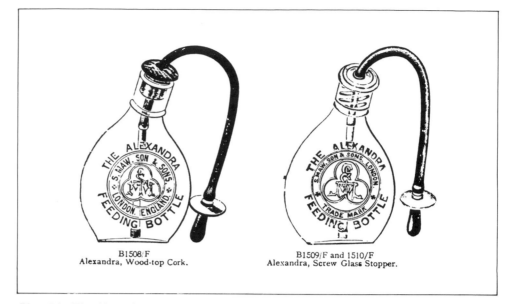

| B1508/F | B1509/F and 1510/F |
| Alexandra, Wood-top Cork. | Alexandra, Screw Glass Stopper. |

Plate 31. The Alexandra Feeding Bottle, which featured in Maw's 1868 Catalogue, and was launched amid the surge of popularity for the new Princess of Wales, who married the future Edward VII in 1863. The long rubber tube which connected the teat with the bottle was a fruitful breeding-ground for germs. Such bottles cost 3/- per dozen. Maw's.

certainty that invisible organisms in the atmosphere caused food to decay) the deadly 'Siphonia' bottle was introduced. Known in some quarters as a 'Murder Bottle', it was later banned in many American States. The long narrow India rubber tube which connected the bottle to the teat was a perfect breeding ground for bacteria, even though it came with its own wire brush for cleaning. Maw's introduced a similar model, patented by O'Connell, which featured in their 1868 *Catalogue,* and similar examples were still being sold as late as 1914. They were popular with working mothers and slovenly nurses alike, since the bottle could be placed next to the baby in the cot, and he could suck from it at will all through the day, allowing the milk it contained to stagnate.

Another chillingly dangerous device, which kept 'the food warm all night and day', and therefore in a perfect condition for bacteria to multiply, was an 'artificial breast', which was supposed to be worn full of milk 'by the female in the position of the breast'.

Questionably less hazardous were the glass feeding bottles which had a glass inner tube, also fiendishly difficult to clean with any efficiency. A typical example of this type was the 'Alexandra' Feeding Bottle, introduced by Maw's during the 1860s and marketed to coincide with the surge of popularity of the maternally-minded Princess of Wales who had married Bertie, the eldest son of Queen Victoria, in 1863.

Developed some time later by Borroughs & Wellcome, was the Thermo-Safeguard Feeding Bottle, which had a thermometer fitted into the glass to test the temperature of the milk.

The sterilisation of feeding bottles by boiling, and the boiling of milk and water to eradicate bacteria, as a result of the work of Pasteur and Koch, did not become widespread until after the end of the nineteenth century.

Something of a breakthrough was the Allenbury Feeder, devised by Allen

Plate 32. The Allenburys Feeder, by Allen & Hanbury's, complete with instructions and wire brush in the original box. Devised in 1900, this popular model, which could be cleaned from both ends, was on sale for around forty years. Cow & Gate.

Plate 33. The Crown Glass Feeding Bottle, of a similar depressed globular shape to that used for pewter examples during the 18th century, c.1920. Cow & Gate.

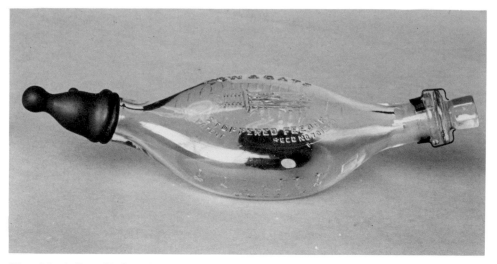

Plate 34. A Cow & Gate Feeder, adapted from the Allenbury's, c.1930.   Cow & Gate.

& Hanbury's in 1900, and in use for some forty years. The boat-shaped bottle had a hole at either end, which made it much easier to clean and regulate the flow of the milk, and was the first feeding bottle to incorporate a teat and valve.

Wide-necked bottles were not introduced until the 1950s, by which time special sterilising fluid was also on the market, along with a whole range of much safer substitutes for mother's milk, and bottle-feeding at last became a safe alternative to the breast. During its heyday the feeding bottle, along with the perambulator, the lavatory, and a host of other household items, was given a series of romantic and grandiose names which included 'The Eugenie', 'The Century' and 'The Darling'.

Goodyear's vulcanisation of rubber occurred in 1839, and in 1845 Elijah Pratt patented the India rubber teat in the United States. This was popularized at the Great Exhibition in 1851 and widely distributed by Maw's, who also made ivory teats. In their 1868 *Catalogue* they advertised black or white teats with apertures in four sizes 'for fluids of different consistency', which were described as 'holes' or 'leech bites', depending on the shape. The rise of the feeding bottle saw the decline of the wet-nurse, although advertisements for them were still carried in *The Times* as late as the 1880s. It was not until Dr Truby King's Mothercraft movement became popular during the 1920s, that the maxim 'Breast-fed is Best-fed' began to gain ground, and gradually breast-feeding came back into fashion.

Manufactured Milk Substitutes

With the gradual development of more hygienic feeding bottles during the second half of the nineteenth century, successful attempts were made to preserve cow's milk, which had hitherto been sold under horrifyingly unhygienic circumstances. Tins of evaporated and condensed milk were bought by mothers to be watered down as substitutes for breast milk. During the 1880s and 1890s manufacturers such as Nestlés and Horlicks, and the Aylesbury Dairy Co. Ltd., later joined by Cow & Gate, marketed mother's or 'Humanized' milk substitutes made with dried and powdered cow's milk, with added cereal and sugar.

Plate 35. The Cow & Gate Upright Feeder, with the well-known 'Smiler' logo, and original box. The wide-necked screw-top bottles were not introduced until 1950. Although Pasteurisation was introduced in 1890, hygienically bottled milk was not widely available until the 1920s, and sterilising fluid was not available until 1947. During the 19th century seven out of eight bottle-fed babies died.   Cow & Gate.

Women freed themselves from the restrictions of the breast pump and the nipple shield with as much gusto as their sisters in the 1960s liberated their breasts from their symbolically constricting bras, and breast-feeding did not enjoy a revival until the successful crusade led by Dr Truby King in the 1920s.

Mrs Panton's advice in *The Way They Should Go,* 1896, sounded a clarion call to the women of the nation. 'Let no mother condemn herself to be a common or ordinary "cow" unless she has a real desire to nurse... women have not the stamina they once possessed'. (So strong, indeed, were her feelings on the subject that she went on 'I myself know of no greater misery than nursing a child, the physical collapse caused by which is often at the bottom of the drinking habits of which we hear so much'.) However, the flip side of all this liberation was the fact that the processed milk foods contained nothing like the amount of vitamins and minerals contained in breast milk, and during the 1870s one-third of the children in industrial cities such as Manchester or London were found to have contracted rickets.

By 1906 it was discovered that cow's milk lacked the vital amines necessary for good nutrition in small babies, but it was not until the 1930s that it became possible to fortify these dried milk substitutes with vitamins during their manufacture.

Along with the patent milk foods, a whole range of cereal products for babies were developed, which were added to the milk, or given by spoon, within the first few months. Dr Ridge's Food was one such preparation. It was advertised, somewhat sickeningly, in the *Illustrated London News* for 1884 as 'so prepared by perfect cooking as to be fit nutriment for the fair, pure body that it helps to build into healthy flesh and bone'. It was available 'From all chemists and Grocers and at the Stores'. Other experts were more selectively cynical about the plethora of new infant foods. The Surgeon who gave his somewhat stentorian 'Advice to Mothers' in *The Englishwoman's Domestic Magazine,* 1859, declared tartly that 'Baked flour, when cooked into a pale brown mass, and finely powdered, makes a far superior food to the others. Prepared groats we may dismiss at once to the other side of the Tweed, or to the category of arrowroot and raw flour.' Robinson's Patent Groats were popular at the time, and other preparations for infants included Mellin's, Kranz's and Liebig's Food.

Colour Plate 1. An illustration from the Arunberg Missal *by the Master of Charles V, Antwerp, c.1520. The scene shows the Birth of St John the Baptist, who is about to be washed in a coopered wooden tub in the foreground, while his mother, St Elizabeth, lies back exhausted on her pillows in the background, attended by her midwife. On the table behind the nurse, who is washing the child, can be seen a spouted and lidded pewter vessel. This no doubt contained a purgative, which was administered to the newborn baby to cleanse its system of the dark green contents of its bowels, known as meconium, which was thought to be harmful. As late as 1748 Dr William Cadogan complained that 'the general Practice is, as soon as a child is born, to cram a Dab of Butter and Sugar down its Throat, a little oil, Panada, Caudel, or some such unwelcome Mess'. The colostrum, or thin fluid, which issued from the mother's breasts for the first two or three days before her milk 'came in' was also thought to be harmful. In fact we now know that this fluid contains vital antibodies which build up the baby's immature immune system against infection.* Sotheby's.

Chapter 4

WEANING
AND TEETHING

Pap-Boats and Pap-Warmers

'Give him his brekefast while I am here, make his pappe, take away that
fier-brand that smoketh for it will taste of the smoke, where is his little spoone?'
(Peter Erondell, 1580.)

'A viscous and crude paste, more proper for binders to bind their books than for
the nourishment of infants'
(M. Ettmuller, 1698.)

'Dance a baby, diddy,
What can Mammy do wid 'e,
But sit in her lap,
And give 'un some pap,
And dance a baby diddy?'
(Douce Ms, c.1805. Reproduced from the *Oxford Dictionary of Nursery Rhymes.*)

Weaning was, as every other aspect of childcare, a matter for extreme argument and contention, on the part of the male childcare experts of the day. In 1651 Nicholas Culpeper, *A Directory for Midwives,* was offering the following advice on weaning. 'If the child be strong and healthy, a year is enough in all conscience for it to suck..., The fondness of mothers to children doth them more mischief than the devil... in letting them suck too long. Unnatural food in their infancy, and cockering in their youth, will (if it were possible) make a devil of a saint'. He goes on, 'When the teeth come forth, by degrees give it more solid food, and deny it not milk, such as are easily chewed... It is best to wean in the Spring and Fall in the increase of the moon, and give but very little wine'.

On the other hand, Dr William Buchan, *Domestic Medicine,* 5th edition, 1776, believed that weaning should begin early. 'After the third or fourth month it will be proper to give the child once or thrice a day, a little of some food that

is easy of digestion; as water pap, milk pottage, weak broth with bread in it and such like'.

Pap was composed of flour or bread, cooked in water, with the possible additions of beer, wine or broth. If the mixture was too thick for a small 'toothless babe' to swallow easily, 'the nurses in taking it into their mouths dilute it with their saliva and place it after that in the infant's mouth'. (M. Ettmuller, *Pratique Spéciale de Médecine,* Lyons, 1698.) In view of this it is little wonder that good teeth were considered a requisite of a wet nurse.

The use of pap had been widespread since the fifteenth century, and as late as 1813 James Hamilton, *Hints for the Treatment of the Principal Diseases of Infancy and Childhood,* wrote 'Panada and pap be now almost universally used for the first food of infants, as a substitute for mother's milk'. It was gradually discontinued during the nineteenth century with the introduction of efficient feeding bottles, and the development of patent foods for infants. Not all childcare experts were happy about its use, however, and in 1783 De Claubry, a French paediatrician, advised mothers that 'pap is the most dangerous of all the foods for infants, that is has caused to perish a great number or has rendered them infirm and diseased for their whole lives'. Things did improve a little, however, during the nineteenth century, when some mothers substituted bread or flour with mashed potato, which was rich in vitamin C, and recognised as a cure for scurvy.

Panada was another popular infant food, made rather like a thick white sauce with flour, bread or cereals mixed with butter and milk, and sometimes the yolk of an egg. Its use was equally controversial. 'The stomach of an infant could digest stones as easily as it could digest panadas, aleberries and gruels. They never fail to produce the most severe and destructive diseases, first in the stomach and then throughout the whole frame', thundered J. Herdman in his *Discourses on the Management of Infants,* in 1807.

The problem was that mothers were anxious, as they are even today, that

Plate 37. A George I silver pap-boat, by Anthony Nelme, London 1718, of plain oval shape, with the initials E.C. engraved on the underside. 4½ in. (11.4 cm). Such pieces are found from around 1710, while later examples had a reeded wire attached to the rim for extra strength. Early 19th century examples are elaborately embossed with shells, gadrooning and wreaths of flowers. Interiors are sometimes gilded to prevent tarnishing.   Sotheby's.

their babies should thrive. Worries were legion; that their milk would run dry; that they would develop an abscess on the breast and be unable to feed; that the baby would weaken and refuse to suck; or that no suitable wet-nurse might be found in an emergency, such as happened all too often in families after a birth. In addition to all these niggling fears, the pernicious spectre of the 'watery gripes' hung over every cradle, threatening to carry the child off if the weather turned warm or the almost non-existent hygiene in the nursery became a little more lax than normal. Unaware, as we are today, of the excellence of breast milk, mothers felt that solid foods would help to 'set' the uncertain contents of their babies' stomachs, and enable the children to grow big and strong, with no fears of under-nourishment. Thus, a régime of almost solid foods, lacking in goodness and too thick for immature stomachs to digest, was embarked upon at an unsuitably early age, and with a degree of gusto which could be alarming, if not fatal. 'Surely it is wrong to put a large boat full of pap into their little mouths, suffering them to swallow the whole of it in a minute, and then from their cries to ply them with another, which is no sooner down than it is thrown up again', pleaded Dr Hugh Smith in his *Letters to Married Women,* 1792. The fact that spoons were listed separately from pap-boats as one of the four methods of 'artificial feeding' itemised by George Armstrong in 1772, *A General Account of the Dispensary for the Relief of the Infant Poor,* along with cow's horns and bubby pots, indicated that the contents of the boats were, indeed, often poured down the infant's throat rather than being always spooned in. This was no doubt sometimes a matter of convenience for the impatient or lazy nurse, and Sarah Pennington, who rebelled against the laborious and time-consuming process in 1767 was not a lone voice: 'Nothing is more unnatural and tormenting than feeding them (babies) with a spoon that must be taken every minute from their mouths to be replenished'.

Although pap had been used in some form for centuries, the oval boat, shaped like a small shallow sauceboat without feet or handle, made its appearance at the beginning of the eighteenth century. Pap-boats were made in a variety of materials to suit all pockets and tastes. A few gold examples are

Colour Plate 2. An advertisement for Nestlé's Food, c.1890, showing a voluptuous, though decidedly unmaternal-looking mother, mixing some 'Milk Food' in a bowl for her infant. She clearly shows the new spirit of the age, when no mother need 'condemn herself to be a common or ordinary "cow" unless she has a real desire to nurse'. Mary Evans Picture Library.

Plate 38. A mid-18th century pap-boat of Staffordshire salt-glazed stoneware. 1½ in. (3.8cm) high, c.1750.
Colonial Williamsburg Foundation.

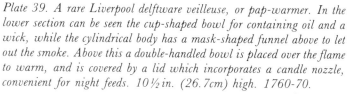

Plate 39. A rare Liverpool delftware veilleuse, or pap-warmer. In the lower section can be seen the cup-shaped bowl for containing oil and a wick, while the cylindrical body has a mask-shaped funnel above to let out the smoke. Above this a double-handled bowl is placed over the flame to warm, and is covered by a lid which incorporates a candle nozzle, convenient for night feeds. 10½ in. (26.7cm) high. 1760-70.
Sotheby's.

known, but silver ones are much more common. The earliest have plain rims, which developed into a reeded wire at the rim for extra strength, which in turn developed into a gadrooned border. Late eighteenth century examples have bright-cut borders, while the more elaborate early nineteenth century examples are moulded with shells and acanthus leaves, and the interiors are often gilt for extra cleanliness. Early hallmarks are generally found near the rim opposite the spout, with later hallmarks at the side. Pap-boats are also found in Sheffield plate, and in pewter, some pewter examples around 1790-1800 being stamped with the initials 'FH', apparently made to raise money by their sale for a Foundling Hospital.

Some recorded makers of silver pap-boats include: William Spackman, 1714; Anthony Nelme, 1718; S. Herbert, 1752; William Sheen, 1767; George Smith, 1782; Thomas Hanwell, 1791; S. Hougham, 1805; John Emes, 1805; William King, 1832. Hester Bateman, Samuel Massey and David Hennell are also recorded as having made pap-boats.

Less expensive pap-boats were made during the eighteenth century in Staffordshire salt-glazed stoneware and in earthenware, which included Leeds creamware. Blue and white printed earthenware from the Davenport, Minton and Spode factories date from the first half of the nineteenth century. These are decorated in typical chinoiserie or pastoral scenes.

Pap-warmers, or veilleuses, as they were called on the continent, were used during the eighteenth and nineteenth centuries to warm up the pap ready for a feed. Porcelain examples were made at Chelsea between 1755 and 1760, but are extremely rare. More common, though still rare, are the Lowestoft examples made between 1760 and 1775 at this provincial east coast factory. They are formed in three parts. The cylindrical body has an opening in the front for the insertion of a small cup or godet, to hold the wick and the oil. The bowl containing the pap fitted above, with flanged sides, and was surmounted by a cover, the knop of which formed a candle nozzle, essential for night-time feeds. Pap-warmers are also found in English delftware and Wedgwood creamware and blue-printed ware. The 1774 Wedgwood Catalogue lists 'Night-lamps, to keep the Liquid warm all night'. Later continental factories also produced pap-warmers.

During the nineteenth century they were replaced by elaborate night-lights which served as feed-warmers also. *The Englishwoman's Domestic Magazine,* 1859, carried 'A Surgeon's Advice to Mothers', stipulating that 'the articles required for the purpose of feeding an infant are a night-lamp, with its pan and lid to keep the food warm, a nursing-bottle, with a prepared teat, and a small pap saucepan for use by day'. The flame from the floating rushlight heated the water in the reservoir above, in which the covered pan, containing the food, floated.

Teething

'Coral . . . is . . . good to be hanged about children's necks, as well to rub their gums, as to preserve them from the falling sicknesse'.
(H. Platt, *Jewel House,* 1653.)

'Corall bound to the neck takes off turbulent dreams, and allays the nightly fears of children.'
(L. Lemnius, *Secret Miracles of Nature,* 1658.)

'Through the house what busy joy
Just because the infant boy
Has a tiny tooth to show!
I have got a double row,
All as white, and all as small,
Yet no-one cares for mine at all.'
(Charles and Mary Lamb, *Poetry for Children,* 1809.)

In spite of the 'busy joy' described in Charles Lamb's verse, the cutting of a baby's first teeth was an event viewed with very mixed emotions by his parents. Even normal healthy children today can find the process of cutting teeth troublesome and painful, with its attendant tummy upsets, snuffles and raised temperatures. Two hundred years ago an attack of diarrhoea or 'the watery gripes', or a high fever accompanied by febrile convulsions, could easily have carried a child off. Added to these problems, scurvy was rife among children, principally due to the lack of fresh fruit and vegetables in their diet. The symptoms, as described by John Arbuthnot, *An Essay Concerning the Nature*

Colour Plate 3. A portrait of Lady Henrietta Stanley (1630-1685), Anglo-French School. She is shown with a coral gum-stick hanging from a white satin ribbon round her neck. The gold mount shows the restraint of the period. She is also wearing a lace-trimmed apron with a bib, and lace-trimmed cuffs over her fashionably ballooned and slashed 'virago' sleeves. A lace-trimmed coif covers her hair, and a single row of pearls completes her sumptuous, yet elegant, appearance, c.1630-31.

Private Collection.

of Ailments, 1731, included 'irritation of the tender nervous parts of the jaw, occasioning inflammation, fevers, convulsions, gangrene, etc.', and these symptoms were, not unnaturally, often confused with the natural process of teething. As a result the whole subject of cutting teeth was approached with considerable trepidation, and *The Female Instructor* or *Young Woman's Companion,* 1815, spoke of teething as an 'evil that sweeps away great numbers; for it is entirely owing to the weakness of their bodies that children cut their teeth with so much difficulty, and that it is attended with fever, convulsions and death'.

Although parents' feelings about teething were ambivalent (it was seen as an important milestone passed when the first tooth was successfully cut), for the baby it involved unmitigated suffering. In 1534, Lady Bryan wrote of her charge, the young Princess Elizabeth, 'God knoweth my Lady hath great pain with her teeth, and they come very slowly forth — which causeth me to suffer Her Grace to have her will more than I would'. To alleviate the pain and allow the teeth to erupt more easily, lancing the gums was a common practice. It was recommended by *The Female Instructor* 'as many might be saved, who daily fall

Colour Plate 4. An early 17th century Dutch school portrait of a child standing in a formal pose, and elaborately dressed in severely adult clothes, clutching a gold-mounted coral teething stick in his hand. The fact that this is a child of high estate is denoted not only by his clothes, but also by the gold chain which attaches his gum-stick to his waist.
Christie's South Kensington.

a sacrifice to those complaints, for the want of it'. However, the methods must be strictly controlled, and readers were urged 'not to depend upon old women, or nurses, who undertake to do it with crooked sixpences and such like ineffectual means'. (A crooked sixpence was said to bring luck, and indeed all crooked objects were thought likely to repel witches or the Devil, hence the need for the interiors of chimneys to be crooked.)

Sometimes leeches could be applied to swollen and inflamed gums to give relief. The parent was warned to take great care with the slippery creatures and to use a leech glass, 'as they are apt to creep down the patient's throat' (*Enquire Within*, 1886). What more terrifying prospect could there possibly have been

Plate 40. A 17th century portrait of the Circle of Van Dyck, showing a young child holding a simple rattle in one hand and a teething stick suspended from a ribbon, in the other. The rattle appears to be of turned wood. Her sleeves are pinned back to save them from spoiling, and she wears a large detachable collar. Her cross-cloth is shown covering her hair. This was a triangular piece of material, tied under the chin or at the back of the head, and worn beneath the coif. Sotheby's.

for an already agonised child save, perhaps, for the remedy of 'an emetic, or enema of salt and water'.

However, less drastic help was at hand. Since classical times coral, which by legend was thought to have originated from the drops of blood which spurted from Medusa's severed head, was held to have magic powers and to ward off evil. Roman mothers hung their babies' cots with strings of coral beads and Mrs Jane Sharpe (*The Midwives' Book,* 1671), recommended that a stick of coral be attached to babies as a protection against evil after baptism. It was also thought to guard against infection, and to change colour with the state of health of the child, turning pale if the baby's life was endangered through illness. It was, therefore, common for babies to be presented with a stick of natural branch coral, mounted in silver, silver-gilt or gold, according to the wealth and status of his family, and to wear it suspended from a red or white ribbon or a chain, round his waist, wrist or neck. Piero della Francesca's painting of the 1470s of the Madonna of Senigallia, shows the Christ child wearing just such a branch of coral, mounted in gold and suspended from a string of coral beads round his neck. Continental and English portraits abound of children holding such sticks from the sixteenth century onwards, and their use was clearly widespread. An imaginary dialogue written in 1580 by Peter Erondell, a Huguenot refugee, describes a mother instructing her nurse, 'You need not yet to give him his corall with the small gold chayne, for I believe it is better to let him sleepe untill the afternoone'.

Such sticks also had a practical purpose. A child could gnaw on the smooth, cool surface of the coral 'gum stick' to exert helpful pressure on the teeth

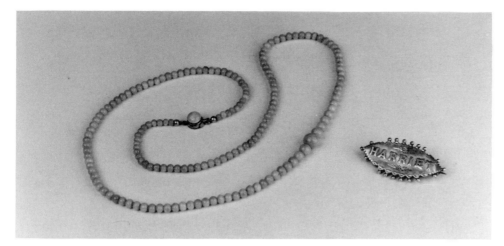

Plate 41. A late Victorian or Edwardian coral necklace of graduated beads, and a silver child's brooch with the name Harriet, Birmingham, 1890.
Private Collection.

attempting to erupt through the painful gums. The design of such sticks changed very little as time went by, with examples becoming, perhaps predictably, more elaborate towards the end of the eighteenth and throughout the nineteenth centuries. A conversation from *Barchester Towers*, by Anthony Trollope, shows that juices could be rubbed on the teethers to make them more palatable. ' "Take his coral my dear", she said, "and rub it well with carrot juice. Rub it till the juice dries on it, and then give it him to play with"... "Not got a coral? How can you expect that he should cut his teeth?" '

As an alternative to coral teethers, strings of teething beads could be purchased. During the shortage of coinage between 1787 and 1797, Basil Burchell of 77 Long Acre gave away copper trade tokens to purchasers of his famous 'anodyne necklace for children cutting teeth', and the tokens were sometimes pierced to be strung along with the beads. For those who could not afford or find Mr Burchell's establishment (from where he also sold 'sugar-plumbs for worms'), such beads could be made at home using the dried roots of henbane and other herbs. These were steeped in red wine, and dusted with 'a dram of red coral, and as much single peony root, finely powdered', before being dried, pierced and strung together. In 1835 when the infant Augustus Hare was sent to his disastrous aunt for adoption at the age of seventeen months, he took with him only two little nightshirts and a coral necklace, and traditionally-minded mothers today still send their little girls to parties wearing a single string of coral beads, little guessing at their ancient origins.

As superstitions regarding coral gradually dwindled away, coral gum-sticks were replaced with silver mounted mother-of-pearl, ivory or bone sticks, often carved in the shape of fishes or cricket bats. (Superstitions lingered longer abroad, however, and as late as the second half of the nineteenth century human teeth were tied to a teething doll, which was supposed to take upon itself the pain of the child). During the latter part of the nineteenth century ivory teething rings were popular, sometimes mounted with a silver rattle or bell, and *The Englishwoman's Domestic Magazine*, 1859, recommended mothers to allay 'the friction of the gums with a rough ivory ring or a stale crust of bread'. During the twentieth century pseudo-ivory teething rings were made in a number of synthetic materials, including celluloid, and Maw's 1868

Plate 42. A Middlesex Copper Trade Token, last quarter of the 18th century. This was used to promote Basil Burchell's 'Anodyne Necklace for Children Cutting Teeth', of which he was the 'Sole Proprietor'. The reverse advertised his 'Famous Sugar Plumbs for Worms', and the edge bears the inscription 'This is not a coin but a medal'. Similar anodyne necklaces were also sold as a remedy for venereal disease, and in Plate V of The Harlot's Progress by William Hogarth a leaflet is seen on the floor promoting their virtues. For decades many 18th century newspapers carried advertisements for a shop at the Sign of the Anodyne Necklace, against Devereux Court outside Temple Bar, where separate necklaces for teething children and syphilitic adults were sold.   Private Collection.

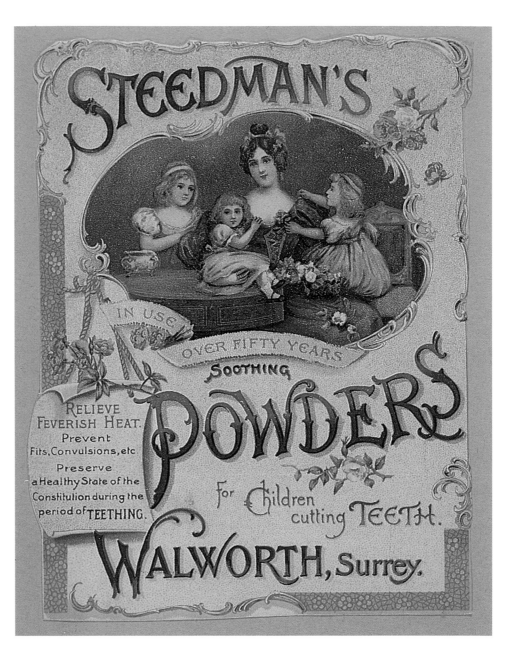

Catalogue advertised 'India Rubber Rings for Children's Gums'.

Little could be done to pacify children left fretful and sleepless from the pain of teething. *The Queen's Closet,* published in 1664, contained a receipt 'To make Children's Teeth come without pain. Proved. Take the head of a hare, boiled or roasted, and with the brains thereof mingle Honey and Butter, and therewith anoint the Child's Gums as often as you please'. By the nineteenth century, patent medicines such as Steedman's Powders or Winslow's Teething Syrup were specifically advertised for the cutting of teeth, and it was common for twenty drops of chloroform to be given to a baby to inhale as his first tooth erupted.

The word 'dummy' was first used in 1845, and in 1901 over sixty different types were being produced, with selling prices ranging from a penny to eleven

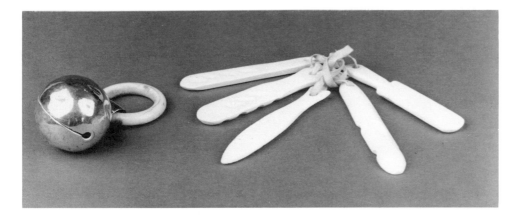

Plate 43. A silver rattle in the form of a globular bell, attached to an ivory teething ring, the silver Birmingham, 1909; and a set of bone or ivory teething sticks, tied together with ribbon, and carved in the shape of a fish, a cricket bat and others.
Private Collection.

Plate 44. A water-colour portrait by Mary Ellen Best, of her son Frank. He was probably between six and nine months old when he was painted in 1841 with his ivory, and probably ebony, teething rings.
Sotheby's.

shillings. Earlier 'pacifiers' had included a 'sugar tit' consisting of a piece of rag enclosing a lump of sugar steeped in rum, or simply a piece of cotton gauze soaked in syrup or honey. In 1859 *The Englishwoman's Domestic Magazine*, edited by Isabella Beeton's husband, Sam, described more dubious means of oral gratification: 'The baby is first indulged with an oyster, the brains of a rabbit, and modicums of toasted cheese, or pieces of pork fat, artfully enveloped in a piece of muslin which, attached to the handle of the cradle by a string, the deluded child may lie and suck, with more than a probable chance of being choked'.

Chapter 5
MEALTIMES

Feeding Bowls and Mugs

'Lord Bless this Food
Which now I take
And make me good
For Jesus sake'
(Embroidered inscription on a nineteenth century linen bib.)

' ''Mama, Why mayn't I when I dine
Eat ham and goose, and drink port-wine?
And why mayn't I, as well as you,
Eat pudding, soup and mutton too?''
''Because, my dear, it is not right
To spoil the youthful appetite.'' '
(Anon.)

Once a child had been weaned from milk and pap, a process which might not have been fully completed until after the age of two, he was introduced to more solid food. The strict Susanna Wesley (youngest of twenty-five children herself, and mother of nineteen, including the evangelical John and Charles), has left us with a description of her children's meals at the beginning of the eighteenth century. 'As soon as they could handle a knife and fork they were set to our table. They were never suffered to choose their meat, but always made to eat such things as were provided for the family. Mornings they always had spoon-meats; sometimes at nights. But whatever they had they were never permitted... to eat of more than one thing, and of that sparingly. Drinking and eating between meals was never allowed'. Breakfast and supper for the young Wesleys was 'broth without bread'.

It is clear, from the evidence that we have, that the diet of most children was inadequate and unhealthy. Knowledge of vitamins and their function was non-existent, and standards of hygiene abysmal. It was of little use for *The Female Instructor,* or *Young Woman's Companion,* to write in 1815 that 'Biscuits, sweet-meats, sugar-plumbs, &c., all which tend to spoil the appetite, are highly improper', when in the same breath, in the same issue, the same 'expert' could propound the following advice on vegetables: 'This food... affords a considerable quantity of slime, which, stagnating in the bowels, serves as a habitation for these little animals' (worms). By the 1880s, the value of vegetables was recognised, and a little 'currie powder' could be added to them if the child was 'flatulent or bilious'.

Fruit had been viewed with grave suspicion in England ever since Eve offered Adam a fateful apple in The Garden of Eden. In Tudor times the sale of fruit was banned in plague years, as the disease was thought to have been carried via the unwashed skins, and maggots in fruit were thought to cause worms in the intestines. *The Female Instructor* cautiously advised that 'Tarts and fruit-pies may be allowed in moderation' along with 'simple puddings'. Scurvy was, not surprisingly, rife and constipation was endemic, punctuated only by the administration of hideous powders or appalling attacks of 'the watery gripes'. The natural laxative qualities of fruit, and the fact that it was generally consumed during the summer when germs proliferated due to the warmer weather, made parents and nurses extremely cautious of giving it to their children. 'From the middle of July to the middle of September, these epidemic gripes of children are so common — that more infants. . . do die in one month than in the other three that are gentle', wrote Dr Walter Harris, in 1693, and as late as 1886 *Enquire Within* was confirming that 'the use of summer fruits appears often to cause most fatal diseases, especially in children'.

Die-hard prejudices against fruit still lurked unchecked at the turn of the twentieth century, and Osbert Sitwell was forbidden by his nanny to eat bananas because she thought they were 'common'. Because the taste of 'forbidden fruit' was so rare, there was no greater treat for children than 'scrumping' apples from a neighbour's orchard, or, in the case of upper-class children, coming down to claim a peach or some grapes during the grown-ups' post-prandial dessert.

By Victorian and Edwardian times the habit of providing inadequate and second-rate food for children had entered the collective sub-conscious, and memoirs of the period abound with descriptions of mutton fat congealed on the luncheon plate, and insipid bowls of bread and milk for supper. Dry bread and milk was breakfast and supper to Charlotte Yonge, and at Castle Howard a hard-boiled egg was cut in half to be shared by two of the children, while Osbert Sitwell described his nursery meals as 'a stodgy eternity of rice pudding' and 'a pale eternity of jelly'.

Knives and forks of small size were made to help children manipulate their food, and the Victorians developed the spoon and pusher to make things even easier. A 'Patent Masticator' was on sale for 2s. 6d. at the end of the nineteenth century to mash-up already mushy food for invalids and small children.

It was not until the beginning of the nineteenth century that plates and mugs began to be made specifically for children. Before that, serviceable and sturdy little mugs in earthenware were made as scaled-down versions of adult examples, with silver ones being given as christening presents. These were sometimes known as 'tooth mugs', not because they were used, as today, as

Plate 45. A group of 19th century earthenware children's mugs. These show a variety of inspiring mottoes such as 'Love and Live Happy', or 'Wish not so much to live long as to live well'. Others were gifts for 'My Dear Boy' or 'A Trifle for William', while some were clearly rewards for virtue. 'Accept this small reward for your Diligence' or 'A Mark of Respect'. Most have printed decoration, while one is decorated with copper lustre. Royal Pavilion, Art Gallery & Museum, Brighton.

part of the teeth-cleaning apparatus, but because they were often given to celebrate the cutting of a child's first tooth. Such an event was viewed with considerable trepidation because of the perils which accompanied weaning, but also as a cause for joy and optimism, since the child had passed another milestone on the dangerous road to adult life.

During the nineteenth century a wide variety of earthenware mugs were given which reflected the attitudes of Society towards children. Many were printed with improving scenes in the robustly naïve style of contemporary children's book illustrations, and showed children involved in acts of charity. Others showed scenes of filial and parental affection beyond the dreams of even the most sentimental Earth Mother, while some were given as Rewards for 'Diligence' or 'Merit'. Yet more had simple, didactic messages of homespun rectitude, 'Love and Live Well', 'Wish Not So Much to Live Long as to Live Well, 'Never Speak to Deceive Nor Listen to Betray' are common examples, while others bore prints illustrating virtues such as Industry or Generosity. Later pieces show scenes from contemporary literature, which has always strongly influenced children's china.

No plates or bowls specifically decorated for children appear to exist before

Plate 46. A small English delftware mug, made in either London or Bristol, the globular body decorated in blue with simply drawn sprays of flowers, in the Chinese style. 3 ¼ in. (8.3cm), late 17th century. Such pieces, which very closely echoed silver examples, would have been in daily use by poorer children, while the more costly silver pieces would have been given as christening presents to well-born children. The squat, globular shape is an eminently sensible one for children's use.
Sotheby's.

Plate 47. A Staffordshire slipware feeding bowl, such as would have been used by a small child, the body inscribed in dark brown and dotted cream slip, with the name IOSEPH and the date 1693. 4 ½ in. (11.5cm).
Sotheby's.

Plate 48. An English delft blue and white porringer, inscribed Mary Miller, 1727. 5in. (12.7cm) wide. Although the titles of porringer and bleeding bowl are liable to confusion, this seems likely to have been used as a porringer, particularly as it bears what is almost certainly a birth date. Such pieces were also made in pewter and silver. Christie's.

the beginning of the nineteenth century. Up until that time small children ate their food from bowls or porringers in cheap and cheerful delftware, thickly-potted slipware, or pewter. Porcelain was reserved for the children of the rich.

Nursery China

From around 1800 the increased publication of children's books, and the belief that children could be educated through all aspects of their daily life, led to some Staffordshire potters producing children's plates with engraved decoration in the centre. Until the mid-nineteenth century the decoration was usually printed in one colour, sepia, black, puce, green or blue, with other colours added later by hand. Printing in more than one colour became popular from around 1850. Some plates were octagonal, the majority circular. The borders were moulded with a wide band of decoration, which included roses and tulips, daisy-heads, animals and insects, fruits, letters of the alphabet, leaves, swags and ribbon bows, and these were often enlivened with bold daubs of colour.

Again, the homespun homilies are found, together with actual quotations from the Ten Commandments, reminding us that this was a time of intense Evangelical activity. Some plates show examples of virtues, such as Attention, Meekness or Politeness, while others show scenes from the Life of Joseph. Others reflect the anxious piety of the age: 'And Can so kind a Father frown/ Will He who stoops to care/ For little Sparrows falling down/ Despise an infant's Prayer'. Engravings adapted from the 1832 edition of Isaac Watts' *Divine and Moral Songs* filled the need for palatable religious instruction at mealtimes, thus nourishing young minds and souls along with bodies. 'How doth the little Busy Bee/ Improve each shining hour/ And gather honey all the day/ From every opening flower'. As in the case of the mugs, good children were rewarded. 'A Present for a Dutiful Daughter' or, less specifically, 'A Good Girl' are typical. Also found are the painfully cloying verses and prints extolling the saintliness of blood relatives, such as 'My Brother' or 'My Grandmother', which were taken from printed sheets published by William Darton Junior, and also used for book illustrations and dissected puzzles. There is even one plate dedicated to 'My Faithful Pony', which would make

Plate 49. Three Welsh earthenware children's plates. Left: The Four Ages of Man, 'Infancy, Youth, Manhood and Old Age'. The printed decoration is picked out in coloured enamels, as is the moulded border, c.1830, marked Baker, Bevan & Irwin, Swansea. Centre: A pearlware plate printed with the inscription 'A Trifle for Jane', probably Cambrian Pottery, Swansea, c.1810. Right: Plate with enamelled and printed decoration, the border moulded with fruit and flowers, the centre with a religious inscription. 'The child that longs to see my face/ Is sure my love to gain/ And thos (sic) that early seek my face/ Shall never seek in vain'.

National Museum of Wales, Cardiff.

Plate 50. Two mid-19th century children's plates, with moulded borders and printed decoration. Left: A somewhat unusual octagonal plate, the border moulded with daisy-heads, and with a print entitled 'Girl Giving Drink to a Thirsty Traveller'. The subject is typical of the Empire-building paternalism, coupled with a strong sense of duty, of the Victorian era. Right: A plate with an uncommon border moulded with a continuous series of hares, greyhounds, a spaniel, a butterfly and a goat. The centre bears a printed scene of a boy seated on his mother's knee and the rhyme 'An Only Son. And Can so kind a Father frown, Will he, who stoops to care For little sparrows falling down, Despise an infants prayer'. Such a verse reflects the anxious piety with which so many Victorian children were instilled, in an age when early death was the norm and Heaven the only hope for grieving parents.

Pauline Flick Collection.

Plate 51(A) (Left). A Staffordshire plate, c.1820-30, printed with a scene showing 'My Brother', and the verse 'At times I own I used to pout, And throw my bread and milk about. Who gave me his, and went without, MY BROTHER'. 6in. (15.2cm). (Right). A mug decorated with an engraving from Mary Belson Elliott's printed sheet 'My Father', published by William Darton Junior, 22nd July, 1811.

Royal Pavilion, Art Gallery
& Museums, Brighton.

(B) (Below). The original printed sheet. Such sheets were pasted onto wood or card for use as 'dissected', or jigsaw-puzzles, or were framed and hung in the nursery to inspire filial devotion.

Sotheby's.

MY FATHER.
by M. Belson.

Who in my Childhood's earliest day,
Before my tongue one word could say,
Would let me with his watch-chain play,
My Father.

Who coaxed me, physic, for to take,
Giving me sugar plums and cake,
If I would drink it for the sake?
Of Father.

When from my Mother's lap put down,
I first essayed to walk alone;
Whose sheltring arms were open thrown,
My Father.

When seated on my Mother's knee,
Who used to play at peep with me
Hiding, where Baby could not see?
My Father.

Who placed me on his foot, to ride
While anxiously my Mother cried,
To hold her Boy, lest he should slide?
My Father.

And as I up to Manhood grew,
Who taught me what was just and true,
As round the fire-side we drew?
My Father.

Who took me in the fields to walk,
And listened to my infant talk,
Making me chains of thistle's stalk,
My Father.

And when my Kite I wished to try,
Who held the string to make it fly,
While pleasure sparkled in my eye,
My Father.

Whose eye, the glistening tear betray'd,
Seeing his Boy was not afraid,
To give a poor black Man his aid?
My Father.

Who bade me never shut the door,
To shun the sorrows of the poor,
Or slight the woes, my power could cure,
My Father.

Should sickness overtake thy age,
My care shall every pain assuage,
And sooth thee, from the Sacred page?
My Father.

If blind, thy smallest wants I'll see
If lame, I'll be a prop to thee,
And every way, thy comfort be,
My Father.

Published February 17th 1811 by Will.m Darton Jun.r 58 Holborn Hill.

68

Plate 52(A). A pair of Staffordshire plates for children, with moulded borders, printed with scenes of a mother and her child taken from the printed sheet 'My Mother' by Ann Taylor. 6in. (15.2cm) diameter, c.1830.   Royal Pavilion, Art Gallery & Museums, Brighton.

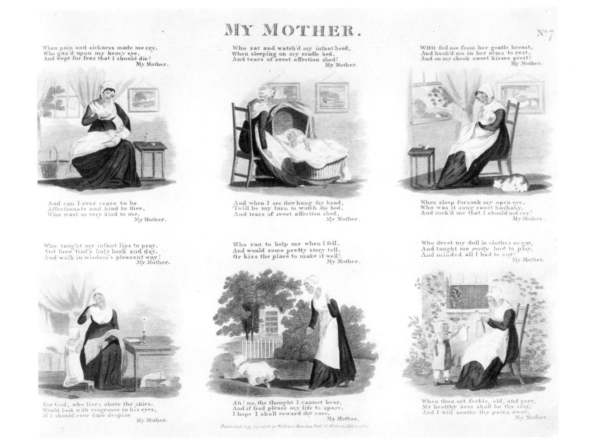

(B). A printed sheet entitled 'My Mother', by Ann Taylor, published by William Darton Junior, imprint dated February 17th, 1812. An accompanying sheet of 'My Father', by Mary Belson Elliott, was also published by William Darton Junior. Such sheets show a sentimentalised idealistic view of family life in a rural setting, in accordance with the Romantic views of the time. They also show the involvement of the mother with her child, including breast-feeding, so much advocated by contemporary child-care writers.   Sotheby's.

Colour Plate 6. A selection of 'Bunnykins' ware, introduced in 1934, and still highly popular today. Described in a contemporary advertisement as 'in fine earthenware of a deep ivory shade', the range was designed by Barbara Vernon, a young nun. She was the daughter of Cuthbert Bailey, who succeeded his father as general manager of Doulton's in 1925, and who recognised the marketing potential of his daughter's anthropomorphic rabbits. Royal Doulton Limited.

even the most enthusiastic supporter of the Pony Club wince with embarrassment. 'To me thou art worth thy weight in gold/ Thy skin is white as driven snow/ Thy pace is not too quick or slow/ MY NOBLE PONY'.

Among the many subjects commemorated on nursery china was the sad death of Princess Charlotte in childbirth, the Coronation of King William IV and Queen Adelaide, Queen Victoria's Coronation, the Birth of the Prince of Wales, and the more mundane 'Opening of the Thames Tunnel between Rotherhithe and Wapping' in 1843. Scenes from the Crimean War were also commemorated, as well as the death of Sir Robert Peel in 1850. By the time of Queen Victoria's Jubilees in 1887 and 1897, cheap commemorative china was being made to appeal to all ages, and was not designed specifically with children in mind.

Makers of relief-moulded plates included Wedgewood (with an 'e' as opposed to Wedgwood); William Smith & Co.; The Stafford Pottery, Stockton-on-Tees, Yorkshire and Edge Malkin & Co., Staffordshire. Some were also made in Swansea, although very few specimens are marked.

By the 1880s these somewhat flimsy plates were being replaced by a more

Colour Plate 7. A selection of Royal Doulton nursery plates, decorated with scenes from the Alice in Wonderland, Nursery Rhymes, Gnomes and Pastimes series. The cartoon trio, bottom left, were Pip, Squeak and Wilfred. Drawn by A.B. Payne, they formed a comic strip which appeared in the Daily Mirror *between 1919 and 1955.* Richard Dennis.

Plate 53. An earthenware child's plate, transfer-printed in underglaze-blue with a boy and girl on a see-saw, and with the legend 'Baby's Plate' on the rim, c.1900, marked Carlton Ware, W. & R., Stoke-on-Trent. Such heavy, thick pieces were eminently suitable for children's use.
Cow & Gate.

Plate 54. A child's hot water plate, c.1925, the printed plate with a pewter base designed to be filled with hot water, to keep the food warm. Cambridge & County Folk Museum.

Plate 55. A late 19th century mug, one of a set of six, made by the Foley China Works, Longton, Staffordshire, c.1896. This is clearly influenced by the work of Kate Greenaway.
Pauline Flick
Collection.

sensible type of bowl for children. With a flat heavy base and straight sides, it was heavy enough not to be hurled to the ground during a temper tantrum, and solid enough to withstand a barrage of attention-seeking raps from a spoon. As a result, many have survived intact, though with some of the coloured printed decoration scratched. Designs included all the popular Edwardian trendsetters, such as Kate Greenaway figures, thundering express trains, Dutch children, seaside scenes, golliwogs, teddy bears, nursery rhymes and Cecil Aldin's dogs. Later appeared the characters of Mabel Lucie Attwell and Louis Wain's cats, who were joined by Doulton's anthropomorphic 'Bunnykins' rabbits, and others. Some of the principal makers included Lawley's Norfolk Pottery, Burslem; Foley Semi-Porcelain; Hammersley & Co., Longton; Grinwade's, Stoke-on-Trent; The Shelley Pottery; Cauldon and many more. Some really crude examples were also imported from Germany.

At about the same time appeared the hot-water plates which were designed to keep food hot on the long journey from kitchen to nursery, and ensured that no food which had been aimlessly pushed around the plate was allowed to remain uneaten because it had 'got cold'. The printed earthenware plate was set into a deeper pewter base, which was filled with hot water through a hole in the side. Such functional plates had been made in China since the last quarter of the eighteenth century.

Since Edwardian times, when a large 'nursery tea' in front of the fire became a ritual, designing children's tableware has been a growth industry, indulged by all the major potters. Doulton's of Lambeth was always at the forefront of nursery design.

In 1903 they introduced a complete tea service decorated with nursery rhymes, designed by William Savage Cooper, a renowned illustrator and

Plate 56. A Shelley nursery teaset, designed by Mabel Lucie Attwell in 1926, the designs adapted from her recently published books featuring 'Boo Boos'. Sotheby's

frequent exhibitor at the Royal Academy. The service was popular in the 1930s, and the biscuit casket, so welcome at nursery tea, was used by Huntley & Palmer to promote their nursery rhyme biscuits.

In 1905 scenes from *Alice in Wonderland* were introduced, and were still in production in 1932. The popular 'Bunnykins' range, depicting scenes in the life of an anthropomorphic family of rabbits, was created by Barbara Vernon, a sweet-faced young nun and daughter of Cuthbert Bailey, general manager of Doulton's from 1925. It is still in production today. Other successes included 'Gnomes', introduced in 1927; 'Into the Land of Dreams', 1919; the 'Pastimes' series, influenced by Kate Greenaway and introduced in 1902; and 'Seaside', 1910.

In 1919 a series based on the cartoon characters Pip, Squeak and Wilfred was introduced. Drawn by A.B. Payne, they formed a comic strip in the *Daily Mirror* between 1919 and 1955. They were vastly popular and had their own fan club known as the Wilfredian League of Gugnuncs.

The 'Pastimes' series was clearly inspired by Kate Greenaway, whose works, including *Under the Window* (1878) and *Book of Games* (1889) were widely read and had a profound influence on children's clothes. Wedgwood and Brownfields also produced nursery tableware based on her illustrations. Rivals used other illustrators. Paragon employed Beatrice Mallett, Hammersley used Tenniel's designs for 'Alice' subjects, and Midwinter employed Heath Robinson to design their nursery rhymes.

Another famous book illustrator whose designs were used on nursery china was Mabel Lucie Attwell. In 1926 Shelley's produced a tea service, the design of which was adapted from her recently published books featuring green elves

Colour Plate 8. A selection of Royal Doulton nurseryware. Top left: *A Gnomes pattern jug (introduced 1927); an Alice in Wonderland bowl and jug (1905); a ewer from a nursery washstand set, 'Into the Land of Dreams' (1919); a Nursery Rhymes biscuit casket in the form of a chest-of-drawers (1903); a 'Pastimes' teapot (1902); and a 'Seaside' jug (1910). Some of the Nursery Rhymes were adapted from designs by William Savage Cooper (1863-1943). He was a frequent exhibitor at The Royal Academy. The biscuit caskets were used by Huntley & Palmer to promote their nursery rhyme biscuits. As large-scale nursery teas became a thing of the past it became the custom once again for children to have just a plate and mug of their own, rather than for a whole service to be ordered for the nursery.* Richard Dennis.

Plate 57. A nursery teaset by Ashtead Potters, c.1930. Each piece is printed with colour designs taken from E.H. Shepard's illustrations for 'When We Were Very Young', 'Winnie the Pooh', 'Now We are Six' and 'The House at Pooh Corner'.   Private Collection.

or 'Boo Boos'. The *Pottery Gazette* rapturously described this as 'a truly irresistible range of nursery ware, altogether in advance of what was usually put before the Trade'. Miss Attwell specialised in a whimsical mixture of stout-legged, rosy-cheeked children with saucer eyes, and coy fairies. The ninth child of a Mile End butcher, she endured a lonely and somewhat neglected upbringing, unromantically retiring to the lavatory to pray that her mother would like her. Her dismal childhood was sublimated in her drawings and her own children. 'All my paintings are the outcome of quaint and beautiful things I have seen at tucking-up time... It is then that I see deep into their little minds, and I am grateful for having the receptiveness of brain to retain the dainty secrets I have seen'.

Chapter 6

FURNITURE

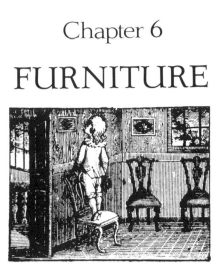

High Chairs

In the sixteenth and seventeenth centuries, high chairs for children were principally made for the child to eat alongside the grown-ups at their table at mealtimes. They lacked the trays or 'playboards' which more modern high chairs provide, and were designed to be pushed hard up to a heavy oak refectory table, thus anchoring the child, who in addition was tied to the chair by his leading strings. A restraining bar was not generally thought to be necessary, but a foot-rest was added, and was adjusted by means of holes in the front legs of the chair.

The earliest surviving examples of children's high chairs, which date from the late sixteenth or early seventeenth century, are massive, heavy oak affairs, often with splayed legs for extra stability. More rarely the high chair takes the form of a small, truncated chair, supported on an adult-sized chair base, which also forms the foot-rest. Panelled examples often have the backs inlaid or carved with a date, initials or other decorative devices, and with carved cresting on the top rails in imitation of adult styles. These chairs are of joined construction with mortice and tenon-joints, and have survived in greater numbers than the turned chairs of the same period which have dowel joints. Turned or 'thrown' high chairs in oak or ash (see Colour Plate 9) are more elegant and fantastic, though they must have been excruciatingly uncomfortable for their small occupants, with their projecting knobs, finials and applied 'buttons'. They were made as virtuoso pieces to reflect the status of the family and the skill of the turner, and definitely not for the comfort of the child.

Another form of joined oak high chair made from the late sixteenth century and throughout the seventeenth for both adults and children had the back, seat and arms upholstered in leather, velvet, or some other rich material. The fabric was secured by heavy brass studs, in a manner used by contemporary cofferers. 'A little chair for a childe, of carnation and green clothe and tinsell', mentioned among the furniture of Robert Sidney, Earl of Leicester in 1588, and valued at twenty shillings, may have been such a piece, the studwork sometimes being replaced with fringeing in metal thread, or braid.

With the development of lighter furniture such as the gate-leg table, high

chairs, too, became lighter and more portable. From the reign of Charles II examples have exuberantly pierced and carved backs, crests and foot-rests, and energetically turned barley-sugar twist legs. During the last quarter of the seventeenth century elegant walnut chairs with canework backs and seats were fashionable. However, these were flimsy and impractical for sturdy toddlers (in spite of the welcome ventilation provided by the canework seats) and few have survived. Some were lacquered in Oriental style, and at Ham House in 1683 were listed 'two chayres for children, the one black and the other japanned'.

During the first quarter of the eighteenth century walnut furniture was all the rage, and some Queen Anne high chairs survive, with sophisticated curves and mellow proportions. The cabriole leg, so popular at the time, did not adapt easily to the high chair, and so styles which would normally have had curved legs look somewhat incongruous as they teeter on long, straight legs. Many an English bulldog of a chair was metamorphosed into a top-heavy greyhound on its journey from the drawing-room to the nursery.

A little later, examples in Chippendale style show chinoiserie fretwork on the legs, although no designs for children's furniture appear in Thomas Chippendale's published drawings. The Hepplewhite style was also reflected in high chairs for children, and these appeared in a wide range of qualities, both urbane and rustic.

Colour Plate 9. An exceptionally fine child's high chair in turned ash, c.1600-30. 42in. (106.7cm) high, possibly Welsh. A virtuoso piece such as this, with loose-turned rings fitted on the back, incised rings and applied 'buttons', reflected the status of the family and the skill of the wood-turner, but must have been supremely uncomfortable for the child. The Shakespeare Birthplace Trust.

Colour Plate 10. A mid-17th century joined oak child's high chair, c.1650, probably made in Gloucestershire. This design closely follows that of an adult panelled chair of the same period. Indeed, the small-size chair has been added to an adult-sized chair base, which projects to form a foot-rest. Such a construction, though not common, is known. Private Collection.

As sets of chairs became fashionable in the dining-rooms of the better-off, so children's high chairs were ordered to match the set. This was particularly true in America, where the more relaxed style of family life meant that children spent more time with the grown-ups in the dining-room and drawing-room, and were not confined for long hours to the nursery, as was the case with English children. The use of restraining bars became more common during the eighteenth century, and was widespread during the more safety-conscious nineteenth century.

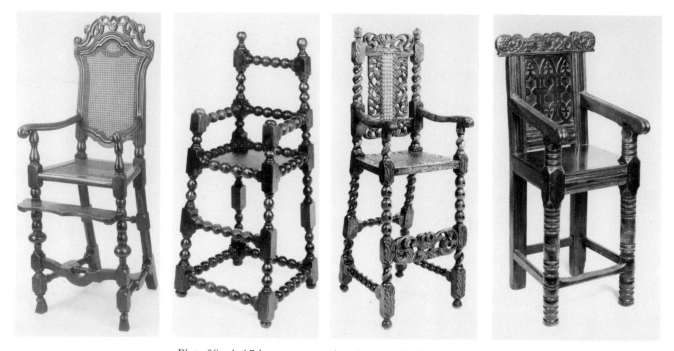

Plate 59. A 17th century carved walnut child's high chair, with caned back and seat and curved foot-rest, c.1680. The carved openwork top-rail is in the bold baroque style of many adult William and Mary chairs. Such pieces were frailer than the more robust chairs made in the reign of Charles II.
Museum of London.

Plate 60. An oak child's high chair, with ball-turned supports and wooden seat, late 17th century. The foot-rest, which in this case is not adjustable, is simply an additional turned bar between the front legs. Even the seat rails are turned in this virtuoso piece.
Christie's.

Plate 61. A Charles II cane and walnut high chair, with exuberantly pierced and carved decoration incorporating crowns and foliate scrolls, absolutely typical of adult chairs of the same period, the legs with barley-sugar twist and ball turning.
Christie's.

Plate 62. A child's early 18th century oak high chair, in the style of earlier pieces, the panelled back carved with Gothic-style motifs, and with the date 1720 carved along the top rail.
Christie's.

Plate 63. A Queen Anne walnut high chair, in the grand manner, with curved arms and foot-rest, upholstered in velvet, early 18th century. 37in. (94cm) high.
Mallett of Bond Street.

Plate 64. One of a rare pair of George III mahogany high chairs, made in the Chippendale style with traces of the Gothick taste in the pierced splats, so fashionable in the second half of the 18th century. The rush seats were a sensible choice for spills and accidents of all kinds, although the unusual boarding above the foot-rests must have come in for considerable ill-treatment from small feet.
Jeremy Ltd.

80

Plate 65. An early 18th century American child's high chair, of simple design, with rush seat.
The American Museum in Britain, Bath.

Plate 66. An early 19th century primitive Welsh stick-back high chair, the comb-back with an uncomfortably narrow seat and foot-rest, c.1820. 39in. (99.1cm) x 14in. (35.6cm). The chair has been painted at a later date. Private Collection.

Plate 67. An American child's Windsor-type high chair, of simple stick-back design. The chair is made of a number of native woods, the seat of white pine, the legs, stretchers and arm supports of maple, and the cresting rail, spindles and arm rail of hickory. Possibly Connecticut, c.1750-90.
Colonial Williamsburg Foundation.

Plate 68. An early 19th century child's high chair in elm and fruitwood, the comfortably shaped seat and spindle back with curved top in the style of contemporary smokers' chairs, which made their appearance c.1825. The height of the seat can be adjusted by means of a screw. The slenderness of the turned legs and the widely splayed position indicate a possible American origin. Christie's.

Plate 69. An early Victorian mahogany and cane bergère chair, on a stand which can be used as a small table. To make a high chair the two pieces are combined by means of a brass thumb-screw which fits into a brass screw-hole in the X-shaped stretcher of the chair, and corresponds to a similar screw-hole in the centre of the top of the table. Sotheby's.

Plate 70. A late 19th century bentwood high chair, with caned back and seat. Designed for comfort and practicality, it has a foot-rest and integral playboard which could be used both at mealtimes and playtime. Its well splayed legs make it extremely stable, an important factor for a piece of furniture designed to hold a sturdy infant. The wheels ensure that it could be wheeled away into a corner when not in use.
Christie's.

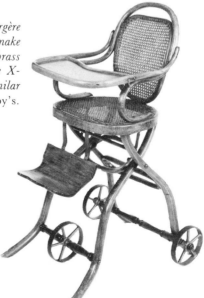

Colour Plate 11. A very fine child's mahogany high chair, with upholstered drop-in seat. The openwork back is of inverted shell form, and carved with flowers and scrolls, the straight, sturdy legs edged with beading, and with a well-worn foot-rest below. 22in. (55.9cm) x 16in. (40.6cm), c.1750. Such a sophisticated piece must have been made to accompany a suite of adult furniture.
Private Collection.

Colour Plate 12. A late Regency mahogany high chair, with elaborately carved cresting rail and top splat. The seat is of cane, no doubt for 'hygienic' reasons, but is covered with a squab cushion for comfort. As with so many 19th century chairs it is fitted with a restraining bar. Like many other chairs of this date it appears curiously unstable, with the legs barely splayed at all, and too fragile for a robust toddler.
Private Collection.

Towards the end of the eighteenth century a new type of high chair was invented. By means of a brass thumbscrew passed through the cross-shaped stretcher of a small armchair, it could, at will, be attached to the top of a small square table to form a high chair. When dismantled, the table and chair could be used separately by the child.

Early in the nineteenth century a rounded mahogany and cane bergère armchair was used in conjunction with a small, square, turned or sabre-legged

Colour Plate 13. A watercolour by Mary Ellen Best of Rosamond and Henry Robinson in their garden at York, 26 July 1833. Their year-old daughter, Ann, who was born in June 1832, is shown sitting in a contemporary high chair, and it is interesting to note that these were used not only at mealtimes, but also for restraining children while out of doors.
Illustration from *The World of Mary Ellen Best* by Caroline Davidson,
published by Chatto & Windus Ltd.

table, and this combination remained popular throughout the nineteenth century. J.C. Loudon illustrates a somewhat plain example in his *Encyclopaedia of Cottage, Farmhouse and Villa Architecture and Furniture,* 1833, and eighty years later J. Eastwood of Prestwich illustrates a similar piece in his *Catalogue,* c.1910, at a price of £1 4s. 0d., in mahogany or walnut. A playboard increased the price by six shillings.

Cheaper and more flimsy high chairs, with cane seats and open or spindle backs, were sold all through the nineteenth century, and were sometimes carved to simulate bamboo. They generally have restraining bars pushed through holes in the arms, and narrow foot-rests. They are usually rickety affairs, with slender and unstable legs. Such pieces, in the style of bedroom or 'ladies tea chairs', appear in Loudon's *Encyclopaedia,* and also in James Shoolbred's *Furniture Designs,* published in 1876, and were often made in stained or painted beechwood.

From the seventeenth, right through the eighteenth and nineteenth centuries, a variety of designs for country high chairs with rush seats and spindle or ladder backs, were adapted for use as children's high chairs. A primitive form of child's chair, found mainly in Wales and its borders, was

Plate 71. A late Victorian illustration showing a child with a baby who is seated in a contemporary high chair, complete with playboard, and mounted on castors for greater mobility. Such chairs were enormously popular, being sold by most of the large stores in various finishes, and often converting to low chairs and tables.
Mary Evans Picture Library.

made by attaching spindles and a top rail to a thick wooden slab which sometimes had its own short, stubby legs, which could stand on its own or be raised to greater heights by being set upon a table or grown-up chair.

Bow-backed wooden-seated Windsor chairs, though more generally found as low chairs for children, or rocking-chairs, were adapted for use as high chairs, one rare type being fitted with a patented base on which a calibrated weighing scale was combined with a spring and handles to enable the child to bounce up and down, perilously but deliciously, and also to be weighed. American examples of the Windsor chair are more slender in design, and with a more pronounced splay to the legs, as is also the case with some Irish examples, which were often painted.

During the second half of the nineteenth century high chairs became more and more complicated and sophisticated. They were featured in many manufacturers' and retailers' catalogues, with a variety of finishes, and often with the word 'Baby' stamped, stencilled, carved or blazoned in poker-work across the back.

The playboard, or attached tray, was a new refinement from the end of the nineteenth century for mealtimes and playtime, and high chairs were at last built for versatility, comfort and practicality. Many models could be converted into several positions, including low chair and table and even a 'go-cart' or rocking-chair.

Wheels ensured that the chair could be conveniently wheeled away into a

Colour Plate 14. An illustration of a child sitting in its simulated bamboo high chair, from At Home, *1881. The child is poking its finger into a piece of bread, by the nursery fire, which is guarded by a typical brass-topped nursery fire-guard. Clearly high chairs were not only used at mealtimes.*
Mary Evans Picture Library.

corner when not in use. Gamages *Christmas Catalogue* of 1913 advertised a 'kindergarten chair' at 11s. 9d. or 14s. 6d., with a pan, while J. Eastwood, of Prestwich proudly displayed a 'Convertible Child's Chair' at 15s. 9d. in his *Catalogue*, c.1910, which could contort itself into four positions. 'The Shuresete', gaining much of its unflinching certainty no doubt from the fact that it was upholstered in 'sanitary leather cloth', was a mass of levers and wheels, and rejoiced in an adjustable foot-rest, playboard, coloured abacus beads and rubber wheels.

Plate 72. *A portrait of Anne, Catherine and Harriet Brydges by Lewis Vaslet, dated 1796. The children are clearly not in their nursery, as the richly patterned carpet and sumptuous armchair show, but a child's table has been provided for their game of cards, and a screen is positioned in front of the door to protect Harriet from harmful draughts.* Sotheby's.

Plate 73. *A portrait of Thomas Smyth, English, early 17th century, standing proudly beside a child's joined armchair upholstered in velvet, with a matching low table. The fluted baluster turned legs are very typical of the date, and the thin overhanging top of the table denotes that it was not made as a stool. However, the use of stools and children's tables was interchangeable at this date.* Leeds Castle Foundation.

Bentwood was used for many high chairs (see Plate 70), and was developed by an Austrian designer, Michael Thonet (1796-1871), who introduced bentwood chairs to England in the middle of the nineteenth century. The height of convenience was illustrated in *The Cabinet Maker's Pattern Book,* published by Wyman in 1877. It was a bentwood high chair with optional commode seat, thus allowing the intake and expulsion of food to be neatly carried out in one sitting.

Low Chairs and Tables

Although many children took their meals seated in high chairs pushed up to the edge of their parents' table, it is clear that from the age of eighteen months or so they also sat at low tables on small-sized chairs to eat and enjoy their playthings. In the 'Litle Dynyng Chamber' at Paget Place in 1552 were listed 'the childrens dynyng table, and 2 squarre little stoles', and in his *Journal* for 24 July, 1732, John Wesley quotes a letter from his mother recounting how she raised her numerous children at the beginning of the eighteenth century: 'At dinner, their little tables and chairs were set by ours, where they could be

Plate 74. A 17th century oak child's stool. Few tables were made specifically for children at this date, and stools often doubled as seats and small tables. Roger Elmesley's Will, *London, 1434, mentions 'a litel tabel peynted trestelwise; also a litel joyned stool for a child', and in the 'Litle Dynyng Chamber' at Paget Palace in 1552 were listed 'the childrens dynyng table, and 2 squarre little stoles'.* Christie's.

Plate 75. A mid-18th century child's side table, the simply turned legs terminating in pad feet, and with a drawer, 17in. (43.2cm) x 18in. (45.7cm). 18th century children's tables are rare, since children usually ate at the table in their high chairs. Sotheby's.

overlooked, and they were suffered to eat and drink (small beer) as much as they would'.

Sadly, few early children's tables survive from the seventeenth century. Early joined oak examples are difficult to distinguish from contemporary stools and indeed the use of the two was certainly interchangeable. Stools were widely used by children, from earliest times, and Roger Elmesley's *Will*, London, 1434, mentions 'a litel tabel peynted trestelwise; also a litel joyned stoll for a child & a nother joyned stoll, large for to sitte on whenne he cometh to mennes state'. Tables proper appear to have had thinner tops, which overhung the legs to a greater depth than in the case of stools, and small children's chairs were made to match, sometimes with backs and seats upholstered in leather or velvet. Home-made boarded Welsh or English chairs, with primitive pierced or carved decoration, were made in rural areas.

Later in the seventeenth century gate-leg tables for children were made in oak, walnut, or fruitwood in imitation of adult examples, and from the eighteenth century drop-leaf and side tables in adult style are to be found. However, the fact was that adult examples could easily be adapted or cut down to make them suitable for children's use, and so purpose-made children's

Colour Plate 15. A William and Mary walnut child's armchair, c.1690, with a typically ornate cresting, carved and pierced in the manner of the period, and with a moulded slat-back, on elaborately turned legs, and with a vigorously carved front stretcher and simple wooden seat, 34in. (86.4cm) high. Private Collection.

Colour Plate 16. A hand-coloured plate from the c.1849 catalogue of Edwin Skull of High Wycombe, showing three children's rocking chairs and a high chair with removable re-straining bar on the right.
High Wycombe Chair Museum.

Colour Plate 17. A mahogany child's armchair, c.1850, with button-upholstered back and seat, typical of high Victorian taste; and a yew-wood Windsor armchair, c.1850.

Private Collection.

tables are rare and hard to identify with certainty.

However, children's chairs have survived in relatively large numbers to this day. Most were made with arms to prevent their occupant from toppling over sideways and falling out, and copied the styles of contemporary grown-up examples. During the eighteenth century, when many English children were segregated from their parents in nurseries for most of the day, fine drawing-room or dining-room chairs for children were much rarer than more crudely made nursery pieces. However, this was not the case in America, where family life evolved along less hierarchical and more relaxed lines, and finer pieces were made for children to fit in with the furniture of the grown-ups, including some upholstered wing armchairs.

Wooden wing rocking chairs were popular from the end of the seventeenth to the beginning of the eighteenth century, and feature in oak, mahogany, walnut, cherry and pine, with the wide skirts of the chairs forming the rockers. They are often found with a hole in the seat to contain a chamberpot, and sometimes with a lid. Decoratively shaped holes in the back form the handles for carrying or suspension. These chairs are found in a wide variety of sizes, to fit children from approximately eighteen months to seven years.

Plate 76. A rustic oak side chair for a child, c.1730, with a shaped crest and a back splat pierced with a design of hearts, and flanked by turned spindles, 34in. (86.4cm) x 17in. (43.2cm). The side drawer may have been used to hold toys, but since adult-sized chairs are also found with such a drawer it seems likely that it was intended to hold a wrapped hot brick.
From the Collection of David Anderson Esq., Welshpool.

Plate 77. An early 18th century American child's armchair, in walnut with walnut veneer, c.1710-30, 30½in. (77.5cm) high. A splendid chair in contemporary adult style, with vase-shaped splat, curved arm-rests and cabriole legs, the tops carved with scallop shells and the seat upholstered in needlework. A good example of a child's piece made en suite with a set of fine adult furniture.
Colonial Williamsburg Foundation.

Plate 78. An American child's walnut chair, of curiously squat proportions, the cabriole legs of an adult chair having been compressed to make a low seat for a child, only 18¾in. (47.6cm) high. The slip seat conceals a fitting for a chamber pot. The chair has suffered several alterations since it was made, c.1760. The original arms have been removed, leaving marks where they would have been. This piece is thought to have been made in the shop of Peter Scott.
Colonial Williamsburg Foundation.

Plate 79. A primitive late 18th century child's chair of ash and elm, 19¾in. (50.2cm) high. This sturdy little piece with its stubby legs emanating from a slab seat could have been stood on a table or adult-sized chair if necessary, to give it height. Sometimes the truncated legs were missing altogether, the wooden slab alone sufficing as a seat.
Sotheby's.

So-called 'Windsor' or stick-back chairs were popular at various centres throughout the country from the seventeenth century, including London, where at least three chair-makers advertised themselves as 'makers of all sorts of "Yew tree, Gothick and Windsor" chairs'. Written references occur from the 1720s. Originally popular for adults at inns and coffee-houses, they were also much used as garden chairs, and were often painted green. Strong, steady, portable and of simple construction, the shaped seat and rounded back made them popular for children, and the design was adapted for low chairs, high chairs and rocking-chairs. They are most often found in beech and yew and were particularly popular in the nineteenth century, as more interest was aroused in rural crafts. Eastlake, that great arbiter of Victorian taste, described them as 'one of the few specimens of honest English manufacture which remains in this country'. The design was also adopted in America, where the

Plate 80. A child's Windsor yew wood chair, probably American, c.1820, 23in. (58.4cm) high. The Windsor chair was one of the most popular styles for children. The wide splayed legs of slender proportions suggest its American origin. Mallett of Bond Street.

Plate 81. A child's version of a smoker's bow chair, the back piece painted with the name Rosamund and dated 1916, the back formed of carved and brightly painted figures of village folk, of somewhat Churchillian appearance. The chair was made as a gift by Ernest Gimson, 18in. (45.7cm) x 16in. (40.6cm). Private Collection.

Plate 82. A George III child's armchair, in mahogany, c.1780. This clearly reflects the contemporary taste in chairs for adults, though with the legs of somewhat sturdier construction than those on a full-size chair. Country styles were infinitely more common than more sophisticated ones for children. Colonial Williamsburg Foundation.

Plate 83. An American child's country chair, of maplewood, with rush seat, c.1760-90. Rush-seated ladder-back chairs were popular for children from the 17th century, being light, stable and easy to wipe clean. Colonial Williamsburg Foundation.

widely splayed legs proved a distinctive feature. The smoker's bow-backed chair was introduced around 1825 for adults. Widely used in offices and kitchens by the end of the century, the shape was also scaled-down for children's chairs.

From the 1840s, when the affluent middle-classes were building showy villas in the suburbs of London and other industrial cities, they ordered children's furniture to match. Well made chairs, and even sofas and couches, in dark mahogany or rosewood, reflected the contemporary bourgeois taste for the solidity and respectability which money could buy, while Berlin wool-work seats and inlaid papier-mâché fulfilled a craving for modest vulgarity. Eastlake wrote disparagingly of 'the upholstering mind', and for many of the *nouveaux riches* the ideals of family life were encapsulated in a drawing-room full of rosy-cheeked children seated by the fire on velvet buttoned chairs, with Papa reading them an improving story, just like the Prince Consort did at Osborne or Windsor.

For the less well-to-do, cane and wicker chairs offered a cheap solution, and the large stores provided a plentiful supply. The Army & Navy Stores *Catalogue* in 1898 advertised children's armchairs for 2s. 6d. and Gamages carried a

Colour Plate 18. A mahogany settee for a child, c.1840, reflecting, in its heavy, solidly-carved mahogany and plump upholstery, the values of early Victorian domestic life. Small versions of single-ended couches were made for children throughout the 20th century. A small couch in Grecian style, made for a girl of two, in 1851, is in the Victoria & Albert Museum, and Gamages showed an upholstered child's couch in their 1913 Catalogue.

Private Collection.

Colour Plate 19. An octagonal inlaid walnut table and eight chairs made for the children of Queen Victoria at Osborne House, their seaside home on the Isle of Wight. Four of the chairs were made c.1846 for the four eldest children, with another four being added around 1854. Each chair has a high back surmounted by a shield inlaid with its small owner's initials. Six smaller rosewood chairs had Berlin woolwork seats embroidered by the Queen's Aunt, the Duchess of Gloucester, as gifts for the royal children during the 1840s.

Reproduced by Gracious permission of Her Majesty the Queen.

Colour Plate 20. A scene of Victorian children at play in a cottage interior by Harry Brooker (fl.1876-1902), signed and dated 1892. The guests at the 'tea party' are sitting on a typical folding chair and four-legged elm stool, of a kind very common during the 19th century in poorer country households. Christopher Cole Fine Paintings.

range of children's basketwork tables and chairs in their 1913 *Catalogue,* from 3s. 3d. to 7s. 9d.

From the latter part of the nineteenth century came small folding chairs for children, often with carpet seats, in the manner of deck chairs, and throughout the nineteenth century small, primitive four-legged stools were used by children in rural areas.

Other Furniture

From medieval times, small oak chests or coffers were used for children to store their clothes and playthings, and Roger Elmesley touchingly bequeathed to his son in his *Will,* London, 1434, 'a litel cofur to putte in his small thynges'. A nursery inventory of 1567 includes 'a chest' and 'a little presser' (wardrobe) for the children's use. Boarded or joined pieces survive from the sixteenth and seventeenth centuries and show a variety of decoration in imitation of adult pieces, which includes chip carving, panelling and cushion moulding. Such

Plate 84. A mid-17th century oak child's chest, simply made, with iron hinges and hasp, and wih two moulded panels for decoration, 16½in. (41.9cm) x 24in. (61cm). Such pieces would have contained the child's clothing and linen. Private Collection.

Plate 85. A child's late 17th century oak chest, the front and sides covered with cushion-moulded panels in a style typical of adult chests of the time, 17in. (43.2cm) x 26in. (66cm). The interior contains a series of secret drawers which would be certain to satisfy a child's natural love of concealment and surprise. Chests of this type are sometimes known as 'mule' chests, the drawer at the bottom being designed to hold 'mules' or slippers. Private Collection.

Plates 86 and 87. A very rare child's clothes press, of painted oak and made in the form of a 'baby' or doll's house. The two wings at each side open to reveal more drawers and shelves, and at the back of the house is space for hanging clothes on pegs. Such a piece of furniture must surely have charmed even the untidiest child to tidy away his clothes. It is dated 1712 and bears the name of its maker, Edmund Joy. 64in. (162cm) high.

Bethnal Green Museum of Childhood.

pieces are now quite rare, and as with tables, adult-sized pieces were often cut down or adapted for a child's use.

One of the most spectacular pieces of furniture made for a child, and unique at that date in the way in which it was constructed to appeal to a child's imagination, is the boarded oak clothes press made by Edmund Joy in 1712 (Plates 86 and 87). Now in the Bethnal Green Museum of Childhood, it is constructed in the form of a late seventeenth century William and Mary house, with Dutch gable ends and classical façade. There are three doors with locks

Colour Plate 21. A fine early 18th century child's walnut veneered bureau-bookcase, the upper part with a mirror set into the door, the lower part with a fall-front above three drawers, and mounted on four turned bun feet, 66in. (167.6cm) x 27in. (68.6cm) x 16½in. (41.9cm). Such fine pieces for children are very rare in England at this date. Private Collection.

Colour Plate 22. A mid-18th century child's bureau, 22in. (55.9cm) x 18in. (45.7cm).
Private Collection.

corresponding to the three sections of the house, the left-hand side containing four shelves, and the right-hand side with four drawers, while the central portion is fitted with wooden pegs for hanging clothes. It is inscribed with the date and the name of the owner in large letters.

English chests-of-drawers for children from the eighteenth and nineteenth centuries are rare, since by that time children were consigned to a life 'above stairs' in the nursery. However, more examples of fine scaled-down furniture for children are found in America, where the quality is sometimes so high that it is difficult to distinguish a child's piece from a cabinet-maker's model.

Desks for children were an important part of the literacy programme, and

Plate 88. A late 17th century child's chest on stand, the deal body decorated in black on a red ground with simulated wood-graining, 48⅜ in. (118cm) high, c.1680-1700. Although of a rather grand and fashionable design, with its 'cup and ball' legs and shaped stretcher, the fact that it is made of deal makes this a sensibly cheap piece for a child, with ample drawer space for his linen and other small belongings. Colonial Williamsburg Foundation.

acted as an encouragement in the dreary letter-learning process. Sixteenth and seventeenth century examples often took the form of table desks, and the style was later adapted for nineteenth century schoolrooms by the addition of legs, with the hinges at the top of the sloping writing slide, and a box-like interior

Plate 89. A late 18th century American child's chest-of-drawers, in cherry wood, with pine drawer linings, probably New England, c.1790. The elegant proportions of this piece confirm the theory that much American children's furniture was of higher quality than English. This was due to the fact that middle-class children mingled far more with adults in the freer atmosphere of 18th century American society, while their English brothers and sisters were confined to the nursery wing, where they had to make do with workaday pieces of furniture. It was only when they were brought downstairs to the drawing-room or dining-room that they had fine furniture made en suite with that of their parents. Colonial Williamsburg Foundation.

Plate 90. An American child's desk in maplewood, the frame and interior of pine, which had originally been painted red. Probably made in New Hampshire, c.1770-1800. 22in. (55.9cm) high, 21in. (53.3cm) wide. Such small bureaux, or 'slant-front' desks as they were known in America, would undoubtedly have been an incentive to literacy, and with their small drawers and pigeon holes would have provided the owner with a delightful measure of privacy and independence denied to most children at that date. Colonial Williamsburg Foundation.

for containing writing equipment and small treasures. During the late seventeenth century the hinges were moved to the bottom of the writing slope, which could then be let down and rested on two 'lopers' at each side, with drawers beneath, and the bureau, which was to remain popular with variations until the end of the eighteenth century, evolved. These were first found in oak, then walnut, and finally mahogany, and in America were known as 'slant-front' desks. Davenports for children became popular at the very end of the eighteenth century and remained in favour for almost one hundred years.

Chapter 7

HEALTH AND 'REGULAR HABITS'

Potty Training

'They (mothers) seem to regard the body as a machine acting upon no fixed principles, and requiring now and then to be driven by some foreign impulse in the shape of medicine. Under this impression they are on the watch to see what they can do to keep it moving, and are altogether distrustful of the Creator's arrangement.'
(Andrew Combe, *Treatise on the Physiological and Moral Management of Infancy,* 1840.)

Before the days of effective bleaches, detergents, disinfectants and washing-machines, the goal of every mother was to instil into her child 'clean and regular habits'. Nappies, or 'tail-clouts' were made of plain linen or linen damask, and were covered with a 'pilch', or thick flannel cloth for extra protection at night. During the eighteenth century an oiled piece of silk was worn over the pilch in an effort to provide a waterproof material, the better to contain 'the disagreeables', as the contents were evasively called. Mary Brudenell, a baby in 1718, was provided with '4 night pilches, 2 dozen and 10 damask clouts', as well as 'a dozen diaper bibs, 5 short stays and 4 lace skull caps', in her layette. A layette of 1825 included six dozen nappies, to ensure that there was always an adequate supply of clean linen, and the immortal words of Mrs Balfour, 'A dirty child is the Mother's Disgrace', echoed in the ears of every parent as a terrible warning of doom and social embarrassment.

John Locke, writing at the very end of the seventeenth century, advocated the idea of telling a child to 'go to stool' at the same time each day to encourage regularity. This was no easy matter when children were denied fresh fruit and vegetables in their diet. Fruit was thought to spread the Plague during the sixteenth and seventeenth centuries, and was later thought, as were vegetables, to be a source of worms in children, because of the maggots and caterpillars which they sometimes contained. The incidence of summer diarrhoea further reinforced the suspicion with which fresh fruit and vegetables, so plentiful in the summer months, were regarded. By the nineteenth century this diet had successfully ensured that the nurseries of England were crammed with children blocked solid with constipation, which was treated with dreaded home-made

Plate 91. A simple Scottish rocking commode chair for a child, of late 18th or early 19th century date, still fitted with its original wooden chamber pot, and with another wooden pot shown alongside. The carrying handles of these chairs are often cut in decorative shapes, such as hearts.
By permission of Birmingham Museums and Art Gallery.

Plate 92. A mid-19th century ash and elm Windsor-type rocking chair, with a hole for a potty in the middle of the seat. Anon.

suppositories made from soap sticks, or enemas of soap and water, helped along by loosening draughts of castor oil washed down with peppermint water. Some remedies were not merely unpleasant, but potentially lethal. Calomel, which was described in *Enquire Within Upon Everything,* 1886, as 'A useful Laxative for Children', was a compound of mercury which is, like arsenic, a cumulative poison.

An unhealthy pre-Freudian obsession with the bowels and their workings was happily perpetrated by nurses and other 'experts'. In 1848 Dr. John Ticker Conquest, *Letters to a Mother,* stated that 'an infant may be brought at a very early age to be so cleanly as to go without any guard, if regularly put on a chair, or if a little pan be placed under it as it lays on the lap'. Andrew Combe recommended permanent watchfulness as 'an attentive nurse can generally discover some indications of what is about to begin and take measures accordingly'. Edward Mansfield Brockbank wrote in 1912 that babies of two months old were to be placed on the pot and 'encouraged' by the nurse. This included 'tickling the anus, or introducing just inside the rectum a small cone of oiled paper, or a piece of soap, as a suggestion of the purpose for which the infant is placed on the chamber'. Henry Ashby, in *Health in the Nursery*, 1898, urged mothers with an almost missionary zeal that 'the stools of the infant should always be carefully watched, as important information... may be gathered from careful and continuous examination'. It is, perhaps, small wonder that the psyches of so many infants were later thought to have been stunted by so much eagle-eyed parental absorption, coupled with the relentless pressure to go on to bigger things.

Small 'close chairs' for children were used from the seventeenth century, or even earlier, with a hole in the middle of the seat to hold a chamberpot. Such chairs are often found as small, wing rocking chairs, with a hole cut in the back to form a carrying handle. No doubt the motion of rocking was thought to be conducive, and occasionally an aperture is found for inserting a hot brick, so that the small occupant would not get cold during what might be a long wait.

During the late eighteenth and nineteenth century Windsor-type rocking chairs came into fashion, and the style was often adapted for children, either as close chairs, high chairs or low chairs.

Sadly the original chamberpots are almost always missing, although some examples exist in pewter or even wood. An inventory of 1688 lists a

Plate 93. A Bristol delft child's chamberpot, 4¾in. (12cm) wide, c.1730-40. Ceramic chamberpots, particularly those made for children, are rare before the 19th century, though examples in Staffordshire salt-glazed stoneware exist. Sunderland lustre examples are fairly common, as are later earthenware pieces with transfer-printed decoration. Christie's.

chamberpot among the nursery silver of the young Prince of Wales. Delftware, salt-glazed stoneware or creamware chamberpots from the eighteenth century are rare, but a number of transfer-printed and lustred examples exist from the nineteenth century for children. Towards the end of the nineteenth century, composition rubber seats were being used to fit onto potties, in order to take the chill away from sensitive young backsides.

Medicines

'Lullaby, oh Lullaby!
Fie, you little creature, fie!
Lullaby, oh lullaby!
Is no poppy-syrup nigh?
Give him some, or give him all,
I am nodding to his fall!'
(Thomas Hood, 1799-1845.)

For loving parents, childhood must have been a time of protracted suspense, when almost all children's illnesses were potential killers. As late as 1900 the advertisments for Fenning's Fever Cure in *Our Nursery Book* were issuing the horrid warning, 'Do not Untimely Die', to mothers and nurses already anxious about their small charges. Without the aid of antibiotics, safe analgesics or adequate disinfectants, even ordinary childhood infections such as measles, croup, or scarlet fever all too often proved fatal, and diagnosis was often a matter of guesswork. Parents suffered paroxysms of anxiety over the more serious infectious diseases such as smallpox, diphtheria and typhus, and the vitamin deficiency diseases of scurvy and rickets were rife. Vaccinations came late, and remedies were, at best, harmless, if ineffectual, and, at worst, tragically misguided. John Aubrey's seventeenth century *Cure for Thrush in Children* directs the mother to 'Wrap a live Frog in a Cloth and place it under the child's mouth until it (the frog) is dead'. The cloth was to prevent the child from swallowing the frog and dying from a 'frog in the throat', the origin of the well-known expression.

Another dreadful remedy involving live creatures was the practice of applying leeches to the afflicted parts, sometimes for as much as three days. First recorded in the second century B.C., these blood-sucking parasitic worms were kept in glass or pottery jars full of water, covered with muslin or gauze, and left in a darkened room until they were needed. Pharmacists often put the fresh day's supply in specially decorated jars. Leeches were used right up until the end of the nineteenth century. Byron's mother spoke distastefully of the 'perpetual leech', and they were thought to ease most childhood complaints. Catarrh, or 'the malignant snuffles', called for a leech to be placed on the nose, and croup for eight leeches on the windpipe. Leeches were set to the abdomen and rectum in 'the watery gripes', and small girls with urinary infections had insult added to injury, in the shape of two leeches placed on the vulva. If the leech was too voracious, a pinch of salt forced it to drop off.

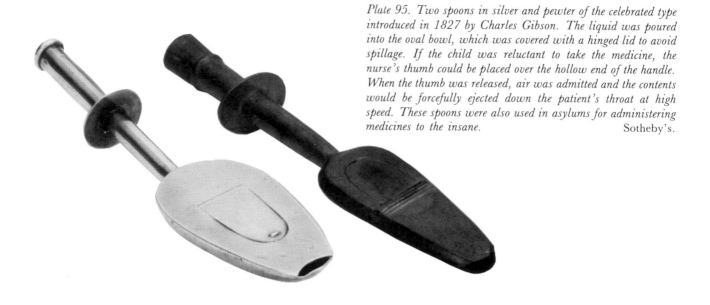

Plate 95. Two spoons in silver and pewter of the celebrated type introduced in 1827 by Charles Gibson. The liquid was poured into the oval bowl, which was covered with a hinged lid to avoid spillage. If the child was reluctant to take the medicine, the nurse's thumb could be placed over the hollow end of the handle. When the thumb was released, air was admitted and the contents would be forcefully ejected down the patient's throat at high speed. These spoons were also used in asylums for administering medicines to the insane.   Sotheby's.

Laxatives and aperients were given at the least sign of a sluggish system, as well as to empty the system after a dose of more serious medicine. Epsom salts and castor oil were great favourites with Victorian parents, though children clearly found them less attractive.

There can be little doubt that most medicines tasted filthy, though things had improved since the seventeenth century, when powdered crabs' claws and ground-up earthworms and snails' shells were incorporated into children's medicines. The cure for a sore throat included 'burnt Alum, the yolk of an Egge, powder of white Dogsturd and some Honey' applied to the throat.

The nineteenth century still had a long way to go. During the 1830s children's tonics included 'steel wine', which was made from two ounces of iron filings 'digested' in two pounds of sherry for a month, and the 'grey powders' of Victorian nurseries were notorious.

Needless to say, the formidable Susanna Wesley had no trouble in impressing her will on her young. 'When any of them was ill there was no difficulty in making them take the most unpleasant medicine. . . for they durst not refuse it, though some of them would presently throw it up'. For the less purposeful mother dosing a child could mean a long and tearful struggle, with a mess of spilt medicine or worse to clear up at the end.

In 1827 help arrived in the form of Charles Gibson's medicine spoon. Made in silver, pewter, Britannia metal or pottery, this device had a hinged lid to cover the bowl, which opened for filling and left a small hole free for administering the medicine. Halfway down the hollow stem was a flange which was covered by the mother's thumb. When this was released, air was admitted and the noxious liquid squirted at high speed down the reluctant victim's 'little red lane'. The use of these spoons rapidly increased, and they were advertised by Maw's in their 1832 *Catalogue* in three sizes, as well as by Dixon of Sheffield.

By the middle of the nineteenth century dosing children had become a national pastime, generally to ensure 'regular habits' on the part of the child, or a good night's sleep on the part of the nurse. 'As soon as she is seated before the fire, she makes up a vicious compound of sugar, water and gin, and complacently proceeds to administer her *nostrum* in teaspoonfuls, wondering in

Plate 94. A group of medicine spoons in silver and pottery including (second from top) the Gibson spoon and (at bottom) an earlier variant, c.1810-60.   I. Freeman & Son, Simon Kaye Ltd.

an hour after, what can have given baby the wind as, with a hiccup that jerks its head forward as if galvanised, the infant expels in spasms the engendered gas from its abused stomach', wrote the 'expert' disparagingly in 'A Surgeon's Advice to Mother' in *The Englishwoman's Magazine,* 1850.

Far more dangerous and sinister were the infant preparations containing morphine or laudanum, which were given to quieten children's screaming and lull them rapidly into a deep sleep. These compounds, which included Godfrey's Cordial, Dalby's Carminative, McMunn's Elixir, Batley's Sedative Solution and Mother Bailey's Quieting Syrup were freely available over the counter from chemists. Some contained as much as half a grain of opium per ounce, and in 1843 such was the demand for Godfrey's Cordial that one pharmacist alone made up thirteen hundredweight of treacle in the elixir. In the same year, 1,600 families in a Lancashire town, where the mothers were forced out of necessity to work in the mills, were regular users of the Cordial. Dr. Hume had claimed in 1776 that it was responsible for the deaths of thousands of infants. Lazy wet nurses looking for a quiet life would rub syrup of opium onto their nipples, and an American physician commented acidly that 'elixirs and syrups... as administered whether by deluded mothers or crafty nurses, have *soothed* many and many a luckless infant into that state of *quiet* that knowns no after-disturbing'. It was for Benjamin Disraeli, in his novel *Sybil,* published in 1845, to help expose on a wider scale the scandal of drug abuse among nurses, who were paid to look after the children of female factory workers during the Industrial Revolution. 'The expense is not great'; he wrote with chilling calm. 'Laudanum and treacle, administered in the shape of some popular elixir, affords these innocents a brief taste of the sweets of existence, and, keeping them quiet, prepares them for the silence of their impending grave. Infanticide is practised as extensively and legally in England, as it is on the banks of the Ganges'.

Chapter 8

SLEEPING

Cradles

'As soon as the child is born it must be swathed; lay it to sleep in its cradle and you must have a nurse to rock it to sleep.'
(Walter de Bibblesworth, late 13th century.)

'Set on the coverlet, now put him in his cradle and rocke him till he sleepe but bring him to me first that I may kisse him; God send thee good rest my little boykin. I pray you Nurse have a care for him.'
(Peter Erondell, 1580.)

The importance of a cradle in the life of a baby cannot be over-emphasized, and his whole pattern of waking and sleeping revolved around this one piece of furniture.

It is difficult for us to imagine the extreme discomfort in which a swaddled baby found itself. Itchy, sore, pricked with pins and stiff with excrement, and denied even the basic movements of kicking, stretching or sucking its thumb, the only way in which he could gain a few hours sleep was by being rocked constantly to and fro. The soothing motion of the cradle lulled him into blessed oblivion, and Susanna Wesley, mother of John and Charles, writing in 1732 of her children's upbringing at the beginning of the eighteenth century, describes the daytime routine. 'The first quarter commonly passed in sleep. After that, they were, if possible, laid in their cradle awake, and rocked to sleep, and so they were kept rocking until it was time for them to awake. This was done to bring them to a regular course of sleeping, which at first was 3 hours in the morning, and 3 in the afternoon; afterwards 2 hours, till they needed none at all'.

Rocking the cradle was clearly a serious business, and N. Brouzet in his *Essai sur l'éducation médicinale des enfants, et sur leurs maladies*, Paris, 1754 (English translation 1755), offers four pages of advice on the rocking of cradles. Rockers, women who were employed for the purpose, assumed considerable importance in the life of the household following a birth, and were often expected to work in shifts due to the long hours demanded of them. After the birth in 1598 of Margaret, second daughter of James I and Anne of Denmark, the doting father ordered a new cradle with four matching stools for the four

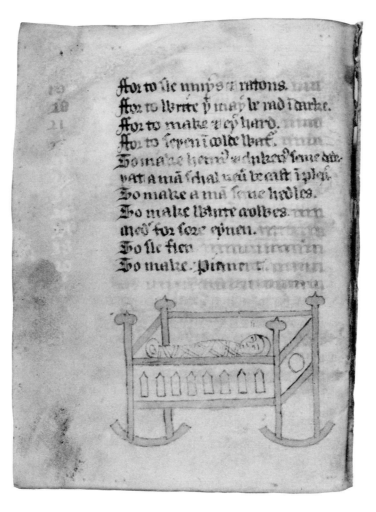

Plate 96. A detail from a late 15th century English manuscript, showing a swaddled baby encased in its Gothic-style cradle.
Sotheby's.

rockers, along with a chair and footrest for the baby's nurse. The cradle was, in medieval times, the perquisite of the rocker, and this may account for the lack of cradles in inventories of the time. However, not all rockers lived up to the trust which was placed in them, and in 1783 Georgiana, Duchess of Devonshire, kept her baby in bed with her and dismissed the rocker when it was discovered that she was dirty and drunk. In poorer households various members of the family took turns to rock the baby, the wooden turned finials which most cradles provided being ideal for the purpose, as well as for winding wool in quiet moments, airing swaddling bands, or tying on 'sugar teats' or other unsuitable morsels of food to keep the occupant quiet while the mother got on with her work.

Numerous superstitions surrounded the cradle and its inmate. It was common for a piece of iron, or some salt to be concealed in the cradle in an effort to ward off the power of evil, and cradles were always supposed to be set near the fire so that the light from the hearth would reveal any evil person or thing which approached. Such a practice could be lethal. Tragically, in January 1658, John Evelyn's 'deare son' was 'suffocated by ye women and maids that tended him and cover'd him too hot with blankets as he lay in a cradle near an excessive hot fire in a close room'.

From medieval times the children of the nobility had two cradles, one a state cradle for daytime use, and another, smaller, for night-time use. These were

richly carved and painted, decorated with gold and silver, and were really miniature versions of the great state beds in use at the time. A cradle of this kind, the earliest surviving in England, is in the Museum of London, and known as King Henry V's cradle. It consists of two upright chamfered posts mounted on trestle feet, and the oak box-like body of the cradle is suspended from iron hooks and rings. It is thought to date from the late fifteenth century and seems to follow closely the 'litell Cradell of Tre' mounted 'on a Forme' which is described in a fifteenth century manuscript in Leland's *Collectanea* (1522), under the heading 'Things that must be had for the Prince's Boddy'. The woodwork of the cradle was to be 'imbroderyd and paynted with fyne Goulde, and devised', with four 'Pomelles of silver and gylte' and five 'Bokelles of silver on eyther side the cradle without Tonges, for the swadle Bands'. (These ensured that the ends of swaddling bands could be passed through the holes in the side and secured to prevent the bedclothes from falling off or, worse, the baby being tipped out during a session of particularly vigorous rocking.) The larger 'Cradle of Estate', described in the manuscript, was to be 'coveryd with crymson cloath of Goulde' and to have pomells or finials 'gylte with the King and Queen's Armes'.

By the seventeenth century most cradles were mounted on wooden rockers, and the swinging cradle had, for the time being, fallen from fashion. Many of these seventeenth century cradles still exist in oak, of joined construction and rectangular box shape, with flat or pointed hoods at one end. These served to protect the baby from draughts and are often shown in contemporary paintings with the bed-clothes thrown over them, either for extra warmth, or in an effort to air the clothes. Sometimes the hood was hinged to allow the baby to be easily lifted in and out, and occasionally a hinged recess at one end would have

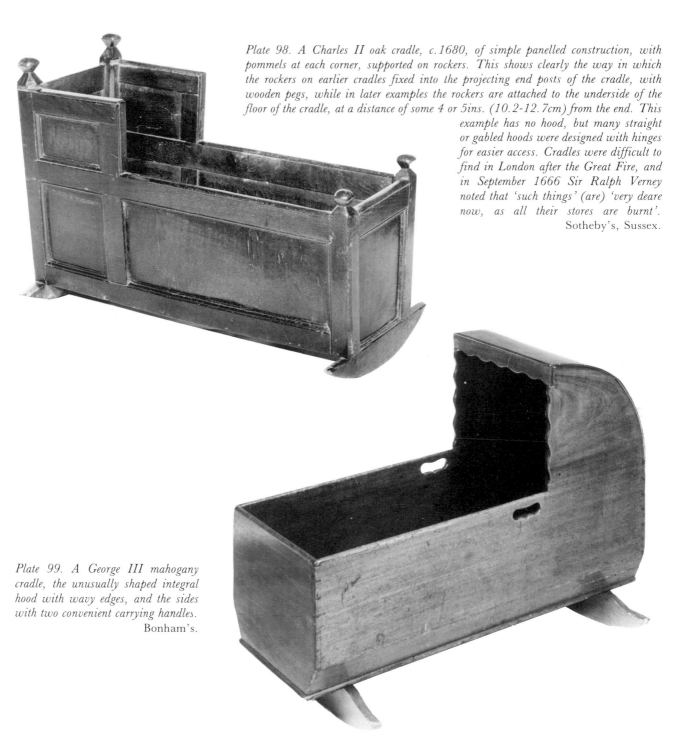

Plate 98. A Charles II oak cradle, c.1680, of simple panelled construction, with pommels at each corner, supported on rockers. This shows clearly the way in which the rockers on earlier cradles fixed into the projecting end posts of the cradle, with wooden pegs, while in later examples the rockers are attached to the underside of the floor of the cradle, at a distance of some 4 or 5ins. (10.2-12.7cm) from the end. This example has no hood, but many straight or gabled hoods were designed with hinges for easier access. Cradles were difficult to find in London after the Great Fire, and in September 1666 Sir Ralph Verney noted that 'such things' (are) 'very deare now, as all their stores are burnt'.
Sotheby's, Sussex.

Plate 99. A George III mahogany cradle, the unusually shaped integral hood with wavy edges, and the sides with two convenient carrying handles.
Bonham's.

allowed a hot brick wrapped in a cloth or a warming-pan, to be inserted to warm the interior. In some cases children slept in a cradle until they were three or four years old, and so a wide range of sizes can be seen in existing examples.

Many cradles are elaborately decorated with panelled sides, sometimes inlaid with foliate and other designs in different woods, or carved in low relief with lozenges, flowerheads or scrolls. Initials and dates sometimes appear. The earlier slits in the sides which took the 'bokelles' for the swaddling bands, were replaced by knobs for securing the bedclothes. In seventeenth and eighteenth century cradles the end posts of the body project downwards, with slits to take the rockers which are fixed up into them. The rockers of later cradles are

simply fixed to the bottom of the cradle 'box', and there are no end posts. Cradles altered little in shape throughout the eighteenth century, though they were generally plainer, with fielded panels and little or no carving, and were made by joiners and carpenters. Thomas Fenton, an Edinburgh merchant in the seventeenth century, supplied fine cradles at four guineas each, but less distinguished pieces were made by local carpenters.

Throughout the eighteenth century pine cradles proliferated, and a little later, mahogany. The cheaper pine pieces were often painted or stained, or grained to imitate oak. Cradles covered in hide, or velvet, studded in brass, or edged in fringeing, were known since the seventeenth century, and were made by cofferers in the same style as contemporary chairs. Such a velvet-covered cradle, now very rare, can still be seen at Badminton House.

During the nineteenth century, the box-shape of the cradle with straight

Plate 102. Pamela Tells a Nursery Tale. *A painting by Joseph Highmore, executed in 1744, as an illustration to Samuel Richardson's novel* Pamela, *or Virtue Rewarded, published 1740-41. Pamela, a virtuous and beautiful lady's maid, is shown after her eventual marriage to her rakish employer in the role of devoted mother. In the foreground is a wicker cradle on rockers, of a type which had been popular since Tudor times. Light and cheaply made, they could be burnt in cases of infection, and easily replaced. John Evelyn records that 17th century cradles were made of plaited lime twigs by rural householders.*

Syndics of the Fitzwilliam Museum, Cambridge.

Plate 103. *A 19th century wicker cradle, in willow. Such cradles, which were often mounted on wooden rockers, or even on wheels, were light, portable and cheap, and the wicker sides provided good ventilation.* Towneley Hall Art Gallery and Museums, Burnley Borough Council.

sides, was replaced by slanting sides, which gave a more fashionable, though somewhat ominous, 'sarcophagus' shape to the cradle, reminiscent of contemporary wine coolers and tea-caddies.

From earliest times basket-work or wicker cradles have been known, and the word cradle derives from the old High German word 'kratto', meaning a basket. Not many now exist due to their fragility, but their use was clearly widespread. Being light, portable and airy, they could also be easily burnt and cheaply replaced in the case of an outbreak of infectious disease. John Evelyn

Plate 104. A portrait by William Hogarth of Gerard Anne Edwards Hamilton in his cradle. This painting, from the first half of the 18th century, shows in the most lively way a baby boy seated in his wicker cradle, which is draped with yards of quilted fabric. In 1717 Lady Grisell Baillie bought 'white Indian quilting' at 4s. 6d. and 5s. 6d. per yard, although it was also laboriously stitched at home by proficient needlewomen. Because of its warmth and durability, it was also much used during the 18th century for clothes, particularly petticoats, and Lady Grisell's infant grandchild had a specially quilted gown included in its linen, which altogether cost almost £200. The rather large doll shown in the painting is contained in a contemporary 'going-chair'.

The National Trust, Upton House, Bearsted Collection.

noted that rural householders made cradles out of plaited lime-twigs, and eighteenth century accounts contain numerous references to wicker cradles. Catherine Naish supplied several such cradles for the children of George III. In 1766 she charged £13 2s. 'ffor a superfine split wicker Cradle very large, a pair of neat mahogany Rockers to do. with Carved Roses', and she supplied another the following year at the same price. Loudon, in his influential *Encyclopaedia of Cottage, Farm and Villa Architecture and Furniture*, 1833, the vade-mecum of the middle-classes, describes a wicker bassinet as being in use for babies up to one year old. It was 'two feet and a half long, the frame of which is made of wicker work, with a hood which falls backwards or forwards as required. It is generally lined with printed furniture, or sometimes with dimity to keep out the draught... a hair mattress stuffed very soft, and a small down pillow complete the bed.'

Early descriptions of bedding for cradles record only the finest examples. Margaret of Flanders, aunt of Edward IV, bought from Jehan de Neauville, a Paris draper, an amazing coral-coloured counterpoint (or counterpane) for her children's cradle. It was embellished with 1,200 ermine skins by a furrier. The Durham Priory Inventory of 1466 lists a quilt embroidered with the four

Plate 105. A 19th century watercolour by John Henry Henshall, showing a child watching his sleeping baby brother or sister. A cane rattle lies discarded on the floor, and the bellows resting on the end of the cradle indicate that this is a fireside scene. There was a tradition that babies' cradles should be placed near the fire as this was very often the only source of bright light in a dark room, which would prevent witches or evil fairies snatching the baby away unseen. Sotheby's.

Evangelists. The rhyme which has been used as an incantation against the evils of the night for many centuries, 'Matthew, Mark, Luke and John, Guard the bed that I lie on', has traditionally been associated with children, and similar quilts may have been made for the cradles of infants. The 'View of the Wardrobe Stuff of Katherine of Arragon' describes bedclothes for a cradle which was probably used for Mary I after her birth in 1516. They include a colourful 'counterpoynte' (counterpane) 'for a cradille paned of yalowe clothe of golde and crymsene velvette lyned with grene bokerhame, havinge single valaunce fringed with blewe and red silke'.

More prosaically, mattresses covered with holland cloth and 'filled with wulle' were also listed. The Shuttleworths of Gawthorpe bought twelve yards of frieze 'for cradle blankets' in January 1613, and in the 1620s the steward at Naworth paid 28s. 7d. for a red flannel cradle cloth with gold lace 'for Mr. Thos. Howarde's child'. A more sumptuous cradle belonging to Charles I and sold after his death was 'covered with carnation vellvet', and realised £3 10s.

Quilted material was very popular during the eighteenth century for bed-covers for both adults and children, and for articles of clothing such as caps, petticoats and stomachers. Either linen or satin could be quilted according to the use required. Two layers of material were sewn together laboriously by hand with running or back stitch often with a layer of cotton wool or down sandwiched between the two layers for extra warmth and padding. Lady Grisell Baillie sensibly bought quilting by the yard in 1717 for her daughter's clothing, at a cost of 4s. 6d. or 5s. 6d. a yard, though many women preferred to do their own work or entrust it to their household servants. It was a laborious and time-consuming process, and outworkers sometimes used as many as fifty stitches to the inch, since they were paid for the thread used rather than the area covered. Quilts have remained popular for children's cots and cradles up until the present day.

A variety of materials formed the mattress, wool being used in some cases, but more usually a straw mattress was placed over a layer of rushes, followed by a sheet or pillow. (Mary Verney wrote to her steward in 1647 and urged him 'to speak to Mrs. Allcock to lett the nurse have a cradle; one of the worst will serve her turne and a hard pillow'.) The rushes could be changed every day, and the mattress refilled as required when it got dirty, but the straw must have prickled and scratched the tender skin of a young child. In 1803, Dr. Buchan in his *Advice to Mothers,* suggested using bran as a filling for the mattress, and this may have been some small improvement.

With the pronouncements of Jean-Jacques Rousseau, the guru of the Age of Enlightenment, *Emile,* 1762, that 'it is never necessary and often harmful to rock children in the cradle', and that swaddling bands must be abandoned, the old-fashioned cradle on rockers gradually fell from favour. Babies were to be allowed to tire themselves naturally, by kicking and stretching with their limbs free, by crawling 'animal-like' on all fours at the right age, and by having access to as much fresh air as possible. The role of the mother was to become more important, and babies were to be stimulated by play and contact with the outside world. Touch and response were vital as the baby's awareness was awakened, and the employment of lethargic nursemaids was a fashionable taboo. 'Banish far the lazy cradle', thundered Hugh Downman, in his 'Didactic Poem', *Infancy, or The Management of Children,* 1774-76. It was 'useless but to give Relief to th'indolent attendant race'. Although some writers acknowledged that the cradle had its uses, many echoed the sentiments of Michael Underwood in his *Treatise on the Diseases of Children,* London, 1789. when he described that he abhorred the violent rocking which led babies to be 'jumbled in the cradle like travellers in a mail-coach'.

Cots, Cribs and Bassinets

Babies. . . 'when they cry or feel Pain, or will not sleep, are to be pacified. . . by singing or by rocking in cradles or hanging beds.'
(The Lady's Delight, 1815.)

Although they had dipped in and out of use, the earlier Gothic type of swinging cot, suspended from two upright posts, or standards, came well and truly back into fashion towards the end of the eighteenth century, when elegant mahogany furniture was popular. This coincided conveniently with the widespread abandonment of swaddling bands, so that hours of rocking were no longer needed, or approved of, to comfort a fractious and uncomfortable infant.

Sheraton's *Cabinet Dictionary,* published in 1803, showed an illustration of 'a

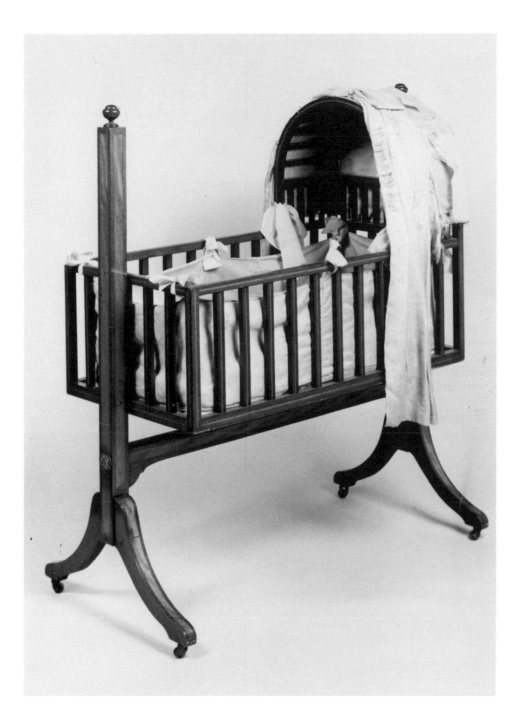

swinging crib bed', a name 'given to the swinging beds lately contrived to lull infants to sleep with'. This elaborate crib or cot had splendid draperies falling from a domed hood like a *baldacchino*. A clock spring was hooked onto 'an iron center screwed to the standard', and by this device (which Sheraton borrowed from a Mr Holinshed, or Holinshade, bedstead maker of 56 King Street, Long Acre), the cot was able to swing by itself. An example in the Victoria and Albert Museum can swing for twenty minutes, and Mr Holinshed had promised a device which would, in time, swing for one and a half hours. Such a style of cot was eminently suited to the emergent neo-classical taste, and

115

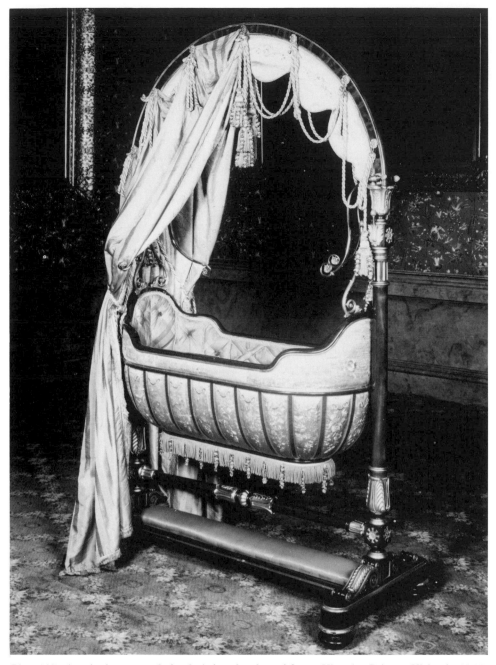

Plate 107. A swinging cot made for the infant daughter of Queen Victoria, Princess Vicky, in 1840. The boat-shaped body has padded mahogany ribs, and is opulently upholstered in buttoned green satin in the manner of contemporary royal railway carriages. It was used by all Queen Victoria's children, and passed on to the Princess of Wales, later Queen Alexandra, and then to the Duchess of York, later Queen Mary. Reproduced by Gracious Permission of Her Majesty the Queen.

Thomas Hope showed a rounded swinging cot with somewhat grandiose Roman decoration in gilt bronze in his *Household Furniture and Interior Decoration,* 1807. It was equally adaptable, apparently, to the Gothic style, and George Smith's *Collection of Designs for Household Furniture,* a year later in 1808, described such a piece as 'suitable to many mansions in this country, and

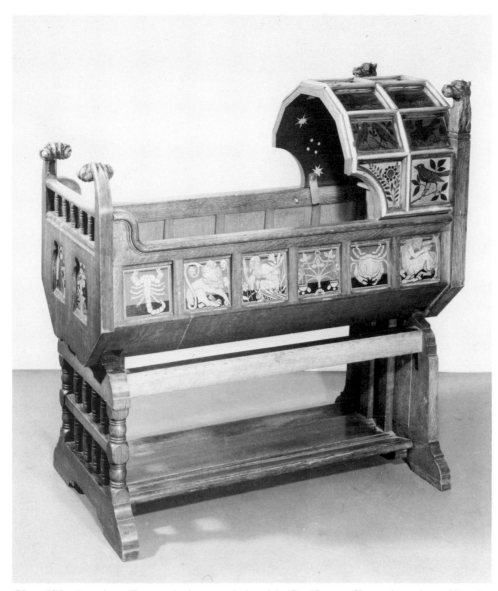

Plate 108. An oak cradle or swinging cot, designed by R. Norman Shaw, the eminent Victorian architect, for Julian Waterhouse, the son of Sir Alfred Waterhouse, in 1867. This is no typical product of a middle-class Victorian nursery, but a highly sophisticated piece of craftsmanship and, like so many Arts and Crafts pieces, it is giddily eclectic. The basic shape is inspired by the idea of a medieval hanging cot. Trustees of the Victoria and Albert Museum.

should be of mahogany or oak, the enrichments carved either plain or gilt; the furniture cotton or silk'.

It was just such a hanging cot which Queen Victoria ordered in 1840 for her first child, Princess Victoria, 'Vicky'. Decidedly neo-classical, and with a distinct feeling of 'Empire', the carved mahogany framework is embellished with architectural motifs such as *paterae* and stiff leaves picked out in gilding. An arch springs from the two standards, and is hung with sumptuous swags of silk and heavy tassels, which must have lent a theatrical sense of drama to the tiny sleeping figure inside. The ribbed sides are upholstered in green silk

Colour Plate 23. A mid-17th century oak cradle, c.1660, the gabled hood with turned supports, and the panelled sides inlaid and carved in the manner of contemporary chairs and chests. In the foot is a drawer which enabled a hot brick to be inserted in order to keep the baby warm on particularly cold days. The pommels on the sides were used to secure the bedding, and the finials at either end were used as an aid to rocking, and also for winding wool or for allowing swaddling bands to air. Tit-bits, of a highly dubious nature, were also attached by a string to 'pacify' the baby. The importance of rocking cannot be over-emphasized, since during the era of swaddling it was the only way of securing relaxation or sleep for a dirty, itchy and pinioned baby, and helped to establish a routine of waking and sleeping. Anon.

buttoned on the interior, somewhat in the manner of contemporary royal railway carriages.

A much more solid, but in its way equally remarkable, hanging cot was designed in 1867 by R. Norman Shaw, the eminent Victorian architect, for Julian Waterhouse, the baby son of fellow architect Sir Alfred Waterhouse.

Colour Plate 24. A late Georgian mahogany hanging cot, c.1820, the hood and sides formed of woven cane-work panels and lined with coarse linen, on turned posts, with splayed feet ending in brass castors. The bases of these cradles are formed either of strong canvas bands or wooden slats to ensure easy cleaning, and the wicker sides allow the hygienic circulation of air.

Cambridge and County Folk Museum.

Giddily eclectic, like so many mid-Victorian pieces, it is made of oak in accordance with the homespun principles of the Arts and Crafts Movement. The basic shape is inspired by medieval hanging cots, with traces of Byzantium in the carved finials. The painted panels of the hinged hood contain elements of Gothic and Japanese art, and the interior is painted with a blue sky and

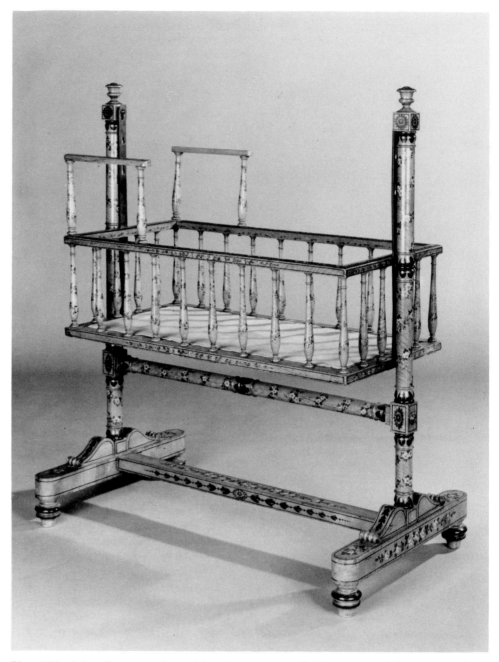

Plate 109. A late Regency satinwood hanging cot, suspended from two upright posts on splayed feet. It is painted with garlands of flowers, the posts surmounted by urns in neo-classical style, 40½in. (102.9cm) wide. Swinging cots became fashionable as swaddling fell from favour, and the need for constant rocking declined.
Christie's.

stars, to give the child an illusion of Heaven. The twelve side panels are painted with the signs of the zodiac in red, black and gold, reflecting the contemporary interest in mysticism and the supernatural. Shaw was responsible, with E.W. Godwin, for designing Bedford Park, 'a little red town made up of the quaintest Queen Anne houses', between 1876 and 1881, while Sir Alfred Waterhouse was a fashionable architect much concerned with all aspects of contemporary domestic design.

Not all hanging cots were so exotic. From the late eighteenth century mahogany swinging cots were made with turned posts, and slatted or cane-work sides for ventilation and easy cleaning, at a time when fresh air and daylight were becoming something of an obsession in childcare. The bases of these cots were made of wooden slats or bands of strongly woven tape, on top of which the mattress could be placed. Often mounted on castors for mobility, the hoods were of 'waggon', pointed or arched ogival shape. The sides, and sometimes the hoods, were lined with padded material to keep out the draughts and protect the baby from the hard surface of the cot. A mahogany and cane-work swinging cot was made by Morgan and Sanders of 16 and 17 Catherine Street, Strand, London in the first decade of the nineteenth century, and in spite of the fact that J.C. Loudon wrote in a somewhat dictatorial fashion in 1833 that 'swinging cribs and cradles are now justly exploded', they remained popular for a large part of the nineteenth century.

Crib was the name generally used to describe a slatted, high-sided child's bed, and derives from the word for a manger. According to the omniscient Loudon, cribs were used when the child was one year old. Supported on high legs, they could be pushed right up to the nurse's bed, with one side of the crib being hinged to let down as necessary. Occasionally three-sided cribs were made, so that when pushed up to another bed they formed a kind of extension, but with the benefit of high sides to stop the child from falling out. The ever-practical and inventive Prince Consort is thought to have designed the cribs in the nursery at Osborne during the 1840s, and James Shoolbred's *Furniture Designs* of 1876 included such cribs. Later examples had sides which slid, rather than hinged, up and down.

It was considered vital that the child's bed should be raised off the ground, and *Enquire Within*, 1886, clearly explains the reasons. 'The most mephitic and pernicious stratum of all in an apartment is that within one or two feet from the floor, while the most wholesome, or atmospheric air, is in the middle of the room, and the inflammable gas ascends to the top.'

With the advent of metal beds in the second half of the nineteenth century, cribs made of iron with mesh sides were common as well as many bassinets, or berceaunettes. Iron was given the approval of the childcare experts because it was hygienic and could not 'harbour vermin'. Painted white, these small, oval, bath-shaped beds had a high hook projecting over the head, from which two floor-length curtains were draped. The bed itself was supported on an X-shaped stand, which could often be folded away when not in use. The hard cold metal was lavishly padded with quilted satin or cotton in pastel colours, and 'dressed' with a profusion of bows, frills and flounces in sateen, lace, muslin or organdie, thus providing an unreal and ethereal setting for the sleeping infant. In the 1860s it was, according to Mrs Beeton, the duty of the monthly nurse to trim the bassinet which could be of metal or wicker, but by the turn of the century many of the large stores, such as the Army and Navy, were selling them ready-trimmed. W. Small & Son, 1 & 2 Chambers Street, Edinburgh, were among the many shops who sold 'Trimmed Bassinettes from

9

Colour Plate 25. An illustration from At Home, *1881, showing small children in their nursery, playing in their drop-sided cribs. Such cots, or 'cribs' as they were generally called, were used after the child had reached the age of about one year. Raised on high legs to about the height of an adult bed, they could be pushed up to the nurse's bed in the nursery if the child was ill or fretful. The hinged side enabled the child to be easily lifted in or out and eventually gave way to the modern form of sliding side. Such cribs were also made in cast-iron, sometimes with wire-mesh sides.*

Mary Evans Picture Library.

122

Colour Plate 26. The New Arrival, *by an unknown artist of the English Provincial School, mid-19th century, oil on canvas, 23½ in. (60cm) x 19½ in. (49.5cm). This shows a baby ensconced in a typical mid-Victorian 'bassinette' or 'berceaunette', the wicker cradle enveloped in a froth of muslin and lace, threaded through and finished with blue satin ribbons. This painting shows the sentimental way in which the Victorians idealized babyhood, and turned babies into ethereal symbols of beauty and goodness. Childhood was a state 'which speaks to us of heaven, which tells of those pure angelic beings which surround the throne of God, untouched by sin, untainted by the breath of corruption'. (Ladies Magazine,* June, 1833.)   Sotheby's.

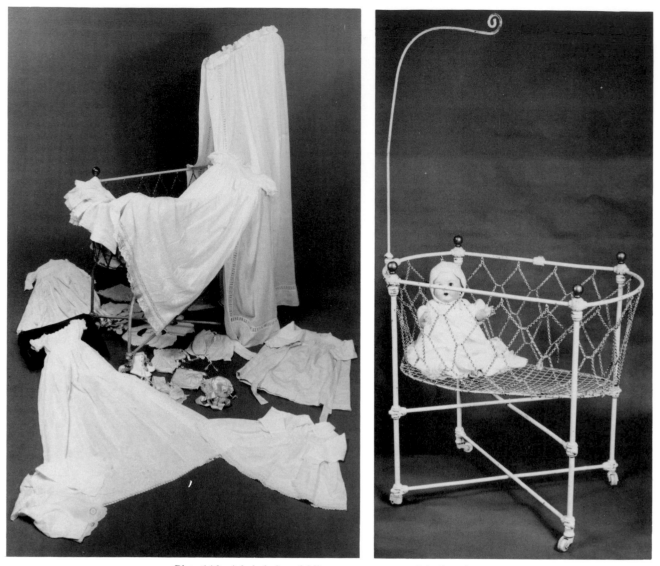

Plate 110. A baby's iron folding cot, complete with its hangings and the infant's first set of clothes. Sadly, this baby, born in 1916, died a few days after the birth and the cradle and layette were never used again. These portable folding cots, on castors, were popular in the small houses and villas of the Edwardian era, when space was at a premium. Such cots were available from the new large stores, and a similar example, lavishly trimmed with satin ribbons, bows and lace, was available from the Army & Navy Stores Catalogue *in 1907 priced at £3 17s. 6d.*

17/6', as well as 'The New Folding Cot, Untrimmed from 15/-, Trimmed 19/6'.

During the early years of the twentieth century, white-painted wooden beds of simple design, and with posts and slats reminiscent of architectural features such as stair banisters and newel posts, became fashionable for older children and were clearly influenced by designers and architects such as Charles Rennie Mackintosh, Lutyens and Voysey.

Chapter 9

NURSERY DECORATION

Day and Night Nurseries

'Poor little things, they are so tired of their own particular sanctum, its sameness,
its dullness, its ugliness'.
(Sylvia's Family Management, A Book of Thrift and Cottage Economy, 1886.)

The concept of the nursery as a room set aside for children is an essentially modern one, dating from the late eighteenth century. Before that, children and grown-ups were segregated in only the most affluent households. Sir William Ingilby's house at Padsidehead contained a 'nurserye' in 1583, and another was mentioned at Ingatestone in Essex a few years later. Inventories of 1567 and 1601 mention trundle beds or mattresses in the 'nurserie', indicating perhaps a separate room where the children slept with their nurse.

Eighteenth century nurseries were inadequate places, generally confined to the top of the house or some other unwanted space or, in the case of the large country houses, in a separate wing. Dr Dewees, *A Treatise on the Physical and Medical Treatment of Children,* 1826, wrote disapprovingly: 'Everybody, almost, in easy circumstances has a part of the house appropriated to what is called the nursery — often the least suitable'. They were frequently cramped and overcrowded, with up to four children of varying ages squeezed into the one room, which had to serve as day nursery, night nursery and schoolroom. Little purpose-built furniture found its way into these rooms — perhaps a baby-walker, cradle or high chair, and the lack of any special features for children reflected the attitude of Georgian society as a whole. Childhood was a necessary evil, but no concessions were to be made to it, and it must be outgrown with all possible speed.

The Victorians found themselves ruled by a young and fertile Queen with the child-bearing constitution of a female ox, and a Consort with a taste for domesticity and drains. As a result, the upbringing of babies and small children was embarked upon in a much more ordered, thoughtful and scientific way than before. Designs for grand houses were conceived with nurseries in light and airy positions, separated from, and yet close to, the living quarters of the parents, so that plenty of healthy parental contact could be maintained. At Eaton Hall, the schoolroom was sandwiched between the twin buttresses of

Colour Plate 27. The Ann Sharp Baby House, the oldest existing English Dolls' House, dating from the late 17th century. 68in. (172.7cm) x 68½in. (174cm) x 21in. (53.3cm) deep. The right hand room on the second floor is the nursery. The daughter of the house and her maid, Sarah Gill, stand centre and left, and a baby lies in a cradle, a point lace cap on her head. A very early silver posset pan stands on the table, to be used, no doubt, for warming pap.

Ann Sharp was born in 1691, one of the fourteen daughters of John Sharp, Archbishop of York. Princess Anne, later Queen Anne, was Ann's godmother and gave her the baby house. As was the custom, Ann Sharp was named after her royal godmother. Private Collection.

the Duke of Westminster's study and the Duchess's boudoir in a self-contained family wing, separate from the grand reception rooms in the main house. At Osborne, Queen Victoria's holiday home on the Isle of Wight, known reverentially as 'Her Majesty's Marine Residence at Osborne', the nurseries were carefully situated on the second floor so that the Queen and Prince Consort could have easy access to their children. In September 1846 Queen Victoria described her visit to the new nurseries. 'Mounting another flight of stairs we come to the children's quarters, nurseries, school-rooms, governess's house etc. All is convenient, spacious and well carried out. Mr Cubitt has done it admirably', she added with a note of satisfaction.

There were separate rooms for day and night nurseries in Victorian houses, which enabled bedding and nightclothes to be thoroughly aired, and allowed children with infectious diseases to be kept apart from their siblings. Fresh air and daylight were essential. 'The windows of the nursery are generally too small', wrote Pye Henry Chavasse in his *Advice to Mothers,* 1839. 'Gardeners are well aware of the great importance of light in the construction of their

Colour Plate 28. A portrait miniature of Lady Howard de Walden with her children, by John Faed, RSA, c.1838. This charming portrait shows the idyllic view of motherhood and family life which was to dominate the Victorian age, which it heralds. Private Collection.

Plate 111. *The night nursery at Osborne, on the Isle of Wight, photographed in the early 1870s.*
The children's beds with their hinged canework sides and upholstered pads acting as 'bumpers' to protect the children, are believed to have been designed by the ever-practical and creative Prince Albert. The chintz-covered screen just visible in the right-hand corner would have afforded protection from beneficial but icy sea blasts. High chairs, a towel rail and a draped swinging cot can also be seen, and between the windows a pair of rosewood chiffoniers, which would have held books, games and toys.
English Heritage.

greenhouses, and yet children, who require it so much, and are of much greater importance, are cooped-up in dark rooms'. The schoolroom was separate again, so that the smaller children would not distract the older ones at their lessons.

Photographs of the nursery at Osborne, taken in the 1870s, show the sensible, solid furniture in use for nurseries at the time, none of it designed to appeal remotely to children's tastes. A pair of rosewood chiffoniers, for holding books and toys, are to be seen between the windows, and prove that much outmoded furniture was relegated to the nursery. J.H. Walsh, in his *Manual of Domestic Economy Suited to Families Spending from £150 to £1,500 a year,* 1879, confirms that 'of late years the rosewood chiffonier has been tabooed, and many thousands have been consigned to the nursery or schoolroom in consequence'. Other nursery requisites included a screen, washstand, large table,

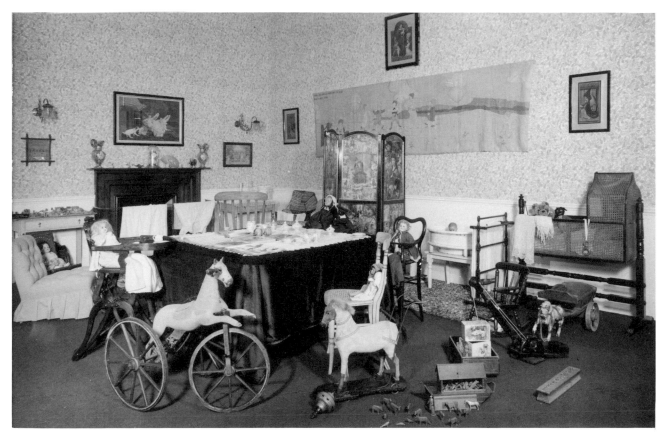

Plate 112. The nursery at Wallington Hall, Northumberland. This shows many features typical of a late Victorian or Edwardian nursery. A colourful frieze pinned onto the wall relieves the somewhat sombre wallpaper, while a white-painted dado below fulfils the contemporary passion for hygiene. (These could also be painted with black paint to provide a blackboard for scribbling and drawing.) The ubiquitous scrap screen stands ready to enfold the baby in his white oval bath, while towels air in readiness on the nursery fireguard. The canework hanging cot is an earlier piece, though the lacy shawl and teething rings hanging over the side are contemporary. A sharp contrast is shown between the flimsy straight-legged balloon-backed mid-Victorian high chair, to the right of the table, and the robust late Victorian high chair with its massive splayed legs opposite. The table itself would have formed the pivot of the nursery, used for everything from copying lessons, cutting out scraps or enjoying a filling nursery tea. National Trust/Edward Gelles.

chairs and high chairs, bath, slop pail, cot, towel rail, fire-guard and bed for the nurse. Walsh advises that furniture (in accordance with nursery food) 'should be of the plainest description. Strong tables and chairs, the latter of various sizes, suitable to children, are chiefly what are wanted... Nothing is so injurious to young children as the constant necessity of restraining their tendency to injure furniture'. In his family budget of £1,701 5s. 1d. only £40 was allowed for the day and night nurseries, and in a lower budget of £670 18s. 6d. a mere £15 was set aside for the children.

There is little doubt that Victorian nurseries must often have been as spartan as they were cosy, particularly if left in the charge of a cold-hearted nurse. As Mrs Beeton pointed out, there were many children 'who... with perhaps the exception of a short half-hour now and then, spend all their time at home in the one room, and Nanny, for good or ill, often reigned supreme'.

Colour Plate 29. A detail of the night nursery at Osborne House.   English Heritage.

Wall Decoration

Wall decoration no doubt attempted to relieve the monotony, and improving texts or nursery broadsheets were framed and hung on the walls. Some of these posed awkward moral questions with which to while away the time. (Question: 'Where Do You Live?' Answer to be supplied from the alternatives of 'In Grumble Corner' or 'Thanksgiving Street'.) Nursery pictures were chosen with care, in accordance with the optimistic advice meted out by Thomas Bull in his *Hints to Mothers,* 1837. 'A fine engraving and a good painting elevate the mind. A taste in early life for everything refined and beautiful purifies his (the child's) mind, cultivates his intellect, keeps him from low company, and makes him grow up a gentleman'.

Many Victorian nurseries were jollied up by 'sanitary paper of some cheerful pattern on the walls', but sadly not all proved to be 'sanitary'. Chavasse recounts a dreadful story in *Advice to Mothers,* 1839. 'Four children in one family have just lost their lives from sucking green paper-hangings'. The seductive green colour which proved so irresistible, was provided by arsenic and copper, and most nursery paints at the time were full of lead.

Plate 113. A late Victorian card printed with verses instructive of good table manners, which no doubt hung in a nursery. It endorses the Victorian philosophy that children should be seen and not heard. c.1880. Cambridge and County Folk Museum.

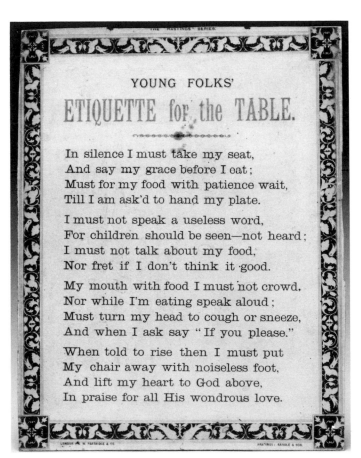

THE "HASTINGS" SERIES.

YOUNG FOLKS'
ETIQUETTE for the TABLE.

In silence I must take my seat,
And say my grace before I eat;
Must for my food with patience wait,
Till I am ask'd to hand my plate.

I must not speak a useless word,
For children should be seen—not heard;
I must not talk about my food,
Nor fret if I don't think it good.

My mouth with food I must not crowd,
Nor while I'm eating speak aloud;
Must turn my head to cough or sneeze,
And when I ask say " If you please."

When told to rise then I must put
My chair away with noiseless foot,
And lift my heart to God above,
In praise for all His wondrous love.

LONDON: W. PARTRIDGE & CO.   HASTINGS: SAVILLE & SON.

Plate 114. A fragment of a nursery wallpaper designed by Kate Greenaway in 1893 entitled The Months. *This was probably the best-known and most highly-regarded nursery wallpaper of the day, inspiring a mass of imitations. It remained in production until the 1930s, so great was its popularity.* Trustees of the Victoria and Albert Museum.

132

But wallpaper and nursery furnishings were soon to become of prime importance. Thanks to the increased mechanisation of the wallpaper industry in the 1840s, and the advances made in colour printing during the 1860s and 1870s, a plethora of children's books emerged during the succeeding decades, with illustrations by celebrated artists such as Kate Greenaway and Walter Crane. Crane (1845-1915) was employed during the 1870s by the publisher, Edmund Evans, along with Kate Greenaway, in illustrating children's books which reflected contemporary aesthetic taste. An educationalist, socialist and dress reformer, Crane was the first President of the Art Workers' Guild, and Principal of the Royal College of Art. He published fifty books between 1865 and 1886, and worked prolifically until the end of the century, upholding the 'Aesthetic' ideals that good art and design should pervade all aspects of everyday life. Most of his wallpapers for the nursery were machine-printed, on surface roller machines, a newly developing process which allowed for mass-production, although his other wallpapers were printed by hand. His nursery designs, which included *The Sleeping Beauty, The Queen of Hearts* and *The House that Jack Built,* found wide acclaim and *The British Architect,* 23 May, 1884, confirmed 'how gracefully and simply Mr Crane tells the tales of fairy kind and nursery rhyme. With the aid of a little intelligent and sympathetic talk nursery walls covered with these designs might be made to live in the lives of children'. Ellen Terry recalled that her children 'were allowed no rubbishy books, but from the first Japanese prints lined the walls and Walter Crane was their classic'.

The reputation of Kate Greenaway (1846-1901) rested on the illustrations for her many children's books, which included *Apple Pie, Marigold Garden* and *Mother Goose,* as well as Almanacks and greetings cards. Her world of nostalgic innocence was evoked by her wallpaper of *The Months,* 1893, which was machine-printed by the Middleton firm of David Walker & Co. It inspired a mass of imitations, but was the best known and most highly regarded nursery wallpaper of its time, remaining in production until the 1930s.

Aesthetic nurseries proliferated, and *The Magazine of Art* declared in the 1880s of the contemporary child, 'He may be said to be something of an art critic 'ere he leaves the cradle and an adept in style 'ere he sees fit to abandon long garments for short — his aesthetic opportunities are innumerable and the matter produced for the gratification of his pampered appetite is perhaps the daintiest ever seen'. There were still some stolidly philistine mothers left with old-fashioned artistic views, and their taste in nursery art was guided by Mary Gardner in *Nursery Management,* 1914. 'Do not choose pictures of sad and depressing incidents, such as a child weeping over its mother's grave, or a faithful dog dying on a gory battlefield. Morbid subjects attract children's attention and do their nerves much harm'.

Nothing could have been less morbid or depressing than the jolly nursery friezes which became fashionable from the 1890s and were designed by artists such as Cecil Aldin, John Hassall or Mabel Lucie Attwell. In their flat, linear style so well suited to the unfolding of narrative, they produced continuous

ARTHUR J. ELSLEY
1909

Colour Plate 30. A painting entitled 'Wake Up! It's Christmas Morning', by Arthur John Elsley, signed and dated 1909. The sleeping girl, in fact the artist's daughter, is shown lying in a typical Edwardian bed. In its simplicity it is clearly influenced by the Arts and Crafts Movement, and its white paint reflects the contemporary vogue for clean, white interiors. It also complies with the requirements of contemporary nursery furniture. 'Furniture for the nursery should have rounded corners, be light, strong and washable. . . Painted furniture can be renovated with a coat of fresh enamel at small cost'.

Sotheby's.

Colour Plate 31. Printer's samples of nursery curtains, c.1917, Mulhouse, France.
Christie's South Kensington.

scenes of children on the sands, animals or nursery rhyme characters, in bold colours and with a robust humour which had been lacking in aesthetic designs. Such friezes, which were usually stuck just out of reach of sticky fingers above a dado of washable paint, made ideal nursery decoration with their humorously drawn scenes in a style reminiscent of contemporary posters or cartoons. Will Owen, one of the most popular designers, had worked as an illustrator for *Punch* and was responsible for the poster showing the immortally scruffy but engaging pair of 'Bisto Kids' inhaling the delicious aroma from their dinner. The illustrators Cecil Aldin and John Hassall worked together and independently on designs for nursery friezes and pictures, with Hassall's designs featuring toys, dolls and Noah's arks among the subjects. Mabel Lucie Attwell too was a popular designer of nursery friezes during the first decade of the twentieth century, before she went on to become famous for her coy, chubby-cheeked children.

The flat, boldly drawn friezes with their large areas of strong colour complemented well the somewhat stark purity of the new nursery furniture. Made of light oak, or painted in white for simplicity and hygiene, the clean lines of beds, tables, chairs, wash-stands and dressing tables were straight, rectangular and uncomplicated, with designers such as C.A. Voysey and Charles Rennie Mackintosh contributing to the style. Some pieces reflected the contemporary taste for artistic calligraphy, and Mary Clive described 'the first real nursery furniture I ever saw' in 1915 as 'hygienic-shaped white cupboards with proverbs like "Waste Not, Want Not" written on them in large blue letters'.

Nurseries were suddenly big business. From being the repositories of

Plates 115 A & B. Two examples of popular nursery friezes.

A. The Sea Shore, *designed by Will Owen in 1912. Such friezes came into fashion during the 1890s.* Whitworth Art Gallery, Manchester.

B. 'Scenes from Nursery Tales', *designed by Mabel Lucie Attwell for Potter, c.1910. An early example of Miss Attwell's work, the chubby-legged, saucer-eyed children have not yet emerged, as they were to do in her work of the 1920s and 1930s.* Trustees of the Victoria and Albert Museum.

Plate 116. An illustration of a 1920s nursery designed by Heal's, showing simple, sturdy furniture, mainly painted white, and a folding wooden playpen.

Reproduced from *The Concise Household Encyclopaedia.*

outgrown bric-à-brac, they became gleaming interiors with every item carefully co-ordinated to amuse and educate the embryonic taste of the small occupants. The large stores were eager to exploit this market and carry the new ranges of nursery rugs, cushions, curtains, furniture and china. Heal's, Liberty's, The Army & Navy Stores, Story & Co., Gillow's and Whiteley's were all to the forefront of taste. *The Concise Household Encyclopaedia,* published in the 1920s, sounded a cautionary note, however. 'It is pleasant to think that the days are gone when anything was good enough for the nursery . . . and that architects and furniture designers have concentrated in producing charming quarters for small children . . . On the other hand, in some of the super-decorated nurseries, specialization is overdone. The colours employed are too glaring, the white furniture is varnished to a dazzling degree, stencilled or painted with strange creatures, while the antics of a medley of grotesques struggle over the walls and screens, appearing on chinaware and table-cloths at meal-times — to say nothing of bibs and feeders — and the down quilt at the foot of the cot at night, all over the linoleum and the cretonne curtains. Mother Goose, in some cases, is even painted flying across the ceiling with favourite characters attendant, to add to the restless effect'. The correspondent

Plate 117. A photograph from Our Homes & Gardens, *1919, showing a contemporary nursery with the usual fireguard guarding the grate and a frieze showing a hunting scene pasted onto the wall at dado height, with washable paint beneath.* From *Our Homes & Gardens,* 1919.

in *Our Homes & Gardens,* 1919, wholeheartedly agreed. 'No gnomes and forest hobgoblins, please. The taste for them is really adult. Nurse has to explain that such things do not really exist, and that there is no need to be frightened at the monsters on the wall, quaint though they may be to the sophisticated'.

Colour Plate 32. The nursery created at Cardiff Castle by the architect William Burges for the children of the third Marquess of Bute in the 1870s. Round the room a frieze of hand-painted tiles tells stories from the Arabian Nights, *Hans Andersen and the Brothers Grimm. Hardly a typical Victorian nursery, Cardiff Castle reflects the taste of the medievalist Burges and his scholar patron.*
Cardiff City Council.

Nursery Tiles

The fashion for nursery tiles lasted from the 1870s until the turn of the century, and was a reflection of the contemporary love of improving illustration coupled with the contemporary passion for hygiene. The flat glazed surface of tiles was easily wiped down with a damp cloth, and provided an excellent surface on which to paint or print designs. They could be incorporated into a nursery bathroom or in the surround of a fireplace, and could be used in pieces of furniture such as wash-stands, or simply framed and hung on the wall.

Potteries at the forefront of tile production included Minton, Wedgwood, Doulton, Maw's and Pilkington. As well as employing their own designers they also used the talents of established children's book illustrators such as Walter Crane and Kate Greenaway. Walter Crane adapted illustrations from his books, *The Baby's Opera* and *The Baby's Bouquet* for Maw's during the 1870s,

Plate 118A. Two Minton nursery tiles, colour-printed with two scenes taken from The Baby's Bouquet *by Walter Crane, first published in 1877. They show 'The Old Man in Leather' and 'The Four Presents'. Impressed marks Mintons China Works. The frontispiece of the same book shows two children in a contemporary 'Arts and Crafts' nursery, with a series of tiles showing nursery rhymes set into the panelling below the dado rail.* Private Collection.

Plate 118B. A pair of Minton nursery tiles, designed by Walter Crane, with the nursery rhyme Jack and Jill, *c.1890. Crane was a distinguished artist and illustrator of children's books, and was employed with Kate Greenaway by the publisher Edmund Evans. He also worked for William Morris at the Kelmscott Press, and in 1898 became Principal of the Royal College of Art.* Manchester City Art Gallery.

and his designs were also used by Minton. J. Moyr Smith, whose work was reminiscent of Walter Crane's, also designed for Minton. Kate Greenaway designed tiles for the firm of T.B. Boote, one of the most popular of which was a set of four depicting The Seasons. Nursery rhymes, fairy stories and scenes from children's literature, as well as *Aesop's Fables,* were favourite themes.

During the Edwardian era Doulton's of Lambeth designed some spectacular tile panels to decorate the children's wards of some of the large new London hospitals.

Plate 119. Two Wedgwood tiles showing May and September from the 'Old English' or 'Calendar' series, produced during the 1880s, and attributed to Helen Jane Arundel Miles. A professional illustrator and artist, she was based at Etruria in the late 1870s, and designed a number of tile series for Wedgwood. The tiles appear in blue, green, brown and polychrome printed versions.

Chapter 10
NURSERY EQUIPMENT

Bath-Time

'In places where bathing of children is used, let it be washed twice a week from
the seventh month till it be weaned'.
(Nicholas Culpeper, *A Directory for Midwives*, 1651.)

Medieval babies are shown in contemporary manuscripts being washed, after birth, by the midwife, in a coopered wooden tub. Salt was often added to the bath water as a safeguard against evil, and babies who were considered too weak to be washed were rubbed in salt or wine. Bath-time for older babies was, in no way, considered a pleasurable activity as it is today, and was usually repeated only once a week, or when strictly necessary. Cold water was considered beneficial and in 1789 Michael Underwood struck a discordant liberal voice in his *Treatise on the Diseases of Children*. 'To see a little infant...

Plate 120. A scene from the Girls' Own Paper, 1885, showing a nurse with her four charges in the nursery. The smallest child is bathed in front of the nursery fire, as usual safely guarded with a brass-topped fireguard, in a tin or papier-mâché bath, the shape of which is still used, in plastic, today.

Mary Evans Picture Library.

Plate 121. A Victorian baby's bath illustrated by Mrs Beeton in her Book of Household Management, *first published in 1861.*

Private Collection.

Plate 122. A Victorian enamel baby's bath, the oval bath-tub supported on a four-legged stand, which incorporates a towel rail and shelf to hold the soap and sponge. By the side is an enamel slop pail with a detachable lid, used for holding dirty nappies, c.1880.

Cambridge and County Folk Museum.

washed up to breast and loins in cold water, exposed for several minutes, perhaps in the middle of winter itself, in one continued scream... has ever struck me as a piece of unnecessary severity'.

Under the Victorians bath-time became an intimate ritual, and washing a baby assumed an aura of cosy sanctity performed in the glow of the nursery fire. Queen Victoria, however, remained a realist and confessed that she disliked 'that terrible frog-like action' of small babies in the bath. Her daughter, Vicky, wore a flannel washing-cap in the bath, and a powder-box and hair-brush were other bath-time accessories. 'Tooth-preservers' were used for brushing the teeth. Towels and night-clothes were hung over the nursery fire-guard to warm while the bath was in progress, and the baths themselves were made of papier-mâché, tin or white enamel, often inserted into a stand which combined a towel-rail and recesses for the sponge and soap-dish.

Night lights

'Are all the dragons fled?
Are all the goblins dead?
Am I quite safe in bed?'

In the days before rooms could be flooded with light at the flick of a switch, night-time held untold terrors for children. Flickering embers in the nursery grate served only to enlarge and distort the shadows on the wall, and a candle guttering or blowing out during a nocturnal sortie must have been a stomach-churning experience for a small child, particularly in view of the fact that contemporary children's literature was obsessed with giants, witches and evil fairies. Hobgoblins and foul fiends must have daunted even the most reckless young hero after dark, and from an early age Lord Byron would search his room and order his servant to check that no-one was hiding under his bed. No reader of *Jane Eyre* can forget the uncontrollable panic of the young Jane's enforced night alone in the red bedroom where her uncle had died.

Added to all these childish fears was the dread of mothers and nurses that a newborn baby might be kidnapped by fairies and replaced by one of their own babies. Unbaptised babies were considered particularly vulnerable, and cradles were always placed near the fire, often the only source of light in a

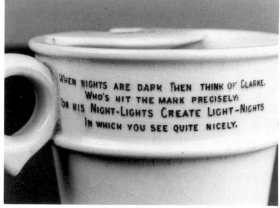

Plate 123. The 'Fairy' night light made by Clarke's 'Pyramid' Night Light Co. Ltd., London, c.1888. This held three-quarters of a pint of water, and cost 5/-. The cup was first filled with water via the channel at the front, then a night-light (which was reputed to burn for nine hours) was floated on the water in safety.
Cambridge and County Folk Museum.

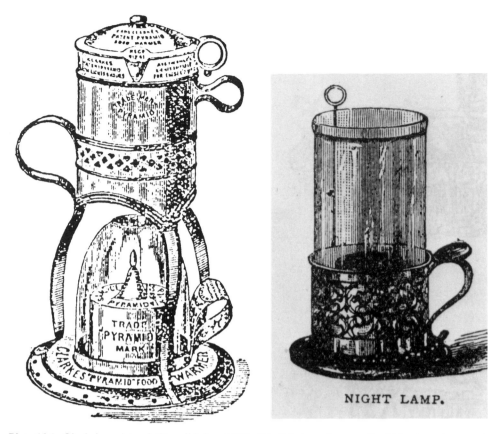

NIGHT LAMP.

Plate 124. *Clarke's registered 'Pannikin', c.1890. 'By this invention any liquid food can be poured out or drunk without scum or grease passing through the spout, and prevents spilling when poured into a Feeding Bottle, so objectionable with all other Pannikins'.*

The Midwives Chronicle and Nursing Notes.

Plate 125. *A Victorian night lamp for a Nursery, reproduced from Mrs Beeton's* The Book of Household Management, *first published in 1861, 1891 edition.*   Private Collection.

darkened cottage parlour. In Scotland the doorposts of a new mother's room were spread with urine to repel such marauding fairies. 'When larks gin sing, Away we fling, And babes new-born steal as we go, An elf instead, We leave in bed, and wind out, laughing, Ho, Ho, Ho'.

Clarke's registered their 'Pyramid' night light, which was reputed to burn for nine hours, in 1888. Their showrooms were at 31 Ely Place, Holborn, and there they also displayed their registered 'Pannikin' which, when fitted over a 'Pyramid' nursery lamp heated liquid such as broth or pap, filtered the 'scum or grease', and allowed it to be poured easily into a feeding bottle. Also on sale were Clarke's 'Fairy' Night Light Holders. The white earthenware cup was first filled with water via the channel at the front, then a 'Pyramid' night light was placed on the water where it floated alight for nine hours. Clarke's pride in their product was undoubted, and was celebrated in the appalling doggerel verse which they printed on the 'Fairy':

> *'When Nights are Dark then think of Clarke,*
> *Who's hit the mark precisely,*
> *For his Night-Lights create Light-Nights,*
> *In which you see quite Nicely.'*

Plate 126. A Victorian scrap screen, c.1880. Such useful pieces protected the young inmates of the nursery from harmful draughts, and sticking on the scraps provided employment during the long winter afternoons. Other screens were decorated with poker-work, painted, or simply hung with pleated cretonne or chintz.

Edward Gelles.

Screens

Situated as they were, at the tops of houses, with windows often flung open so that the small inmates could fill their lungs with life-giving draughts of fresh air, Victorian nurseries would have been swept by a maelstrom of sub-Arctic gales. Screens were essential to protect new-born or sickly children from catching a 'chill', and were no doubt a boon to the shivering governess as she sat for hours trying to instil the rudiments of education into her recalcitrant charges. Although new-born Victorian babies were carried on cushions by their nurses in front of open windows to take the air or suspended in trays and baskets attached to the sills, draughts were another matter and considered altogether harmful. Folding portable screens were *de rigueur,* and could be made of pleated cretonne or chintz nailed onto a wooden frame, or of wood painted or decorated with poker-work. Many such screens were covered with scraps, cut out and pasted on by small fingers during the long winter afternoons, and then finished with a coat of varnish.

As late as the 1920s the *Concise Household Encyclopaedia* was advising that 'a cot should be on castors and should not be placed between a window and the fireplace or between a window or door without the protection of an efficient draught screen'.

Plate 127. *A Denby stoneware child's hot water bottle, c.1930, modelled in the form of a Gladstone bag and with the initials B.E.D. on one side, 9in. (22.9cm).* Private Collection.

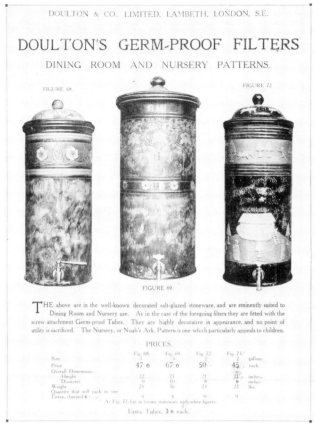

DOULTON & CO. LIMITED, LAMBETH, LONDON, S.E.

DOULTON'S GERM-PROOF FILTERS
DINING ROOM AND NURSERY PATTERNS.

THE above are in the well-known decorated salt-glazed stoneware, and are eminently suited to Dining Room and Nursery use. As in the case of the foregoing filters they are fitted with the screw attachment Germ-proof Tubes. They are highly decorative in appearance, and no point of utility is sacrificed. The Nursery, or Noah's Ark, Pattern is one which particularly appeals to children.

Plate 128. *A Doulton hot water bottle with relief-moulded animals and birds, and the word 'Baby', c.1910.* Royal Doulton Ltd.

Plate 129. *Water filters were a standard piece of domestic equipment to the late Victorians and Edwardians, who became increasingly health-conscious and anxious to avoid diseases like cholera, typhoid and diphtheria from which so many children had died earlier in the 19th century. Doulton's of Lambeth made 'Germ-Proof Filters' in salt-glazed stoneware, with a relief design particularly made for the nursery featuring Noah's Ark. It sold for 50 shillings.* Royal Doulton Ltd.

Hot Water Bottles

Fending off the cold had always been a problem in draughty, unheated houses, and babies and small children were notoriously vulnerable to chills and fevers. It was traditional for babies to be warmly wrapped, with layer upon layer of coverings to the cradle, which was placed in front of the fire. Seventeenth and eighteenth century cradles were warmed by the insertion of a hot brick wrapped in flannel, or of a warming-pan, but during the nineteenth century stoneware hot water bottles were produced. By the early twentieth century some fifty factories were making stoneware hot water bottles, the four main factories being Doulton's of Lambeth, the Fulham Pottery, Bourne's Pottery, Denby, and Lovatt & Lovatt in Nottingham. Some were made specifically for children's cots, blue or green Doulton examples being charmingly decorated with the word 'Baby' and with applied reliefs of cockerels, hens and figures. Always a pottery to meet the needs of the public as they arose, Doulton also made hot water bottles specially for perambulators, and breast warmers for mothers. After the 1930s stoneware bottles were replaced by rubber examples.

Chapter 11

FIRST STEPS

Baby Walkers

'When it is stronger, let it not stand too soon, but be held by the nurse, or put into a go-chair, that it may thrust forward itself, and not fall'.
(Nicholas Culpeper, *A Directory for Midwives*, 1651.)

A child's early attempts at walking are always fraught with accidents and falls. To our ancestors a toddler's tumbles could have had disastrous results — down a narrow flight of steep, dark stairs, against a heavy piece of carved oak furniture or, horror of horrors, into an unguarded fire. Attempts at walking were embarked upon at a much earlier age than we try today, since a crawling child reminded its parents too poignantly of his bestial nature and the attendant concept of original sin. 'What was thou being an infant but a brute, having the shape of a man? What is youth but an untamed beast?' 'Animal-like' crawling on all fours was, therefore, a natural phase which was nevertheless often missed out in the past, and babies of the sixteenth, seventeenth and early eighteenth centuries were thrust prematurely into the world from the comfort of their nurses' arms onto rickety little legs which were often unable to bear their weight.

Wheeled wooden structures to enclose a child and support him on his first teetering steps were thought to have been introduced from the Low Countries. They have been known since medieval times, and appear in innumerable contemporary woodcuts and manuscripts. A drawing of the Holy Family, at Chatsworth, by Giulio Romano, shows Joseph the Carpenter presenting a square wooden baby-walker to the infant Jesus, and The First Steps of the Virgin was a favourite theme of medieval art which sometimes included a primitive baby-walker.

None appear to have survived before the seventeenth century, although several appear from the eighteenth and nineteenth centuries. They were known by various intriguing names, which include go-carts, go-gins, going-stools or chairs, baby-runners or baby-walkers. Seventeenth century examples comprise a circular wooden ring, banded in iron, to hold the baby securely round the waist, which was often padded for comfort and upholstered in leather or velvet, depending on the status of the owner. This waist ring was hinged so that the child could be easily lifted in and out, and fastened with an

Plate 130. A detail from a late 14th century embroidered orphrey panel, depicting The First Steps of the Virgin, *who can be seen faltering uncertainly in a rudimentary three-wheeled wooden baby-walker, watched anxiously by her parents. Such simple structures, more akin to our modern walking-frames for the elderly, were known since medieval times.* The Burrell Collection, Glasgow.

Plate 131. An oil painting, English School, c.1650-60, showing a small boy standing in a contemporary painted baby-walker, the four supports of bobbin-turned wood leading to a square base supported on four wooden castors attached to striped wooden balls. The iron hook fastening can easily be seen. Even though indoors, the child wears a lace-edged coif, a plain bib and apron, and matching cuffs, to protect his dress. Leading strings, with which to steady him, or restrain him once the baby-walker is discarded, hang from his shoulders. A silver-gilt rattle with coral teething stick is tied to a ribbon round his waist, and he wears a string of teething beads round his neck for double measure. Norwich Castle Museum.

iron hook and eye arrangement. The hinged supports were widely splayed for stability, and also to prevent the child approaching too close to tables alluringly covered with food, candles and other, possibly deadly, temptations. These supports ended in large wooden or brass castors, which became progressively smaller in size as time went by, and were fitted onto a wooden stretcher, usually square, which could be turned, moulded or plain.

During the eighteenth century examples became lighter in weight and design, with walnut, beech, yew, ash or mahogany being used alongside oak. Sometimes baby-walkers were painted in red or green, and examples with traces of the original paint survive.

The simple square-based structures of the seventeenth century gave way to more elegant circular or hexagonal examples, with correspondingly shaped stretchers. Some 'going-chairs', very like the examples shown in contemporary

Plate 132. A portrait of three children, called the 'Children of James I', inscribed with the date 1611. The ages of the children are given as five, two and four years. The two-year old in the centre sits on an oak child's chair, with elaborate carving, and wears a coral teething stick on the end of a ribbon, as well as leading strings which are held by his sister. To the right of the picture is a baby-walker, with a comfortably upholstered waist ring covered in velvet and studded in brass.
Formerly North Mimms Park Collection. Photograph: Courtauld Institute of Art.

Plate 133. A late 17th century baby-walker in beechwood and walnut, very similar to the one in Plate 131, with its square base and large flat castors with ball finials. Although light and sturdy, with fine turning, it must have proved to be a very unwieldy shape, with its sharply angled corners, and it is no wonder that later examples adopted a circular or hexagonal base. Christie's.

Plate 134. A late 17th century baby-walker in elm and sycamore, still partially covered with the original dark green paint. A very simple design, although the scrolled curving supports are an unusual feature. Again, the hook and eye fastening is clearly visible, as are the large iron hinges. Smaller castors denote a date around 1700, as does the simply moulded circular base. 20½in. (52.1cm) high.   Hereford City Museums.

Plate 135. An early 18th century walnut baby-walker, with iron bandings round the wooden waist support rings, and a very plain hexagonal stretcher. This baby-walker is very unusual in having an additional upper ring which can be adjusted to fit the height of the growing child. 27½in. (69.9cm) wide.   Sotheby's.

Plate 136. A late 18th century baby-walker, c.1790, of rather flimsy appearance, the support with turned knops to simulate bamboo, and with a waist-ring padded and upholstered in leather. The small brass castors are typically much smaller than those in use a century or so earlier, and have leather disc inserts. 19in. (48.3cm) high.   Cambridge and County Folk Museum.

Colour Plate 33. A most interesting 18th century painting by a member of the Circle of Gawen Hamilton, (c.1697-1737), showing a mother with her two small children. She hands a coral on the end of a ribbon to her older child, who is sitting in a winged wooden seat, known as a 'go-chair', which is complete with a play-board, wheels and a carrying handle. Such pieces are very often of continental, usually Dutch, origin. A chamberpot or hot-brick could be concealed inside the chair. The baby linen tumbles in disarray out of a layette basket on the table, while the baby is loosely wrapped in a linen cloth, with a simple cap to keep his head warm. Phillips Fine Art Auctioneers.

Colour Plate 34. A portrait of John, 14th Lord Willoughby de Broke, with his family, by John Zoffany, c.1766. The two boys, John and George, aged about four and three, are shown still in their skirts (breeching usually took place around the age of five or six in the 18th century), and with long blue silk ribbon leading strings falling from their shoulders. These were used to restrain and guide toddlers while they were learning to walk, and still unsteady on their feet. Clear distinction was made between 'going frocks' for toddlers and 'carrying frocks' for immobile babes-in-arms.
Private Collection.

Dutch paintings, were constructed as winged wooden seats enclosed in a kind of wooden box on wheels, with a tray in front, but these appear to have been rarer in England than on the continent. Hot bricks or braziers could be inserted inside the contraption to keep the child's extremities warm, and a chamber pot placed underneath the seat for more pressing needs.

As the eighteenth century progressed, baby-walkers became more and more slender and lightweight, with some simulated bamboo examples reflecting the contemporary chinoiserie taste of the last years of the eighteenth century and the Regency. Others were made of willow, none of which, sadly, seem to have survived. In 1707 Lord George Hay described how his nephew, Thomas, 'runs up and down the room in a machine made of willows, but my lady the Countess takes care that he does not stress himself with walking too much'. More than a century later, J.C. Loudon, *The Encyclopaedia of Cottage, Farm and*

Plate 137. An early 19th century Anglo-Chinese going chair, made of bamboo in typical Chinese style, the seat supported on wheels and with a sliding tray in the front. 24in. (61cm) high.

Sotheby's.

Villa Architecture and Furniture, 1837, talks of 'a go-cart which is frequently made of willow rods but is here shown as a piece of carpentry standing on casters... children learn to walk by these machines without danger of falling'. Walter Crane illustrates a toddler in a wicker 'going-chair' in a typically Aesthetic interior as the frontispiece to his book, *The Baby's Bouquet,* published in 1877.

Baby-walkers were usually made by turners, sometimes in the carpenters' workshops of the great country estates, as was the case with dolls' houses and many other items of everyday children's equipment. The Howard Household books record a payment for two days' work to a servant in making a 'going-cart' in 1620, and in 1828 they were reported to be sold by 'toy' shops all over London, but particularly by the turners of Spinning Wheel Alley, Moorfields. During the seventeenth century they were imported into Scotland from England in considerable quantities. On 19 July 1666 David Gillie's ship, *The Margaret,* sailed into Leith harbour with 'six go-carts' for James Ochterlony, a local merchant. Demand was obviously high, and three weeks later on 3 August, a further six arrived for Ochterlony in the ship, *The James.*

By 1879 J.H. Walsh was able to report in *A Manual of Domestic Economy* that 'the old-fashioned go-cart is quite out-of-date but why I know not... It is merely a circular light frame-work supported on legs and casters and raised to

Plate 138. An early 19th century child's earthenware plate, showing a child being guided by his grandmother with the help of the leading strings attached to his clothes. The plate is inscribed with the verse 'Who when a Babe in Leading Strings/Would haste to me on pleasure's wings/And brought me many pretty things/My Grandfather'.
Brighton Museum and Art Gallery.

the level of the child's waist so that being in the middle, a fall cannot take place'. In fact, such structures, with very little modification, and made of plastic and metal rather than wood, are still used today.

Other aids to walking included small box-like carts, which the child could stand behind and push forward.

Dress changed with the onset of mobility, the infant's 'carrying frocks' being exchanged for 'going frocks', which were shorter so that the child would not become entangled in the voluminous folds of his skirt while attempting to toddle. This was known as 'short-coating' and occurred around the age of nine months to a year. 'Pudding' hats with a padded band round the edge which somewhat resembled a black pudding, were tied under the chin to protect the infant's tender pate during the inevitable tumbles and spills.

Leading Strings

Leading strings were made of strong material and sewn onto the shoulders of the child's dress, and could be used to restrain, balance or propel him by his nurse. Until around 1630 the leading strings were incorporated into the actual sleeves of the dress, and were known as 'hanging' sleeves, though Mary

Colour Plate 35. A very unusual mid-19th century baby-cage, the top with a large tray for toys edged with a gallery of turned spindles, below which is a seat for the child. The top is attached to the quatrefoil base by four turned columnar supports, and with ceramic castors below. This is of unusually complex design, incorporating as it does a circular table top for the child's amusements, and a seat. Such a device, which the nurse could have pushed from room to room, would have anchored the child safely with his toys while she busied herself elsewhere.

The Bowes Museum, Barnard Castle, Co. Durham.

Queen of Scots, a prolific needlewoman, is known to have embroidered a pair of leading strings for her son James. They were worked in gold and silver thread, and touchingly inscribed 'God hath given his angels charge over thee: To keep thee in all thy ways'. As a rule, leading strings were made of worsted or silk, and Alexander Campbell, a seventeenth century Edinburgh merchant, paid seven shillings to a colleague in London for six pairs of silk leading strings.

They were worn for a surprisingly long time, proving how pitifully bent and unstable the ravages of childhood rickets had left so many toddlers' legs. Five or six years was not uncommon, and Lady Anne Clifford noted in her diary for 1617, 'Upon the 1st (May) I cut the child's strings off from her coats and made her use togs alone, so she had 2 or 3 falls at first but had no hurt with them'. The little girl was three, and John Verney was almost four when his mother wrote in 1715, 'Pray desire Cousin Peg to buy me a pair of leading strings for Jack, there is stuf made on purpose that is very strong for he is so

Plate 139. A simple ash baby's walking frame, or baby-cage, which confined the baby but allowed him to stagger from one end to the other within the sliding waist ring, which ran along between grooves. This example dates from the end of the 18th century, but 17th century examples are known. Sometimes a shallow rectangular tray was provided at either end to contain some simple toys. 17in. (43.2cm) x 60in. (152.4cm) x 18in. (45.7cm). Cambridge and County Folk Museum.

heavy. I dare not venture him with a common ribin'.

With the advent of the perambulator in the nineteenth century leading strings became a thing of the past, although leather harnesses with straps, and sometimes bells, were in common use until the 1950s or so. Plastic and nylon leading reins are still used by mothers to restrain their wayward toddlers.

Baby Cages, Baby Minders, Play-pens and Jumpers

'On Wednesday last, an inquest was held at the Eagle Public House. . . . . . . on view the body of Tryphena Camp. It appeared that on Friday morning the deceased child, who was about two years old, went to take the lid off the kettle on the fire, when her clothes caught fire. She was soon enwrapped in flames and ran into the street. The poor girl was so severely burnt that she died the following morning.'
(Hertfordshire Mercury, 27 November, 1852.)

With mobility comes the stage which most mothers of small children delight in and yet dread. Children who are old enough to move around freely, yet have no instinct for danger, embark, at the toddling stage, upon a series of suicidal adventures. Some form of restraint is, therefore, vital to prevent them from hurting themselves, and to preserve maternal sanity. Such restraint was even more essential in an age when the naked flames from unguarded fires flickered seductively in the corner of every room, and even for adults fire was a continual hazard. ('Hearth-death' was a common cause of death among women who cooked over open fires, wearing long skirts and petticoats.) Dogs brawled noisily in most houses, and floors were alive with all kinds of dirt.

One of the most ingenious kinds of 'baby-cage' had an open rectangular frame supported on four splayed legs. A wooden waist-ring held the child securely, and slid along between the grooves in the top side rails, allowing the

Plate 140. A rare late 17th century oak baby-minder. A pivoting iron rod was attached to either end of an octagonal post, one end of which was embedded in the ceiling, the other in the floor. An oak arm protruded at right angles to the post, with an iron waist band to secure the infant attached to it. The height of the arm was adjusted by slotted wedges above and below the central post. Length of post 71¼in. (181cm).
Shakespeare Birthplace Trust.

child to stagger from one end to the other. Wooden trays were sometimes fitted at each end for small toys, and the child was effectively contained, and yet able to practise walking at the same time. Such frames were made in oak, beech or walnut from the end of the seventeenth century to the beginning of the nineteenth, and can be seen in Stranger's Hall, Norwich, the Hereford City Museum and the Cambridge Folk Museum.

Yet more inventive is a seventeenth century oak 'baby-minder' in the kitchen of Shakespeare's Birth Place in Stratford-upon-Avon. A pivoting iron rod was attached to either end of an octagonal oak post, one end of which was thus embedded in the ceiling and the other in the floor. An oak arm protruded at right angles to the post, with an iron waist-band to secure the infant. The height of the arm could be adjusted by slotted wedges above and below the central post. The child could only move round and round the post, rather like a gerbil in a wheel.

Various forms of play-pen were in use from a very early date, and Bartholomew Metlinger in *A Regimen for Young Children,* 1473, advised parents to construct 'a little pen of leather' when the baby showed signs of mobility, and various forms of wooden contraption were made more or less to fit the purpose. However, with the vogue during the second half of the nineteenth century for fresh air and exercise, these began to be marketed at a more sophisticated level, particularly in the United States. The childcare 'expert' in

Plate 141. *A view of an 18th century American kitchen showing, next to the table, a contemporary red-painted wooden playpen of primitive type. In the days of open fires and unguarded hearths it was vital to restrain a toddling child for its own safety.* American Museum in Britain, Bath.

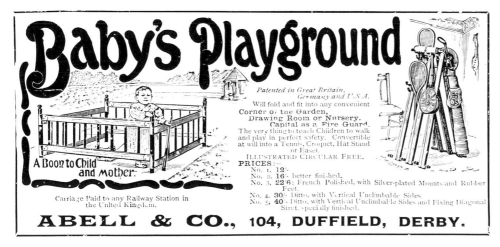

Plate 142. *A 1902 advertisement for a play-pen known as 'Baby's Playground', which was designed to fold away when not in use. Prices started at 12 shillings, rising to 22s 6d for a french polished model with silver-plated mounts and rubber feet. This seemingly miraculous contraption was 'convertible at will into a Tennis, Croquet, Hat Stand or Easel'.*

Mary Evans Picture Library.

Plate 143. A baby jumper, from the middle of the 19th century, clearly showing the harness-type suit, with a small skirt added to ensure that the major part of the baby's legs were covered. The Victorian obsession with legs meant that, for reasons of delicacy and modesty, even the legs of grand pianos were sometimes draped to avoid giving offence.
Courtesy of the National Trust, Snowshill Manor.

Sylvia's Family Management, depressingly sub-titled *A Book of Thrift and Cottage Economy,* warned that 'to keep infants constantly in arms cramps their heads and bodies, stops the free circulation of their blood and often makes them weak in standing'. Luther Emmett Holt, *Care and Feeding of Children,* New York, 1894, asserted that 'a nursery fence two feet high, made to surround a mattress, makes an excellent box stall for the young animal'. The 'Baby's Playground', advertised in 1902 by Abell & Co., Derby, was an ingenious

Plate 144. An amusing illustration depicting The Happy Family *from George Cruikshank's* Comic Almanack, *1849. Both father and children are shown hanging contentedly in their new elasticated harnesses which hang from the ceiling. Dr John Ticker Conquest, in his* Letters to a Mother, *London, 1848, recommended Roger's 'Patent Infant Gymnasium' or 'Baby Jumper', which had been recently introduced from America.* Mary Evans Picture Library.

wooden play-pen designed to fold away when not in use. Prices started at twelve shillings, rising to 22s 6d for a french polished model with silver-plated mounts and rubber feet. This seemingly miraculous contraption could be metamorphosed at will into a tennis, croquet or hat stand or easel.

Another ingenious device imported from the New World in the 1840s was the 'Baby Jumper'. A canvas and leather harness enclosed the infant in a seat, and was then hung by a strong elastic spring from the door frame or ceiling, at a height from which the child could just touch the floor. This enabled him to bounce happily and safely in one place. Dr Conquest, *Letters to a Mother on the Management of Herself and Her Children in Health and Disease*, 1848, recommended Roger's 'Patent Infant Gymnasium', or 'Baby Jumper'. Since this was the age when legs spelt unforgivable indecency, a 'modesty apron' in the form of a little skirt was attached to the seat of the jumper to preserve the decency of the child and the sensibilities of the onlooker. In 1849 George Cruikshank's *Comic Almanack* illustrated a whole family bouncing contentedly from the ceiling. Baby jumpers are still in use today, though sometimes suspended from a self-supporting metal frame. This was the case with S. Fawkner Nicholls' 'Baby Care Taker and Exerciser' which was advertised at the turn of the century. Described as 'Thoroughly substantial' and 'very handsome', it was considered suitable 'For use in any room — the lawn — the sands, &c.,' and was available 'Handsomely japanned' at thirty-five shillings or 'Superior in brass' at fifty-five shillings.

Chapter 12

BABY AND TODDLER CLOTHES

Layette and Short-coating

'Your little boy goes on very well, and has just got shoes and short petticoats'.
(Letter from Lady Grantham to the Marchioness of Grey, 1784.)

'Pull off his shoes. Pull off his frock and petticoat. Put on his nightcap. Lay his head on the pillow. Cover him up. Goodnight'.
(*The Child's Spelling Book,* Massachusetts, 1798.)

'The clothing of infants should be warm, light and loose... that kind should be employed which may seem best adapted to secure the equal and tranquil diffusion of the blood throughout the system'.
(Webster's *Encyclopaedia of Domestic Economy,* 1844.)

'All the clothes provided for the advent of the little stranger are made entirely on a false principle, and calculated to produce a baleful influence on its future development.'
(Madame Roxey A. Caplin, *Health & Beauty, or Woman & Her Clothes,* 1864.)

The preparation of a layette, which consisted of a newborn baby's immediate needs, as well as its first clothes up until 'short-coating', helped to occupy a mother during the long, uncertain months of pregnancy, and to take her mind off the impending trials of labour and childbirth. It is clear that some mothers let this enjoyable and anticipatory process go to their heads. The intellectual Margaret, Duchess of Newcastle, railed in the seventeenth century against the unnecessary expense to which women put themselves, and in the eighteenth century Lady Grisel Baillie's daughter, Rachel, spent nearly £200 on clothes, bed linen and equipment for her new baby. In 1821, 'Paris, Brussels, London and Vienna had been ransacked', at a cost of nearly £2,000, for the layette of the future fourth Marquess of Londonderry, by parents who apparently had more money than sense.

Many mothers preferred to sew their own baby clothes, as a labour of love as well as an exercise in thrift. In 1605 Mary Coke wrote to her husband, 'I thank God that I can certify you that I am in health and comfort, and do spend

Plate 145. An 18th century baby's linen shirt, with insertions of Holliepoint lace, and trimmed with bobbin lace. Shirts were worn beneath the swaddling bands, and finely worked examples such as this may well have formed part of a special christening set.

part of my time in making baby's clothes'. A pragmatic approach to the business was taken much later by *Harper's Bazaar* in 1893. 'They (baby clothes) are made precious by the needle work that is put into them. The first baby usually has a good deal of... handwork about his clothes, and the second generally wears out his elder brother's dainty garments. Further children must depend upon the sewing machine for the stitching of their frocks.'

As well as the swaddling bands, bibs, caps or biggins, shirts, mittens and sleeves, 'tailclouts' or nappies were of obvious importance. Usually made of unbleached linen or calico, some thrifty mothers, such as the seventeenth century heiress Lady Anne Clifford, used their husbands' old shirts for the purpose. Mary Thresher, née East, included 106 nappies in the List of her 'Child Bed Linning' in 1698. They included '12 Large figured damask Clouts, 18 small flower'd damask Clouts, 24 fine holland Clouts and 4 dozen and four diaper Clouts'. (Diaper, a formal chequered pattern linen, was used, like damask, for bibs and clouts, hence the American use of the word for nappies.) At night the clouts were covered by a flannel 'pilch' for extra protection, and sometimes a piece of oiled silk helped to reinforce the minimal waterproof effect.

In 1707 Madame de Maintenon wrote of English children that she had observed, 'when they are 2 or 3 months old are no longer tightly swaddled, but under their dress they wear a wrapper and a loose nappy, which are changed as soon as they are soiled'.

At the age of around four to eight weeks seventeenth and eighteenth century babies were 'short-coated' or 'shortened', by having their swaddling bands removed and replaced by wrappers and bellibands worn with a shirt, tailclout,

163

Plate 146. A portrait of the children of Sir Lionel Tollemache, Bart, English School, c.1600-10. Lionel, the baby, who became the second Lord Tollemache, is shown lying on a cushion, wrapped in swaddling bands, which are enclosed by a velvet cover richly embroidered with pearls. His arms are left free, the wrists encased in detachable lace-trimmed cuffs. His two caps and stiff head-dress are similarly edged in lace. The two little girls in the centre of the painting are shown wearing bibs, aprons and cuffs, which were designed to protect their smart and expensive dresses.

The Lord Tollemache, Helmingham Hall. Photograph: Courtauld Institute of Art.

Plate 147. A portrait of Lady Mary Ogilvy, daughter of James, third Earl of Findlater, at the age of nine months, painted by an unknown artist of the Scottish School, 1664. The formal pose shows the attitude of 17th century society to children, who were forced into an adult mould at the first possible opportunity. She wears a lace-edged cap, a bib, apron and detachable collar and sleeves to protect her long frock, garments which she would have assumed after 'short-coating'.

Private Collection.

Plate 148. A late 18th century oil portrait of Mrs Oliver and her sleeping child, by George Romney (1734-1802). This charmingly tender portrait reflects the new ideas, inspired by Rousseau and Locke, of bringing children up naturally, surrounded by love and affection rather than constant rigid discipline and punishment.

Sotheby's.

and flannel petticoat over a frock. During the 1660s, Harry Harper, an Edinburgh merchant, supplied to the 3rd Duchess of Hamilton 'carrying frocks' for babies and 'going frocks' for those who were on their feet. Their baby's bibs were replaced by a more grown-up pinafore, an apron that derived its name because it was pinned to the front of the gown, and in the sixteenth and seventeenth centuries an aptly named muckinder, or handkerchief, was pinned to the child's waist for extra protection. In 1625 the Coke family accounts record: 'Pd. for 3 blue aprons. . . for 2 yards of cobweb laces for Bess (the child)' and in 1629 17s. 4d. was paid 'For 13 yeardes of Scotts (a type of linen) for aprons for little Mrs. Marie and Mrs. Elizabeth Howard'. These were necessary to preserve their ankle-length dresses, worn by boys and girls alike, from dirt and 'slobber'. Quasi-adult dress was worn until the 1760s and 1770s and it was not until the enlightened writings of Jean-Jacques Rousseau, who advocated loose and flowing garments, allied with the growth of imported muslins in the second half of the eighteenth century, that small children's clothes allowed for any freedom of movement at all. Mrs Papendiek describes

Plate 150. A painting of John Ruskin at the age of three and a half, painted by James Northcote (1746-1831), in 1822. 58⅛ in. (122.3cm) x 49⅛ in. (99.4cm). This shows the typical muslin dress worn by boys and girls at the end of the Georgian period, with the low neckline leaving the shoulders bare, puffed sleeves tied up with ribbons, and a high waist echoing the Empire style so fashionable for women. The two rows of tucks round the bottom sensibly allowed for letting-down as the child grew up, and the leading strings made of ribbon enabled the child to be restrained. Sotheby's.

the clothes of her one-year old in 1784: 'We made her four white frocks and two coloured ones, with the skirts full and three tucks and a hem; the bodies plain, cut crossways and the sleeves plain with a cuff turned up'. Fabric for baby clothes of 1785 included 'muslin for 3 common frocks; long lawn for 1 doz. shirts, Cambric for 6 caps; calico for 4 or 5 bedgowns, & flannel for 3 undercoats'. John Ruskin was painted in 1822 at the age of three and a half by James Northcote (1746-1831), at his studio at 39 Argyll Street in 'a white frock like a girl, with broad, light-blue sash and blue shoes to match... These articles of my daily dress were all sent to the old painter for perfect realisation'. White muslin, cotton or calico was invariably used for baby clothes, and similar white dresses for both sexes were worn until the age of five or six, not only because it suited their delicate colouring, but also because there were few colour-fast dyes and those available were thought to be poisonous. The fashion for these loose and comfortable dresses with their simple sprigs of embroidery, which expressed the love of freedom and the response to nature of the Romantic movement, was not to survive far into the nineteenth century.

By the end of the eighteenth century, when infants were allowed to crawl before they could walk, short-coating did not occur until between six and nine months, since infants were no longer thrust onto their feet at such an early age. Until 'shortening', babies of the nineteenth century were swathed in ostentatiously long robes which 'help to keep the feet of the infant safe from cold air... and give a nurse a good hold of a child'. However, they were not to be so long as to 'trail on the ground, or to float with every move made by the nurse, so as to reach the bars of the grate'. Once the requisite age had been reached, small Victorian boys and girls were squeezed into alarmingly *decolleté* dresses which exposed their necks and shoulders to the elements. Dr J.F.

Plate 151. A baby's dress in cambric, the sleeves and Empire style bodice with diagonal bands of inserted needlepoint lace, the hem with a border of white embroidery, c.1819.

Trustees of the Victoria and Albert Museum.

Plate 152. An early 19th century baby's frock, with a waist so high that it is parallel with the armpits. The hem and sides are edged with borders of simple whitework embroidery.

Trustees of the Victoria and Albert Museum.

South, *Domestic Surgery,* urged his readers to 'have your girls' chests covered to the collar bone and their shoulders in, not out of their dresses'. In 1854 Mrs Merrifield, *Dress as a Fine Art,* deplored the fact that 'Girls are suffered to shiver at Christmas, in muslin dresses with bare necks and arms', which only defied gravity in staying up because they were tied so tightly round the waist. At a time when so many children suffered from 'weak chests', and the cough of consumption haunted every household, it seems a strange fashion indeed.

In 1808 *The Lady's Economical Assistant* had decreed that 'it is now so much the fashion to dress children, both boys and girls, in pantaloons instead of petticoats', and during the 1840s and 1850s when skirts shortened and were stiffened out, these became decoratively covered in rows of tiny frills, all the more to cover the legs successfully, the sight of which was now socially unacceptable. Although white frocks had been used for boys and girls until the age of three or four, stiff dresses in plaid wool or velvet became fashionable in the 1840s and 1850s.

Plate 153. From around the 1830s, the simple Georgian styles of dress for babies and children were superseded by more showy and elaborate examples, with skirts sometimes more than one yard long, richly embroidered, and with voluminous flannel and silk petticoats worn underneath for warmth. This cambric example, with a central insertion of Ayrshire whitework embroidery, dates from the middle of the 19th century. Trustees of the Victoria and Albert Museum.

Plate 154. This mid-19th century baby's robe, with cotton embroidery on cambric with drawn work and needlepoint lace fillings, displays the typical Victorian V-shaped bodice and the extravagantly long skirt worn at that date by babes-in-arms. The length of the dress is 45½ in. (115.6cm), and was designed to be shown off as the baby was carried about. Most Victorian babies were 'short-coated' around the age of six to nine months, when an interest in crawling began to be expressed.

Plate 155. An English primitive painting from the middle of the 19th century, showing a young child wearing a muslin dress. The V-shaped bodice has by now taken over from the high waist of the Empire style, and the fine sprigged embroidery has been superseded by broderie anglaise, interspersed with large, and practical pin-tucks. Bonham's.

Plate 156. A miniature watercolour portrait on ivory, signed Nicholas, of Ellen, Alice and William Cooper, showing clearly the unsuitable decolleté styles for children of the mid-19th century. Bare shoulders and cleavages were socially acceptable, but modesty ruled below the belt. Pantaloons ensured that the minimum amount of leg was allowed to show. The younger two children are wearing dresses trimmed with the newly fashionable broderie anglaise. Bonham's.

During the 1870s the popularity of the perambulator peaked, and the awareness of the benefits of fresh air meant that warm woollen and flannel clothing became fashionable for children. Woollen clothing generally received a tremendous boost at this time, when Dr Gustav Jaeger's Sanitary Woollen System exploded into England. Meriting a leader in *The Times* in 1884, it was hailed as 'a new gospel' and acclaimed by *The Lancet* and *The British Medical Journal.* Dr Jaeger became a hero for his invention of 'combination drawers and vest', otherwise known as 'coms'. The fashionable intelligentsia, including Oscar Wilde and George Bernard Shaw, pressed wool to their bodies like a long-lost lover, and the Great Lover himself, Rupert Brooke, dubiously rhapsodized in verse over 'the rough male kiss of blankets'. The Rational Dress Society, founded in 1881, also advocated the use of healthy, sensible clothing, and Aertex and Viyella came into being soon after, in 1888 and 1891. The Society advised that a sensible layette should include '4 woollen binders, 4 woollen vests, 4 flannel or cashmere robes, and 48 Turkish towelling nappies'. *The Gentlewoman's Book of Dress* advocated 'wool next the skin' for babies and recommended Jaeger's 'daintiest little woollen shirts for babies in

Plate 157. A small child's frock from the 1880s, of princess line, and decorated with diagonal rows of pin-tucking, and borders of broderie anglaise. By this time broderie anglaise was machine-made, and provided cheap trimmings for children's clothes.

Christie's, South Kensington.

Plate 158. A 17th century child's knitted shirt and mittens. Very finely knitted, with decorative border patterns, these may have been used as part of a christening set. Knitted garments are very rare at this date, and seldom appear in contemporary paintings. The Rational Dress Society, founded in 1881, and Dr Jaeger's Sanitary Woollen System, introduced into England in 1884, resulted in a tremendous rise in the popularity of woollen clothing for children and babies.

Museum of London.

the finest and softest of wool'. During the early twentieth century knitted woollen baby clothes achieved enormous popularity, although Edwardian children were still literally 'dolled' up by stores such as Harrods and the Army and Navy in silk cream jackets trimmed with lace, and cashmere and alpaca cloaks trimmed with jap silk embroidery. Children's clothes were readily available from manufacturers such as Chilprufe at all the large London stores, and mothers no longer had to spend their pregnancies in stitchery.

Plates 159 and 160. Princess Daisy's Layette, which accompanied the English wax doll of that name, which was exhibited at the International Exhibition in Amsterdam in 1895, and was later presented to Queen Mary. The layette is of great interest because it comprises 'a complete outfit of everything necessary for a royal layette'. Even at such an early age Princess Daisy had frocks for morning and afternoon, as well as a white silk pelisse and a pink satin cape for outdoor appearances. A complete list of the contents of Princess Daisy's Layette, which is in the Bethnal Green Museum of Childhood, is included on the opposite page. Such excesses had their parallel in real life. In 1821 it was recorded that 'Paris, Brussels, London and Vienna had been ransacked' for the layette of the future fourth Marquess of Londonderry, at a cost of nearly £2,000.

172

Princess Daisy's Layette, circa 1895.

1 Christening Frock of real Valenciennes lace	24 Squares
1 white Satin Undergown	24 fine Towels
1 Christening Cap of real Valenciennes lace	6 Pairs of first Drawers
1 Christening Cushion	12 Pairs white Stockings
1 Christening Cover	6 Pairs silk Bootikins
4 Morning Frocks	6 Pairs silk Mittens
2 white Negligées	*1 Cradle* complete with:-
with one pink silk underfrock (long sleeves)	4 embroidered Sheets
4 Afternoon Frocks	4 under Sheets
with one pink satin underfrock (short sleeves)	4 embroidered Pillow Cases
1 white silk Pelisse	1 pink satin Pillow
1 white silk Bonnet with real lace veil	1 pink satin Quilt, &c.,
1 pink satin Cape	*1 Basket* complete with:-
1 Dressing Gown	1 ivory Powder Box
1 Woollen Jacket	1 ivory Hair Brush, &c., &c., &c.,
1 Shawl	1 silver Hot Water Bottle with 4 flannel Covers
1 Flannel Head-square	*Princess Daisy's Christening Presents*
2 Woollen Hoods	1 Necklace in real pearls and diamond clasp
1 silk Hood	1 Gold Bracelet
6 hemstitched Chemises	1 Gold Brooch
6 flannel Vests	1 Real Silver Mug
6 woollen Vests	1 Real Silver Rattle
6 Night Gowns	1 Real Silver fork and 2 spoons
6 swansdown piqué peticoats *(sic.)*	1 Real Silver Porridge Bowl and Spoon
6 flannel Squares	1 Real Silver Food Boat
6 white Peticoats *(sic.)*	

Baby's Layette from *The Gentle Craft*, by Thomas Delaney, 1597-1600.

Soap	Tailclouts (nappies)
Candles	Mantles
Beds (wrapping cloths)	Hose
Shirts	Shoes
Biggins (caps)	Coats
Waistcoats	Petticoats
Headbands	Cradle
Swaddlebands	Crickets (low stools for the
Crossclothes (forehead bands)	attending midwife)
Bibs	

At the Foundling Hospital, founded by Captain Thomas Coram in 1742, newly admitted babies were issued with the following layette:-

4 linnen biggens (bonnets)
4 linnen stays
4 linnen caps (worn under the bonnets)
4 linnen neckcloths
4 linnen shirts
12 linnen clouts (nappies)
1 grey linsey mantle (cloak)
1 Pr. of grey linsey sleeves (detachable woollen sleeves)
2 white bays blankettes
One rowle (roller)
2 double pilches (thick pieces of flannel worn over the clouts at night for extra protection).

Baby's Layette, 1843. (Cunnington family correspondence, quoted in *Costume for Births, Deaths and Marriages* by Phillis Cunnington and Catherine Lucas, 1972.)

4 nightgowns	3 whittles (large white shawls)
4 day caps	6 shirts
5 long robes	2 flannel caps
4 day gowns	2 short chemises
8 pinafores	Baby linen, basket and cover
24 napkins	Powder Box
3 flannel barrows (wrapping petticoats)	Pincushion
9 back wrappers	Feather for bed, and blanket
4 flannel belts or soft binders (band of fabric tied round baby's abdomen for warmth and support)	Sponge
	Soft Hairbrush

The layette for a newborn baby recommended by the Army & Navy
Stores in 1907 consisted of the following:-

	£	s.	d.
6 lawn Shirts @ 1/9		10	6
3 " " @ 2/8........................		8	0
4 Woven Linen Swathes @ 8½d.		2	10
3 Flannel Swathes @ 8½d.		2	1½
4 Night Flannels @ 0/10d.		7	4
4 Day " @ 3/4		13	4
6 Night Gowns @ 3/0		18	0
3 Day " @ 4/6		13	6
3 " " @ 5/9		17	3
3 Doz. Linen Towels @ 10/6	1	11	6
6 Flannel Pilches @ 1/2		7	0
2 Waterproof Pilches @ 1/2		2	4
4 Pairs wool Boots @ 1/0		4	0
4 Fancy Bibs @ 1/0		4	0
2 " " @ 1/6........................		3	0
4 long Slips @ 3/8		14	8
1 embroidered head flannel...............		8	9
1 Robe, trimmed, embroidered		14	6
1 " " lace	1	1	6
1 " " "	1	15	6
1 Cashmere Cloak	1	10	0
1 silk hood	1	10	6
	£14	0	1½

Baby's Layette from Harvey Nichols' *Catalogue*, circa 1936.

6 Wrapover vests
4 long flannels (wrapping petticoats)
4 long petticoats
6 day gowns
6 cotton nightgowns
2 Chilprufe nightgowns
6 nun's veiling nightgowns
2 robes of muslin, organdie, or net
6 knitted jackets
1 wool shawl
2 lightweight wool shawls

1 silk matinée jacket
6 embroidered muslin bibs
36 Turkish squares
36 Harrington's squares
2 pairs of cot blankets
6 linen pillowslips
2 embroidered muslin pillowslips
1 down quilt
Cot hangings
Layette Basket

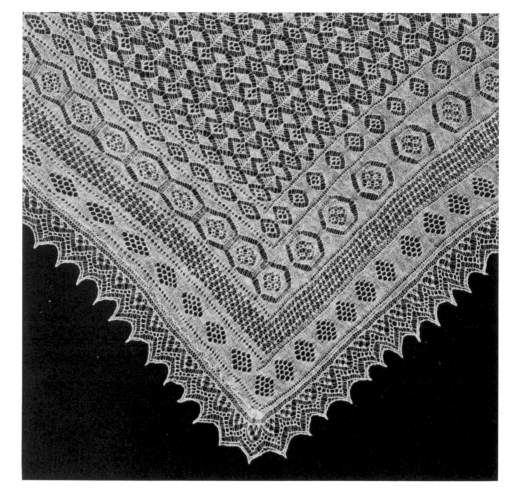

Plate 161. An Edwardian baby's shawl knitted in Shetland wool. The baby was wrapped for the first weeks of his life in a shawl of hand-woven cashmere, knitted wool or silk. Such filmy garments were known as 'zephyrs' or 'whittles', and many were worked by the mother herself. During the 19th century 'veils' of fine Shetland wool were worn over the baby's face to protect it from the cold.

Shawls

By the 1830s the young baby was carried around in a flannel square, or a fine knitted shawl. These were sometimes known as 'zephyrs' because of the airy lightness of the lacy hand-knitting, or 'whittles' (Old English 'white mantles') and were often made by the mother of the baby, while awaiting the birth of her child. Soft Shetland wool was used for knitted examples, and alternatives were to be had in woven cashmere with white embroidery and fringeing. By the 1840s the town of Paisley in Scotland was developing the manufacture of shawls with elaborate woven designs of colourful oriental inspiration, which were sometimes used for carrying babies out-of-doors.

Mothers who preferred frills and furbelows to sensible clothing sent their infants out to the park in cloaks or pelisses trimmed with swansdown and broderie anglaise. In some circles shawls were regarded as vulgar, working-class garments, and in 1896 Mrs Panton, in *The Way They Should Go,* felt that she should attempt, albeit half-heartedly, to correct such prejudices. 'That mother is wise who simply buys a charming shawl and sends out her baby wrapped in that. I know, for naturally one recollects with a shudder the people and babies one often sees in connection with these garments, but Liberty's sells such charming white soft shawls, that I think if effort in the right direction were made, it would not be so dreadful after all'.

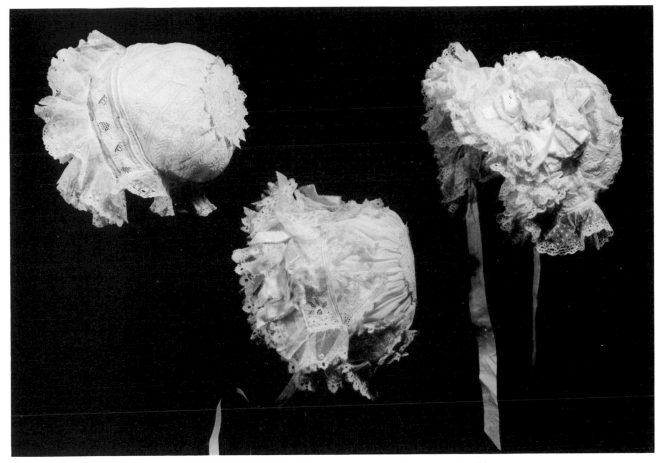

Plate 162. Three extremely elaborate 19th century muslin and lace caps, lavishly trimmed with ribbons and with a plethora of tucks and frills, all embellished with white embroidery. Items such as these were clearly intended for special occasions, their layers of filmy white muslin designed to show off and frame the tiny face at their centre. Coloured ribbon was often used to enhance the effect, or perhaps a lining of pale blue or pink silk which glowed softly through the white. From the middle of the 19th century machine-made laces meant that bonnets became even more elaborate.

Museum of London.

Caps and Bonnets

Caps were always considered of great importance, since they were thought to prevent heat loss from the head and help regulate the baby's body temperature. Fear of 'chills' meant that all babies and small children wore caps both day and night, indoors and out. In 1633 Dr Chambers, in a letter to King Charles I about the illness of his son, wrote, 'He stood late looking out at the bedchamber window in the hands of one of his rockers, without either hat upon his head or neckcloth to his neck, which myself did see and reprove the rocker'. Until the end of the eighteenth century two caps were worn by babies, a plain one, covered by a lace-edged or embroidered one over the top. Pamela, in Samuel Richardson's novel of the same name (1740), describes a baby, as 'triple-crowned like a young pope with covering upon covering', and as late as 1799 *The Lady's Monthly Magazine* advised that 'two caps should be put on the head until the child has most of its teeth'.

Caps, coifs or biggins, as they were called, feature regularly in seventeenth

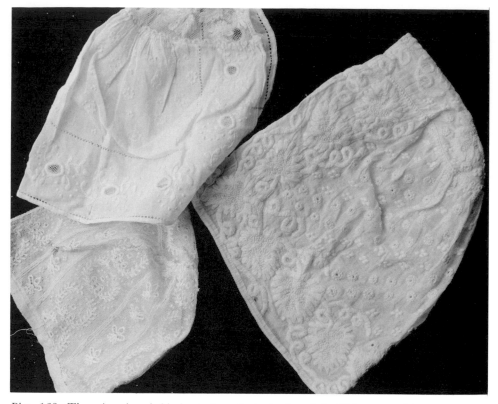

Plate 163. Three American babies' caps from the beginning of the 19th century. Two are of cotton muslin with white embroidery, the third of embroidered net, with a pink silk lining, Philadelphia area. These sprigged designs are typical of early 19th century work, c.1800-20.

The Henry Francis du Pont Winterthur Museum.

century layette lists and account books. They were usually of plain linen, with a border of vermicular embroidery in laid cord, 'lac't', edged with lace, or 'cruel', crewel-embroidered. A 'cross-clothe' was a triangular piece of linen worn under the caps and tied under the chin or behind the head.

In the eighteenth century caps became more decorative, with tiny insertions of Holliepoint lace, showing geometric devices such as stars, flowers or hearts, and with a date or initials sometimes added. Holliepoint (thought to derive from the words Holy point) is a form of needlepoint lace related to detached button-hole stitch, with the pattern formed by tiny holes left in the tightly knotted rows. The geometric motifs, particularly the stars, have the same naïve simplicity common to much primitive art and seen in folk patterns as diverse as Fair Isle knitting or Turkish rugs. Such caps were particularly worn at christenings, with dates from the 1730s to 1770s predominating. Very often the holliepoint panel was removed as the child grew up, to be re-used in other baby's clothes.

During the colder weather, caps and other baby clothes, in quilting, were worn. 'Italian' quilting, used particularly on babies' caps, was patterned by a piece of linen cord being inserted with a bodkin between two parallel lines of back stitch. Two layers of linen were stitched together in this way, sometimes with a layer of wool between.

Towards the end of the eighteenth century bonnets became more flimsy and elaborate, with several layers of lace sewn onto the muslin, creating an effect

178

Plate 164. A black chalk and watercolour portrait of Lady Henrietta Elizabeth Cavendish, younger daughter of the fifth Duke of Devonshire, by Elizabeth Royall, later Mrs Surtees, after John Russell, R.A. Lady Henrietta (known generally as Harriet) was born in 1785, and is shown here wearing one of the elaborate lace-trimmed caps so typical of the 1780s. With its high 'balloon' crown, it reflects the interest in hot air ballooning, which surrounded the ascent of Lunardi's balloon in 1784. It is this style of cap, together with the long mittens which late 18th century little girls wore 'to preserve the arm in beauty for womanhood' which Kate Greenaway revived in her pretty, innocent illustrations of the 1890s.

The Devonshire Collection, Chatsworth. Reproduced by permission of the Chatsworth Settlement Trustees.

of white froth around the baby's face. For formal occasions flowers, or ribbons, which matched the colour of the sash of the dress, could be added to the already heavily-frilled cap. *The Young Gentleman's and Lady's Polite Tutor* for 1770 stipulated that headwear should include 'For young ladies from three to fourteen years old a Feather, a Flower, Egret or Ribband or Pompon. These are proper for dancing in', and in 1789 Mrs Papendiek described her daughters in her *Diary* 'in their new pink sashes and new caps with ribbon to match'.

Her first daughter, Charlotte, wore a cap with a blue bow at the age of one and it is worth noting that 'pink for a girl and blue for a boy' is a tradition

Plate 165. An oil painting by Daniel Gardner, c.1810, of a young girl wearing an elaborate lace-trimmed cap, and holding a rattle, 18¼in. (46.4cm) x 15¾in. (40cm). As usual in the case of little girls, the cockade in this painting is placed in the front of her cap. Sotheby's.

shrouded in superstition and mystery, which appears to have crept into use during the late nineteenth or early twentieth century. It was certainly not adhered to during the eighteenth or the main part of the nineteenth centuries. There were, however, other ways of distinguishing the sex of a child. *The Workwoman's Guide,* 1838, while describing hoods, confirms that 'a rosette of satin ribbon is worn on the left side if a boy, and in front, if a girl'.

As the eighteenth century gave way to the nineteenth, caps and bonnets became ever more elaborate. Susan Sibbald described a two-month old baby, circa 1811-12, with 'a bare neck and a cap like a sunflower, with a scarlet cockade to match the ribbons of the robe' and Fanny Kemble's father, circa 1810, arranged to have 'an especially pretty and becoming lace cap at hand in the drawing room' for when visitors called.

By the mid-nineteenth century new ideas about hygiene and fresh air lead to indoor caps falling from favour, though Mrs Beeton was firm in the 1860s that 'the infant during the first month must not be exposed to strong light, or much air; and in carrying it about the passages, stairs, &c., the nurse should

Colour Plate 36. A baby's cap with holliepoint lace insertions, late 18th century.
Museum of Costume, Bath.

Colour Plate 37. A portrait miniature on ivory by Andrew Plimer (1763-1837) of a little girl wearing a frilled cap with a blue cockade and decolleté, Empire-style dress, 2⅞in. (7.3cm), c.1800. Around her neck is a string of coral beads, worn by children for centuries, and by small girls until the present day.
Private Collection.

always have its head-flannel on, to protect the eyes and ears from the currents of air'.

In 1854 Mrs Merrifield in *Dress as a Fine Art,* wrote 'Caps with their trimmings of three or four rows of lace and large cockades which rivalled in size the dear little round face of the child are discontinued almost entirely within doors, though the poor child is still overwhelmed with cap, hat and feathers in its daily airing'. This was because the advent of the perambulator meant that the focus of fashion had turned from the long carrying robes of the first half of the nineteenth century to the head of the child, which was now becomingly framed by the hood of the pram. Competitive mothers and nurses looked now to the headwear of the baby to gauge the status of his parents, and bonnets decorated with frothy layers of Buckinghamshire or Valenciennes lace were popular. Edith Wharton, writing of her childhood in New York in the 1860s, described her white satin winter bonnet, 'patterned with a pink and green plaid in raised velvet'. 'It was all drawn into close gathers..., and thick ruffles of silky blonde lace under the brim in front. A gossamer veil of the finest white Shetland wool hung down over the wearer's cheeks and like the white paper filigree over a Valentine'.

During the early twentieth century knitted and crocheted bonnets in fine wool were fashionable.

Chapter 13

CHILDREN'S CLOTHES

Breeching and Boys' Clothes

'Joy to Philip, he this day,
Has his long coat cast away,
And the childish season gone,
Put the manly breeches on.'
(Anon.)

'Sunday, November 1, 1801. Hartley breeched — dancing to the jingling of the
money — but eager & solemn Joy, not his usual whirl-about gladness'.
(Extract from the *Notebooks of Samuel Taylor Coleridge.*)
(Hartley was born in 1796.)

At the age of three or four in the seventeenth century, and five or six in the
eighteenth century, it was customary for a small boy to take the important,
symbolic and exciting step out of the ankle-length frocks or 'coats' which he
had worn since short-coating, and be dressed in the manly attire of breeches.
Many contemporary portraits appear of a young boy wearing breeches and
standing in a precociously commanding attitude, with his hand on a sword or
dagger hilt, and with a short cloak or cape over his shoulders. A Stuart
breeching in the North household is described in *The Lives of the Norths,*
published in 1890, by the boy's grandmother. 'Never had any bride that was
to be drest upon her wedding night more hands about her, some the legs and
some the arms, the taylor buttoning, and others putting on the sword, and so
many lookers on that had I not a ffinger amongst them I could not have seen
him'.

The breeches assumed at 'breeching' were a carbon copy of adult male
dress, and it was not until 1780 that a garment designed exclusively for
children made its appearance. This was the 'skeleton suit', which consisted of
ankle-length trousers in Nankeen or cotton drill, which were easily washed.
The trousers were buttoned onto the parallel rows of buttons on a tight-fitting
jacket, with a soft lawn frilled shirt worn underneath. It allowed for freedom
of movement in accordance with the new Romantic love of nature, and in its
similarity to the trousers worn by seamen and some labourers appealed to the
Revolutionary and egalitarian sentiments of the day. Such a 'skeleton suit' was
described by Dickens in *Sketches by Boz* (1838-39) as 'one of those straight blue

Colour Plate 38. A portrait of three young girls, by a member of the Circle of Robert Peake, c.1600-20. This enchanting triple portrait shows the finery, all of it in a very grown-up style, with which well-born small children of the late Tudor period were arrayed. The costly orange and scarlet damask gowns are lavishly trimmed with gold lace, with head-dresses, cuffs and ruffs in 'punto-in-aria' lace. The padded 'wings' or shoulder pads cover the seams of the sleeves, which were probably detachable, and the little girl's leading strings can clearly be seen attached to them at the back. These could be used to tie her into her high chair at mealtimes, and to restrain and guide her while learning to walk. All the children are wearing coral jewellery as a protection against evil and disease. The middle child wears a ring attached to her wrist with a black cord, so that she will not lose it.

As a child, Mary Queen of Scots, born in 1542, numbered among her wardrobe shot red and yellow taffeta for dresses, dresses of gold damask, canvas and buckram to stiffen the dresses, orange taffeta petticoats lined with red serge, rose leaves of gold thread for caps, and gold and silver paillettes to be sewn onto her clothes, as well as jewelled buttons and other items of jewellery.

Private Collection.

cloth cases in which small boys used to be confined... an ingenious contrivance for displaying the symmetry of a boy's figure by fastening him into a very tight jacket with an ornamental row of Buttons over each shoulder and then buttoning his trousers over it so as to give his legs the appearance of being hooked on just under the arm-pits'.

Skeleton suits remained the fashion until the 1830s, when pantaloons were worn by boys under a tunic or frock. Such tunics had tightly fitting bodices and full, pleated skirts, and were frequently trimmed with frogging, braid and gimp. They are yet another confirmation that the Victorian era was indeed the

Colour Plate 39. A portrait of James Cecil, fourth Earl of Salisbury and his eldest sister, Lady Catherine Cecil, by John Michael Wright, c.1668. Lady Catherine, although four or five years old, is still wearing leading strings to match her lavish pale blue frock, which is shot with silver thread. To protect it she wears a trimmed apron, with a bib of gros point de Venise. *Her small, though regal, brother, wears a V-shaped stomacher bib over his white and silver frock. There is little childish innocence in this state portrait, which combines symbols of classicism with emblems of wealth to produce an icon of power and noble blood.* The Marquis of Salisbury.

Colour Plate 40. A portrait of the Croft Children, 1803, attributed to Sir William Beechey (1753-1839). Frances, seated second from the left, aged three, is shown wearing a lace-edged muslin cap, embroidered in white and trimmed with a blue ribbon to match the sash of her muslin dress. Although blue, the rosette is placed firmly in the front, denoting her sex. Thomas, aged five, bottom right, is dressed in a fashionable 'skeleton' suit. Herbert, aged ten, top right, sadly died in 1803, while at Westminster School, and there is a family tradition that his portrait may have been painted in posthumously. Certainly there is an air of sadness about him not seen in the lively expressions of the younger children, and his figure is set slightly apart by the painter. The children's father, Sir Richard Croft (1762-1818) was physician to King George III. He attended the Prince Regent's only daughter, Princess Charlotte, who died in childbirth in 1817 at the age of twenty-one.

The Lord Croft.

Colour Plate 41. An oil portrait of Sir Edward St. Aubyn, Bt. by Samuel Lane. The young boy, born in 1799, is shown wearing a fashionable 'skeleton suit'. Worn since the 1780s, boys were dressed in these after the age of four, and the fashion declined during the 1830s. For the first time small boys were dressed in childish clothes, and not in miniature versions of the breeches, coat and waistcoat of their elders. The revolutionary trousers, so much more practical for childish pursuits, were made of easily washed cotton, with a cotton or lawn shirt with a soft frill buttoned on above the waist, which became acceptable in adult male dress around 1825. Hair was short and simple, and the good sense of the whole style was in direct response to the egalitarian teachings of Rousseau, and the Romantics' liking for a more natural way of life. Private Collection.

Colour Plate 42. A boy's tunic or frock, c.1858, of plaid wool with woollen braid trimming, the jacket, bodice and skirt all in one. Until the age of five or six there was very little difference in the frocks worn by mid-Victorian boys and girls. Such frocks would have been worn with trousers beneath, or drawers. The checked plaid anticipates the fashion for Highland dress popularized by Queen Victoria. Private Collection.

Colour Plate 43. A watercolour portrait of Charles Graham and Edward Curteis Graham, by George Richmond, signed and dated 1835. The older boy wears a fashionable white-collared tunic with a full skirt over his practical trousers. Private Collection.

Age of Upholstery, and must have given stout small boys something of the appearance of a button-backed *chaise longue*. Heavy checked plaid materials (a loose translation of authentic tartans), were fashionable and were a reflection of the contemporary taste for Caledonia witnessed in the novels of Sir Walter Scott, and the romance with which the public, including Queen Victoria, regarded all things from north of the border. *The Lady's Newspaper,* 1849, mentions 'those dark chequered woollen fabrics, now in general use for children's clothing', and in November 1844 Cecilia Ridley described how Matt 'and little Eddy are both in plaid frocks and really look very nice'.

By the 1860s knickerbockers had become popular and the use of trousers again became widespread.

Colour Plate 44. An Edwardian oil painting, entitled Under the Christmas Tree, *by Edmund Kregczy, signed and dated 1902. This shows two children opening their presents on Christmas morning, the girl dressed in a white frilled pinafore and coral necklace over her red dress, the boy in a sailor suit with knickerbockers. This style of dress was made popular after the Prince of Wales, in his sailor suit, was painted by Winterhalter in 1846, and has remained popular ever since.*
Private Collection.

Sailor Suits

'A boy before he rises to the dignity of trousers and jackets is never so happy as in a middy suit or a Jack Tar, and these suits are now selling in thousands.'

On 26 August, 1846, Lady Lyttleton, in charge of the royal children, wrote 'Princey quite at home in his sailor's dress — ''Je suis un petit mousse''. It seems to please all the people who see it — John Bulls and Jack Tars. It was a good notion of Her Majesty'. The sailor suit in question had been made at the Queen's command by a ship's tailor on board the Royal Yacht, the *Victoria and Albert,* for her eldest son, Prince Albert, later Edward VII. The following month, on a cruise off the Channel Islands, 'Bertie put on his sailor's dress... When he appeared, the officers and sailors, who were all assembled on deck to see him, cheered and seemed delighted with him'.

Not only the loyal members of the Queen's Navy were delighted. The vogue for nautical dress for children spread rapidly after the five year old Prince of Wales was painted by Winterhalter in his sailor suit in 1846. It was to be an enduring fashion. In 1874 his own children were photographed in sailor suits, and in 1879 *The Queen* magazine confirmed 'sailor suits are always popular... and ever since the Prince of Wales's two sons have adopted naval uniform the preference has increased'. (The two Princes, Eddy and Georgie, the latter to become King George V, were sent in 1877 to continue their studies on board the *Britannia* for two years.) There were many variations on the nautical theme with, generally speaking, white blouses for summer and navy blue for winter.

Ada Ballin, *The Science of Dress*, 1885 declared that 'a very pretty and nice dress for boys when breeched is the sailor's suit which, by its looseness, allows free movement, and is very durable and covers all the limbs... it may be worn until the boy is old enough to wear ordinary trouser suits'.

However, not all was sweetness and light. Compton Mackenzie, describing his childhood in the 1880s wrote 'By now I was always in a sailor suit. The hated petticoats had gone for ever some months before, but my knickerbockers instead of being kept up by braces were buttoned to a sort of red flannel corset. This was a source of grief to me, and I longed for braces'.

In fact, with its wide trousers or knickerbockers, and loose open-necked shirts which were equally comfortable in cotton or wool as the season demanded, the sailor suit was one of the most sensible of children's fashions and was easily adapted for girls by the replacement of the trousers by a pleated or gathered skirt. On cold days a nautical reefer jacket could be worn on top. Boys and girls still dress in sailor suits for weddings and smart parties today.

Highland Dress

Another enduring children's fashion to be instigated as a result of Queen Victoria's holiday travels, was that of Highland dress. In 1849, her children were painted at Balmoral by Winterhalter wearing kilts. In 1852 *The Lady's Newspaper* warbled enthusiastically that 'the costume worn by the Prince of Wales, when at Balmoral, has set the fashion of adopting the complete Highland costume'. A craze for velvet jackets and waistcoats, sporrans and Glengarry caps swept the nurseries of the nation. But as always there was a dissenting voice. The formidable Ada Ballin, an authority on 'Rational Dress', and editor of the magazine, *Baby,* blasted off in vehement terms against the kilt in her *Science of Dress,* stopping short only of condemning them as works of the Devil. 'Scotch suits for boys, which are so fashionable, and so much admired, are an abomination owing to the way in which they expose the legs'. She continued her tirade by quoting the dreadful case of a six year old boy who had not grown since the age of three because his legs were thus 'exposed'. In spite of her diatribe, kilts for children are still fashionable today, for children's parties, weddings and other social events.

An account from Meyer & Mortimer, 'Navy and Army Contractors, Tailors

Colour Plate 45. A portrait of the Hon. James Charles Plant Murray by Sir Edwin Henry Landseer, c.1824-26. Although some years before the fashion for dressing children in the costume of Highlanders became the rage, this shows the kilt and its accessories adapted for children's wear. In 1849 Queen Victoria's children were painted at Balmoral by Winterhalter in just such a costume and The Lady's Newspaper *of 1852 confirmed that 'the costume worn by the Prince of Wales, when at Balmoral, has set the fashion of adopting the complete Highland costume.'*
From His Grace the Duke of Atholl's Collection at Blair Castle, Perthshire.

& Clothiers to Her Majesty & the Royal Family, Royal Clan-Tartan Warehouse, 105 George Street, Edinburgh, and at 36 Conduit Street, London' includes the following entry for October 23rd, 1847:

'Saxony wool shepherds check kilt and scarf   £2 12s. 6d.
For his Royal Highnefs Prince Alfred
Black silk velvet Doublet,
lined with silk & trimmed with silver braid   £4 14s. 6d.'

Colour Plate 46. A watercolour of The Little Visitors *by Caroline Paterson, which clearly shows the influence on children's dress of the book illustrations of Kate Greenaway, who, it was said, had 'dressed the children of two continents'.*
Phillips.

Aesthetic Clothes

'Mama: ''Who are those extraordinary-looking children?'' Effie: ''The Cimabue Browns, Mama. They're Aesthetic, you know'' '.
(Gerald du Maurier cartoon, *Punch.*)

During the 1870s and 1880s the Aesthetic Movement swept across England, leaving in its wake a band of devoted followers with addresses in 'Passionate Brompton' and other fashionable quarters, their drawing-rooms filled with peacock feathers, 'art embroideries' and Japanese screens, a sunflower wilting in a blue and white vase on every windowsill. Things ancient and foreign were *de rigueur*, bright colours were considered 'unartistic', and fashionable women dressed in loose, flowing gowns in drab colours. 'Greenery-yallery' silk or 'cobwebby grey velvet with a tender bloom like cold gravy' were the order of the day. For their children, the work of book illustrators such as Kate Greenaway provided the inspiration for similarly loose garments in a quaint, bygone style. Walter Crane, too, took a keen interest in children's dress and drew some designs for the journal of the Healthy and Artistic Dress Union, between 1893 and 1894.

Colour Plate 47. A girl's dress in ivory wool, possibly by Liberty's, with smocked yoke and cuffs, lace trimmings and gold bows, embroidered with flowers in shades of gold, c.1880. This is an example of the agricultural smock turned Aesthetic. The gold of the bows and embroidery is typical of the love for 'greenery-yallery' colours, and was a favourite of the 1880s. Liberty's store in London was the Mecca of the aesthetically-minded. Private Collection.

Mrs Oscar Wilde remarked in *Woman's World,* 1888, 'it is probably owing to artists having turned their attention to matters of dress that we see so many picturesquely dressed children around us'. More robust and philistine members of the Establishment were merciless in their criticism of 'aesthetic dress', and found a champion in Gerald du Maurier's cartoons for *Punch* of little Monna Givronda Cimabue Brown. Her intellectually precocious siblings exposed themselves to ridicule by flagrantly preferring the National Gallery and Bach's 'glorious Passionmusik' to an outing to the Zoo or a pantomime.

E. Nesbit, a typically 'modern' woman, wrote in 1885 of one of her daughters, 'I dress Iris (an Aesthetic-sounding name based on the vogue for poppies, lilies, sunflowers and other tall flowers capable of wilting artistically) in a kind of loose gown now — it comes a little below her knees and she looks so aesthetic and pretty in it. It is old gold colour'. Bright colours were 'out' for children as well as their mothers, and Ellen Terry recalled with a shudder that when her daughter, Edy, born in 1871, was given a doll 'dressed in a violent pink silk', she refused to play with it and said it was 'vulgar'.

The Kate Greenaway look was another symptom of the Aesthetic movement. A hugely successful illustrator of children's books, her first book, *Under the Window,* was published in 1878. In 1883 the first Kate Greenaway *Almanack* appeared, and sold a staggering ninety thousand copies in England, America, France and Germany. Her influence on children's dress was profound, and it was said that through the pages of her books 'she dressed the children of two continents'. Little girls were dressed up in *fin-de-siècle* interpretations of late eighteenth century and Regency fashions, with a particular emphasis on large frilled caps and bonnets, flounced tippets and fichus, high-waisted dresses and mittens. *The Queen,* 1890, trilled that such a dress 'recalls the good little women and men in Hoppner's pictures, with its high-waisted slip of a bodice'. Lady Harberton, president of the Rational Dress Society, disapproved of these somewhat frivolous fashions. Miss Greenaway, she asserted, 'clothed the children of her fancy in "pretty" garments totally unsuited to the practical needs and comforts of boys and girls'. But mothers knew best, and adored the innocent, sentimental appearance which such clothes gave to their children. In short, they made them look 'good'. Enid Starkie, born in 1897, gave the child's eye view. 'My mother treated us like a pair of dolls, always picturesquely dressed in full-length Kate Greenaway frocks with fichus and wide sashes, and we wore large poke bonnets... I hated all picturesque clothes and I longed to be dressed like other children'. In fact, she longed for a sailor suit 'perfect in every detail, down to the whistle on a white cord tucked into the breast pocket'. But her mother 'thought such a dress too ordinary'.

By the end of the 1870s, smocked dresses in cotton and linen became fashionable for children, as a result of the nostalgia for old country crafts generated by the Arts and Crafts Movement. Loose and comfortable, they were closely modelled on the smocks worn by agricultural workers, and in 1880 *The Ladies' Treasury* informed its readers that 'the fancy of the moment is for

Colour Plate 48. A portrait of Maud Amelia Cassell, painted by Anders Zorn in 1887 when the sitter was seven years old. Her full, waisted dress in 'old gold' silk was typical of the fashion for 'aesthetic' clothes in murky colours and allowing scope for movement. Private Collection.

Colour Plate 49. A child's scarlet twilled cotton smock, c.1890-1900, with silk embroidery to the yoke, collar, pockets and cuffs. These smocked cotton or linen dresses, so loose and comfortable for children to wear, were a by-product of the Arts and Crafts Movement and its interest in the revival of traditional skills. They were closely modelled on the smocks worn by agricultural workers.

Private Collection.

Plate 166. A silver print photograph of a young girl and a baby, late 19th/ early 20th century, showing the plain linen clothes worn by the children of the poor.

The Shaftesbury Society.

children to wear the new provincial smock made exactly like carters' or waggoners' dowlais frocks... They are decidedly not becoming to little folks'. However, by 1888, *Woman's World* could exclaim, 'How pretty are those old English smock frocks that have of late years become so fashionable for children of all ages', and in 1890 *The Queen* cooed that 'Pretty blouse-waisted frocks for boys and girls are made either in pink, blue or white, smocked at the throat, and with the short skirt composed simply of a 9 inch flounce of embroidery'. For smaller children, 'Nothing could be daintier for a damsel of one or two years old than a little smock of white washing silk'.

Arthur Liberty, head of Liberty's, the London store which had become the Mecca of the aesthetically-minded, joined forces with E.W. Godwin, the architect and designer, who was a costume historian, Honorary Secretary of the Costume Society and had been described by Oscar Wilde as 'the greatest aesthete of them all'. Between them, they set out to 'establish the craft of dressmaking upon some hygienic and intelligible basis' in the Costume Department at Liberty's. The 'Mab' smock was one of their most popular lines in the early years of this century, and small girls still wear smocked dresses from Liberty's 'for best' today.

Chapter 14

GOING OUTSIDE

Perambulators

'One of the most extraordinary inventions of the age'.
(J.H. Walsh, *Manual of Domestic Economy,* 1873.)

'But where do you live mostly now?'
'With the Lost Boys'.
'Who are they?'
'They are the children who fall out of their perambulators when the
nurse is looking the other way'.
(J.M. Barrie, *Peter Pan and Wendy,* 1911.)

'My aged friend, Miss Wilkinson,
Whose mother was a Lambe,
Saw Wordsworth once, and Coleridge, too,
One morning in her pram'.
'This was a three-wheeled vehicle,
Of iron and of wood,
It had a leather apron,
But it hadn't any hood'.
(Walter de la Mare (1873-1956), *The Bards.*)

In the days before the advent of the perambulator, nurses and mothers who were tired of carrying babies about in their arms often resorted to all kinds of wheeled vehicles in order to give their aching limbs a rest. For the children of the nobility such a thing was always managed in the grand manner, and William, the young son of the future Queen Anne, was presented by the Duchess of Ormonde with a miniature carriage drawn by ponies the size of dogs. The earliest known surviving baby carriage in England was designed by William Kent and made for the children of the third Duke of Devonshire in 1730. An elaborate and splendid construction, made in the shape of a scallop shell and with entwined snakes which echo those of the Devonshire family crest, forming the towing bar, it was designed to be pulled by an animal, such as a goat, small pony or large dog. With its carriage lamps, upholstered interior and leather hood, it is very reminiscent of a contemporary carriage, and such pieces were indeed made by coach builders on the great estates.

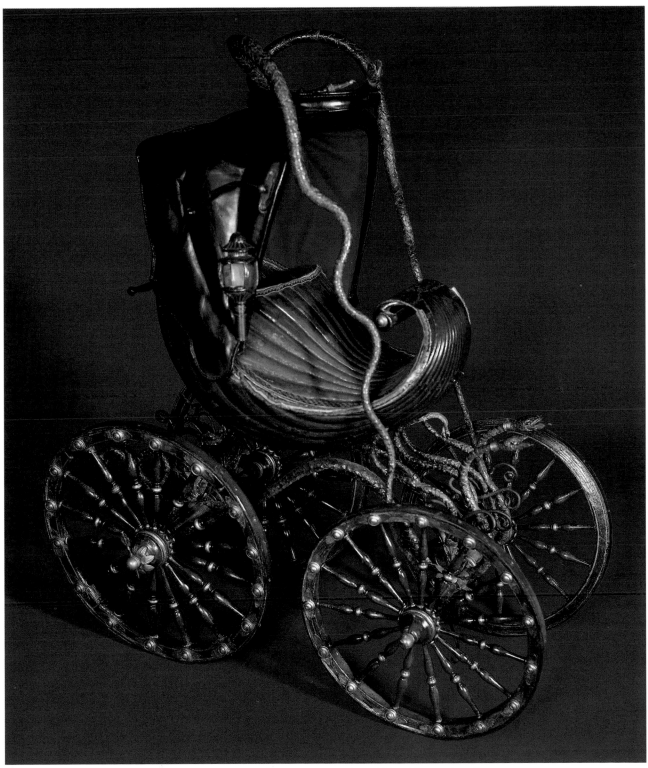

Colour Plate 50. The earliest known baby carriage in England, designed by William Kent and made for the children of the third Duke of Devonshire in 1730. The body is shaped like a shell, inspired no doubt by classical representations of Venus riding in her scallop shell, and is complete with a canopy with carriage lamps and an apron which is incorporated into the design as the interior of the shell. Such an object speaks volumes about the importance attached by noble families in the 18th century to displays of rank and wealth.

Other baby carriages of the period figure in contemporary paintings, and are often no more than a seat fixed to a platform, which is mounted on wheels with a towing bar at the front. Richly decorated mid-eighteenth century rococo examples, lavishly carved and gilt, or painted with the family crest, can be seen in paintings such as the *Graham Children* by William Hogarth, now in the Tate Gallery, or the *FitzPatrick Children* by George Knapton, at Woburn Abbey. These have tow bars, and were designed to be pulled along by a liveried manservant, or perhaps by an older brother or sister. The larger wheels were always at the back, as in horse-drawn carriages, to allow for a tighter turning circle. A baby carriage made for Lady Georgiana Cavendish in 1784 at Chatsworth is raised on four C-springs with a rotating front axle for greater comfort and mobility.

The children of the poor were, at this date, transported where necessary in a stick or spindle wagon, of the type used by hop-pickers and farm workers since early times. Wyclif refers in the fourteenth century to 'waynes' being used for the 'carriage of little children'. Although these boxes on wheels were vastly uncomfortable and draughty, with no springs to cushion the extremities of the children from a bumpy ride over rutted cart tracks, they were reasonably safe, since the child was protected by the high sides from falling out, a major hazard in more assuming baby-carriages.

The demand for a more satisfactory method of transporting small children

Plate 168. An early 19th century drawing by John Alfred Giles showing a family group of five children. The baby is enjoying an outing in a sophisticated cross between a baby carriage and a stick wagon, which is being pulled by a rope, rather than a wooden handle. Such early carriages had to be pulled since they were built by coach and carriage makers, and were therefore unsatisfactory because the mother could not watch her child. No safety straps were fitted to restrain exuberant toddlers.
Bonham's.

Plate 169. 19th century print entitled A Day's Pleasure, The Journey Out, *showing a father pulling his children in a stick wagon.* Jack Hampshire's Pram Museum.

out-of-doors arose as the healthy preference for fresh air developed into a cult during the first half of the nineteenth century. Babies were suspended in little trays from window sills to inhale the life-giving draughts, or carried in their nurse's arms before an open window. The windows of nurseries were flung open with alarming zeal, and governesses were urged to wear their coats indoors if they felt the cold.

In 1840 the first factory opened which specialised in small carriages for children. These were three-wheeled contraptions, designed to be pushed by the perambulator (in other words, the person doing the pushing, although this word came in the next decade to refer to the vehicle itself). They were suitable only for children who could sit up by themselves, and were not intended for tiny new-born babies. By the end of the nineteenth century this type of pram (as we shall now call them), was known as a 'Victoria'.

The royal seal of approval was given to these new vehicles which were loosely based on the design of contemporary invalid or 'Bath' chairs, when Queen Victoria bought three at a cost of four guineas each from Hitchings Baby Stores of Ludgate Hill, London, E.C., in 1846, for her growing brood. Such vehicles soon became the rage. In 1853 a patent for a pram was taken out by Charles Burton of Regent Street, and in the same year a Mr Frampton in Trinity Street, S.E., patented a three-wheeler pram with metal, rather than the more expensive wooden, wheels. His business flourished and he retired to the

Colour Plate 51. A painting of John, fourth Duke of Atholl, with his family, by David Allan, 1744-1796, 48in. (121.9cm) x 51in. (129.5cm). This charming conversation piece, painted in about 1782, illustrates the difficulty of transporting small babies in the days before perambulators. The house is clearly some way off, and the baby has had to be carried to this idyllic rural spot, complete with voluminous robes and rattle. It is obvious that the tradition of blue for a boy and pink for a girl is a thing of the future, since John wears a pink sash to his dress, while his sister Charlotte wears a blue one.

From His Grace the Duke of Atholl's Collection at Blair Castle, Perthshire.

continent with a fortune in the 1880s. In 1854 Scott's Perambulators, of Soho Square, produced a larger version with a basket seat for children up to seven years old, and in 1856 there were four perambulator shops close to Burton's, supplied by some twenty makers. By the end of the 1860s there were around thirty pram-makers in London, and soon a trade gazette was started, distinct from *The Journal of Domestic Appliances,* known as *The Journal and Pram Gazette.*

In July 1855, the Reverend Benjamin John Armstrong, Vicar of East

Colour Plate 52. A painting by Arthur Devis (c.1711-1787) of Sir Thomas Cave, Bt., and his family in the grounds of Stamford Hall, Leicestershire, signed and dated 1749. The group of three children to the left of the picture have as their focal point a painted wooden baby carriage, which is in reality little more than a seat attached to a four-wheeled platform with a towing bar, and yet bears traces of the style of contemporary carriages, particularly the elegant family crest painted on the side.
Private Collection. Photo: Sotheby's

Dereham in Norfolk, wrote in his diary, 'The streats *(sic)* (of London) are full of Perambulators, a baby carriage quite new to me, whereby children are propelled by the nurse pushing instead of pulling the carriage'. There were obvious advantages, since the nurse could now watch over her charge and prevent him from falling out. But there were other dangers, colourfully depicted by Pye Henry Chavasse in his *Advice to Mothers,* first published in 1839. 'These wretched perambulators', he spluttered, 'are dangerous in crowded thoroughfares. They are a public nuisance, in as much as they are wheeled against and between people's legs, and are a fruitful source of the breaking of shins, of the spraining of ankles, or the crushing of corns, and of the ruffling of tempers of all the foot passengers who unfortunately come within their reach, while in all probability gaping nurses are staring the other way,

Plate 170. *An illustration from* Marmaduke Multiply's Merry Method of Making Minor Mathematicians, *J. Harris, London, c.1817, showing two children in a baby carriage with a towing bar.*
Sotheby's.

Plate 171. *An oil portrait of the Dyson children, c.1820, by an anonymous English artist. The baby, George William, is being trundled about by his elder brother, Richard, in a child's wheelbarrow. Such makeshift forms of transport were not uncommon before the advent of the perambulator.*
Private Collection.

Plate 172. *A Galloper push chair, mid-19th century, 48in. (121.9cm) x 51in. (129.5cm). The three-wheeled chair has a reed-work seat and is attached to a pair of dappled horses which rock to and fro as the chair is pushed along. Such carriages were very popular until as late as the mid-1920s, and one was ordered by Queen Victoria for use in the Royal Nurseries.*
Private Collection.

Plate 173. An early child's Victoria, or three-wheeled baby carriage, with leather hood and upholstery, 'C'-springs and metal spoked wheels, 40in. (101.6cm) x 39in. (99.1cm), c.1870-80.
Private Collection.

and every way indeed but the right'. (It was in fact against the law to wheel a four-wheeled vehicle along the footpath, hence the three wheels of the earliest perambulators.) This sounds like a typically male prejudice, and other writers were delighted. The *Dictionary of Daily Wants,* 1860, described the perambulator as 'one of the most useful inventions of the day... The great advantage of the perambulator is that it permits children to be out in the open without subjecting the nurse to any fatigue. It is as well, however, to lift the child out occasionally and to allow them to exercise their limbs until they feel tired, when they can be placed in the perambulator again. In cold weather this is especially necessary as children being subjected to the exposure of the keen air in a state of inactivity are liable to be affected with cramp, rheumatism and other painful affections'.

In fact, the perambulator was to have profound and far-reaching social effects. In an atmosphere of increased wealth and keen commercial and social competition, it was considered *infra dig* for a mother to wheel her own baby to the park. Where they had once been carried in a plump and friendly pair of arms, babies were now kept, literally, at arms' length and removed from their mothers' supervision in the home, perhaps for hours on end. In the households of the *nouveaux riches* servants were, almost, two a penny, and E.L. Linton in *The Girl of the Period,* 1883, writes in uncompromisingly withering terms of the not-so-*riche* household. 'Here, the woman who once had one nursemaid now has two... the shabbiest wife with her two financial ends gaping, must have her still shabbier little drudge to wheel her perambulator'. The consequences

could be far from successful. As the *Dictionary of Daily Wants* outlined, it was the practice for 'nursemaids to wheel their young charges to a certain spot, and to leave them sitting in their prams by the hour together, so that they may be spared the trouble of looking after them, and enjoy their gossip uninterrupted'. But there was much worse. Ada Ballin writing in *From Cradle to School, A Book for Mothers,* 1902, must have made the flesh of many housebound mothers creep with her stentorian warning, 'Many a horrible case of disease has arisen through the indiscriminate kissing of babies by men in the park, who are paying attention to the nursemaid, and I know of one dreadful incident in which such a man took up the baby's bottle and sucked it, thus transmitting a loathsome disease to the infant in whose mouth it was next placed'. The imagination reels, and it would seem that kissing babies was not, at that time, part of the repertoire of politicians running for election.

Some writers advised mothers to pay unexpected visits to the park to make sure that all was well, but others went still further. Marion Harland in *Common Sense in the Nursery,* 1886, daringly suggested that her readers should 'take an

Colour Plate 54. A painting by John Singleton Copley of The Three Youngest Daughters of George III, *104½ in. (265.4cm) x 73¼ in. (186.1cm), signed and dated J.S. Copley RA, 1785. Princess Mary, shaking a tambourine, is pulling along a baby carriage, in which sits little Princess Amelia, clutching the hand of Princess Sophia. During the sittings for this magnificent portrait, dogs, parrots and children grew 'equally wearied', and the King complained to Benjamin West, who assured him that 'Mr. Copley must be allowed to proceed in his own way, and that any attempt to hurry him might be injurious to the picture, which would be a very fine one when done'.* Reproduced by Gracious Permission of Her Majesty the Queen.

Plate 174A. An early bassinet with canework sides, mounted on four wheels, c.1880. Although light and cheap, these were considered difficult to clean and to manoeuvre, but they did allow the small baby to lie flat and sleep, rather than contorting him into a sitting position.

Jack Hampshire's Pram Museum.

Plate 174B. A coach built pram, with solid wooden panels, painted in dark green with outlining in yellow in a style reminiscent of contemporary carriages. It has a shallow footwell, and is mounted on shackled 'C' springs, with a black porcelain handle. c.1890.

Jack Hampshire's Pram Museum.

early breakfast yourself, and arrayed in lawn, percale or modest gingham, brave public opinion by tending your darling in person. To wheel a perambulator' she urged, 'is a crucial test of your moral courage and innate ladyhood'.

There was one major disadvantage to the three-wheeler pram. Pye Henry Chavasse wrote 'it is painful to notice a babe of a few months in one of these new-fangled carriages. His little head is bobbing about, first on one side and then on another, at one moment it is dropping on his chest, the next is forcibly jolted behind: he looks and doubtless feels, wretched and uncomfortable'. Mothers wanted a pram in which it was possible to take a really young baby, not yet able to sit up unaided, out into the air. The bassinet on wheels was developed as a direct response to mothers' anxieties. Babies could lie down while being pushed about, and even though four-wheeled vehicles were not strictly allowed on the footpath until 1875, the law appears to have turned a blind eye to these babies' baskets on wheels, perhaps fearful of the weight of public opinion. Bassinets on wheels were generally made of basketwork backed by American cloth. Though light and attractive, these reedwork bassinets were in fact flimsy, difficult to clean and to steer, with springing of the most basic kind. This was remedied by William Wilson, a perambulator spring smith and inventor, who patented a 'Hammock Sprung Pram' with two 'c' springs from which a metal fixing suspended the body. When his factory was burnt down in 1898 he moved to a larger works, which he re-named 'The Silver Cross', and which still survives today. As time went on the original inadequate reedwork body was replaced by tougher, more practical, materials such as wood, metal, papier-mâché, wire-mesh and hard leather. Most of these

THE   "GROS-
                                                                   VENOR."

light, strongly constructed carriage, painted dark blue or green claret,
best elliptic *steel* springs, brass-jointed reversible hood, mounted on 23 in.

Plate 175. 'The Grosvenor' pram from Harrods 1895 Catalogue. It is described as 'A light, strongly constructed carriage, painted dark blue, green or claret, best elliptic steel springs, brass-jointed reversible hood, mounted on 23in. back and 18in. front India-rubber bicycle wheels, upholstered in Crockett's leather cloth...59/6 or woollen carriage cloth...69/6'.
Jack Hampshire's Pram Museum.

carriage prams had folding hoods, many of which were reversible. Nor was it uncommon at this date in the 1880s and 1890s to find prams with a set of handles at each end. Because the footpaths were narrow, and roads were crowded with carts, carriages and other traffic, it was often awkward to turn the pram round, so the baby was lifted out, turned round, the hood reversed, and the nurse walked round to the other side of the pram for the journey home.

Carriage prams in the last two decades of the nineteenth century were, as we have seen, status symbols, and a subject of discussion and envy in the parks of London and other big cities. *Myra's Journal,* 1884, describes the new type as 'the larger, safer and more comfortable four-wheeled carriage for 1 or 2 children, in which babies can often sit up and enjoy a good view of the world around them, or lie down and sleep as comfortably as if they were in their own snug little beds at home'. There were so many models to choose from in the many catalogues of the day (it is estimated that over 250 pram-makers, some producing more than twenty-five models a year, were in business at this time), that the various models were given suitably grandiose names to describe their qualities. The Elysian, The Ascot, The Queen Mab, The Paragon, The Albany, The Grosvenor and The Parisian smacked of a cosmopolitan and sophisticated yet virtuous aristocracy, while The Khartoum and The Ayah were redolent of Empire. The Victoria and The Landauette betrayed the origins of the baby carriage in the coachbuilders' workshops. Indeed, just like the coaches on which their designs were based, prams could be ordered with a crest or monogram painted on the panels at 10s. 6d. extra, and with attractive 'lining' in a contrasting colour. Designer accessories included a

209

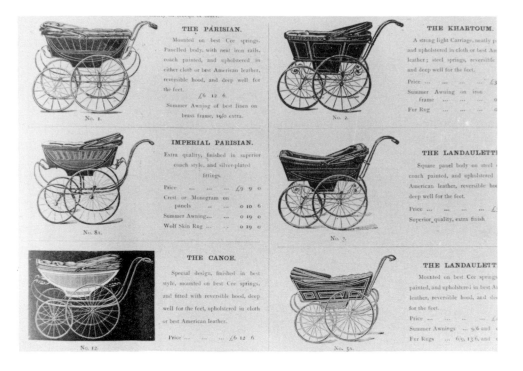

summer awning or sunshade, giving the pram something of the appearance of a 'Surrey with the Fringe on Top', or a sumptuous-sounding wolf-skin rug. Both these luxuries cost an extra 19s. 0d. In fact, the makers of these super de luxe vehicles almost all had other, more mundane, interests, which ranged from pails to sewing machines, mangles and bicycles.

From the 1870s until more or less the outbreak of the First World War, it was fashionable for chic toddlers to be pushed in a curious adaptation of the double-handled mail cart used by postmen since Rowland Hill had established the penny post. Such two-wheeled vehicles, with stabilisers at the back, remained within the law, which until 1875 forbade the use of four-wheeled vehicles on the footpath, and were cheaper and lighter than prams. They were originally intended for older children, who often sat back to back, but clearly mothers could not resist bundling small babies into them too. Ada Ballin complained that 'It is a pitiful sight to see, as one does every day, infants strapped into these vehicles, sitting all in a heap, with their spines and legs bent, their chests contracted and the strap pressing against their stomachs'.

Around 1886 a 'Convertible Mailcart', capable of being converted into a flat-bedded pram, was devised, and when kerbstones were introduced, to separate the road from the pavement, a set of small back wheels replaced the earlier stabilisers, which tended to catch on the stones and break off. The long double handles of the mailcarts were invariably made of ash, since this could be easily bent into the required curved shape when steamed. In *The Hardware Trade Journal* of March 1900, Simmons & Co. of Tanner Street, London, S.E., advertised a range of mail-carts with romantic names beyond the range of anything a modern advertising copy-writer could dream up. These included: The Radiance, The Beauty, The Protean, The Universal, The Popular, The Fay, The Hindu, The Empire, The Parsee, The Welcome and The West End. Priced at between £1 16s. 0d. and £5 10s. 0d., they were extremely popular

Colour Plate 55. A nurse pushing her two charges in a perambulator on an outing to the park, c.1870. This type of three-wheeled carriage evolved in design from the invalid chair, and later in the century came to be known as a Victoria. P.H. Chavasse warned that 'They (perambulators) are a public nuisance, in as much as they are wheeled against and between people's legs... while in all probability gaping nurses are staring the other way, and every way indeed but the right'. This is clearly the case in this illustration from Aunt Louisa's Welcome Gift. Mary Evans Picture Library.

211

Plate 177. A late 19th century mail-cart, painted in blue, 58¼ (148cm) wide. This probably had a hood, which is now missing. The mail-cart enjoyed huge popularity for some fifteen to twenty years, and was adapted from the single two-handled carts which postmen had used for their deliveries since Rowland Hill established the Penny Post. The two small back wheels were added to cope with kerbstones. This model has a well for the occupant's feet, and was designed for an older child. The curved handles of mailcarts were made of steamed ash.   Christie's.

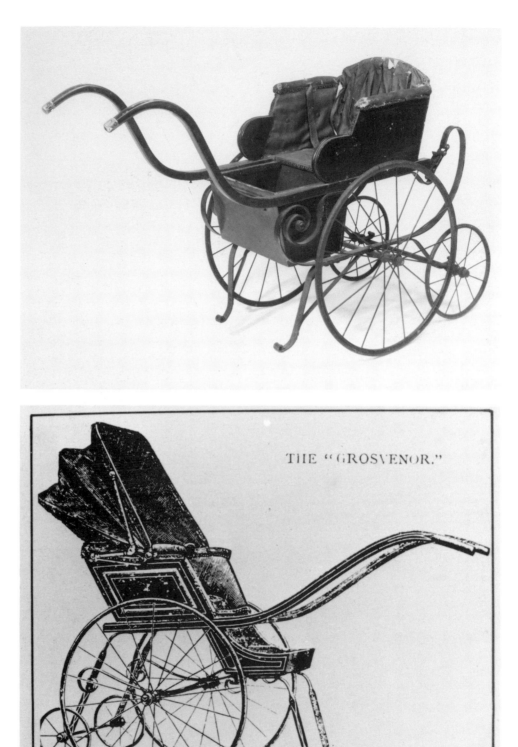

THE "GROSVENOR."

Plate 178. The Grosvenor mail-cart, by Star Manufacturing of Goodinge Road, Holloway, London, made of wood, painted and lined in tan and cream. Its fixed footrest makes it suitable for a toddler who can sit unsupported only, and not for a baby who needs to lie flat.

Jack Hampshire's Pram Museum.

in the colonies, particularly those with bodies decorated with shells, scrolls and arabesques in reed-work against a background of American cloth. Simmons described how 'the canework bodies are produced at Tanner Street, a special department being established for this class of work. Some excellent patterns are turned out and at prices which are bound to command attention'. Indeed, many highly decorated American reedwork prams or 'cars' were imported at this date, with attractively upholstered interiors, but the flimsy bodies, inadequate springing and lack of weatherproofing made them a short-lived craze. The account of Simmons' factory in *The Hardware Trade Journal* revealed that in some cases the 'worked-up' reeds were imported from America, made into 'complete carts' and 'returned to the States'. The sartorial taste in prams at the turn of the century was also described: 'Fond mamas may be tempted to buy a mail-cart or perambulator with a navy-blue body and red under-carriage, or with blue bodies and primrose under-carriages. Others again are

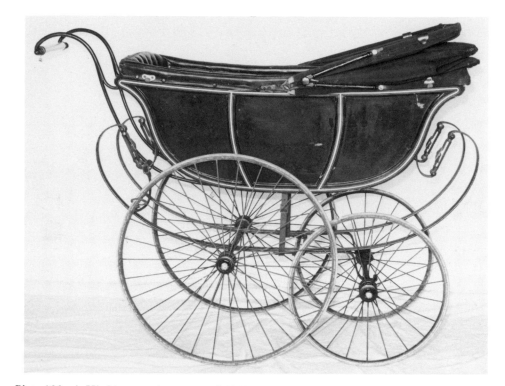

Plate 180. A Hitchings carriage pram of 1912, coach painted in black with outlining in white. It is strap hung on C-springs, and fitted with a clip-on brake. (Brakes were not a standard fitment until the late 1920s.) The fittings are made of brass, and the handles have a pushing bar made of Ivorene. (Earlier handles were made of porcelain.) Queen Victoria purchased three prams from Hitchings Baby Stores of Ludgate Hill in 1846, and the company was in production until the mid-1950s. A very similar model to this elegant Edwardian example, the Princess Patricia, was still being produced in the early 1920s, though prams became deeper at this date.

Jack Hampshire's Pram Museum.

Plate 181. A Marmet pram from the 1920s showing the tubular steel chassis invented by E.T. Morriss in 1912. This cut down repair bills and gave a smooth ride, and was popular until the 1950s, when it was replaced by the more traditional strap hung 'C' springs. Marmet's patent 'Glyda', a chassis-less pram with 'Sponge Rubber Buffer Suspension' was also popular. The deep shape was typical of the 1920s, when there was much concern over babies falling out of prams, but was later thought to harbour germs.

Jack Hampshire's Pram Museum.

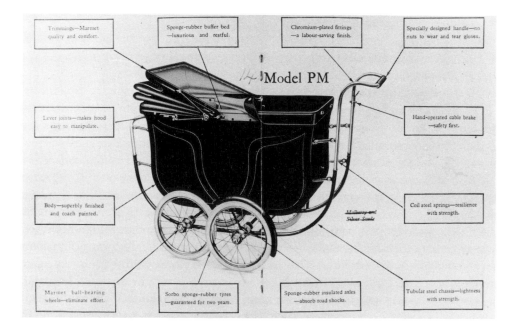

Plate 182. The Frontispiece of Marmet's 1927 Catalogue, showing a typical pram and pushchair of the period. Jack Hampshire's Pram Museum.

adorned with navy blue bodies and ivory white interiors, whilst for those who like something perhaps more delicate still, a pure white exterior associated with a pale blue interior is offered'. Even the most upwardly-mobile of nannies would have been pleased.

Indeed, the advent of the Edwardian era saw the joint ascendancy of these two Empire-building forces, the nanny and the perambulator. The refinements to prams grew ever more elaborate in the early years of the twentieth century. Buttoned leather upholstery, umbrella carriers, waterproof covers and mudguards turned them almost into nurseries on wheels, while improved springs, wheel rims, handles and gears ensured a much more comfortable ride for the child and push for the nurse. Fitted brakes, however, were not standard equipment until the late 1920s.

During the 1920s prams became much deeper with smaller wheels, owing to the danger of babies falling, like Barrie's *Lost Boys,* out of the shallow, if elegant, Edwardian models. This decade saw several developments, including pressed steel rather than coach-built panels, and E.T. Morriss's new pram chassis which combined springs and wheels all together. His company, Marmet, (an anagram of his parents' initials), was located in 'the open country in one of England's healthiest localities' (Letchworth) and, together with Pedigree and Westline, Silver Cross, Dunkleys and Hitchings, was one of the biggest pram-makers in the country.

As was the case with virtually every aspect of childcare, one generation revolted against the decisions of the previous generation, and so it was with prams. Deep prams were considered, in the 1930s, to be unhealthy and airless, and Dr Truby King proclaimed that 'one of the most pitiable and exasperating sights of modern babyhood is the spectacle of an unfortunate infant sweltering and sweating under an American leather pram hood'. During the 1920s and 1930s the hierarchical culture which surrounded the pram rapidly altered. Built now for safety and comfort rather than elegance and luxury, they were

Plate 183. A folding Victoria-type pushchair, with slatted wooden back, carpet fabric seat and leather arm rests, c.1915. Folding pushchairs were hired out for a penny to day-trippers at seaside resorts and railway stations.   Jack Hampshire's Pram Museum.

pushed by tidy mothers in neat garden suburbs rather than by regiments of nannies in the fashionable purlieus of South Kensington and Knightsbridge.

Folding prams had been in use since the turn of the century. Around 1905 the Sturgis Folding Car was introduced from America, and around 1908 folding wooden pushchairs were popular. These could be hired from railway stations or seaside pram shops by day-trippers and holiday-makers for a penny a day. With the growth of the motor car and the gradual demise of the nanny after the First World War, prams eventually came to be replaced by folding carry-cots and eventually by baby 'buggies'.

Chapter 15

DEPORTMENT, DISCIPLINE AND EXERCISE

Stays and Corsets

'What with chin-stays, back-stays, body-stays, forehead cloths, rollers, bandages &c., an infant had as many girths and strings to keep head, limbs and body in one exact position as a ship has halyards'.
(*Englishwoman's Domestic Magazine,* Vol.7, edited by S.O. Beeton, 1859.)

When a baby was finally released from his swaddling bands at the age of four to six weeks, the confining process was sadly not at an end. 'Stays' or stay-bands and rollers were *de rigueur* for most babies, and consisted of thick corded or quilted material, tied tightly round the body to prevent umbilical hernias and provide the required shape. Later on, long strips of flannel fulfilled the same purpose. Older girls, and boys until the age of four or five, wore leather bodices or stays stiffened with cane or whalebone, while, during the eighteenth century, younger children wore a frilled and vertically-tucked slip, known as a 'tucker' between their dress and stays. Thus a small child with his 'best bib and tucker' on was ready to receive company.

At first worn for reasons of health, stays became necessary for a fashionable figure, a practice with frightening results which were described by John Bulwer in 1650, in *The Artificial Changeling.* 'They (young girls) reduce their Breasts into such streights, that they soon purchase a stinking breath . . . (and) to that end . . . shut up their wastes in a whale-bone prison or little-ease, they open a door to consumptions, and a withering rottennesse'. Such stays were one of the main targets of Jean-Jacques Rousseau, in his efforts to secure better conditions for children generally. In *Emile,* published in 1762, he protests, 'the limbs of a growing child should be free to move easily in his clothing, and nothing should cramp their growth or movement'. Disease, he felt, would increase because 'the stagnant humours, whose circulation is interrupted, putrify in a state of inaction'.

However, their use was widespread. Molly Blundell's father spent £1 10s. 9½ d. on 'material and whalebone for stays' in the first decade of ·the eighteenth century, when she was only three years old, and in *The General*

Plate 184. A pair of child's stays of green worsted, lined and piped in unbleached linen, and with vertical boning, c.1740. Once swaddling had been abandoned at four to six weeks, babies were confined by tightly tied stay-bands and rollers, which helped to prevent hernias and were also thought to keep crooked limbs straight. They gave way to stays and corsets once the child was mobile.

Colonial Williamsburg
Foundation.

Advertiser, 11 February, 1784, a Mrs Parsons advertised her 'stays for girls that are crooked or inclined to be so, either by falls, rickets, sickness'. William Buchan's *Advice to Mothers,* 1803, noted with a sigh of relief that 'we no longer see the once familiar spectacle of a mother laying her daughter down upon a carpet, then putting her foot on the girl's back and breaking half a dozen laces to give her a slender waist'. However 'diagonal bandages or ribands fastened across the breast and shoulders with straining violence' still caused 'an unnatural prominence before' and 'frightful indentation behind'. In 1840 Cecilia Ridley recorded that 'Alice has been afflicted with a pair of stays with bones which cause infinite trouble and dismay to the whole household'.

Gradually the pernicious stays died out, though babies were still encased in 'rollers' and 'binders' until the first part of the twentieth century, and women had to endure the limitations of corsets until the 1920s, when the flapper fashions rescued them from the literally straight-laced fashions of the time.

Deportment

'Children, you are very little,
And your bones are very brittle,
If you would grow great and stately,
You must learn to walk sedately.
(Robert Louis Stevenson, *A Child's Garden of Verses,* 1885.)

During the nineteenth century appearance, particularly among the upper classes, mattered quite desperately. 'The distinguishing mark of gentility consisted in a certain grace and ease of deportment proceeding from an early and continued cultivation of the figure and action alike, remote from vulgarish constraints', wrote an early nineteenth century observer. Good deportment was a visible and incontrovertible sign of good breeding, at a time when rickets warped the figures of vast numbers of the population, and Prince Pückler-

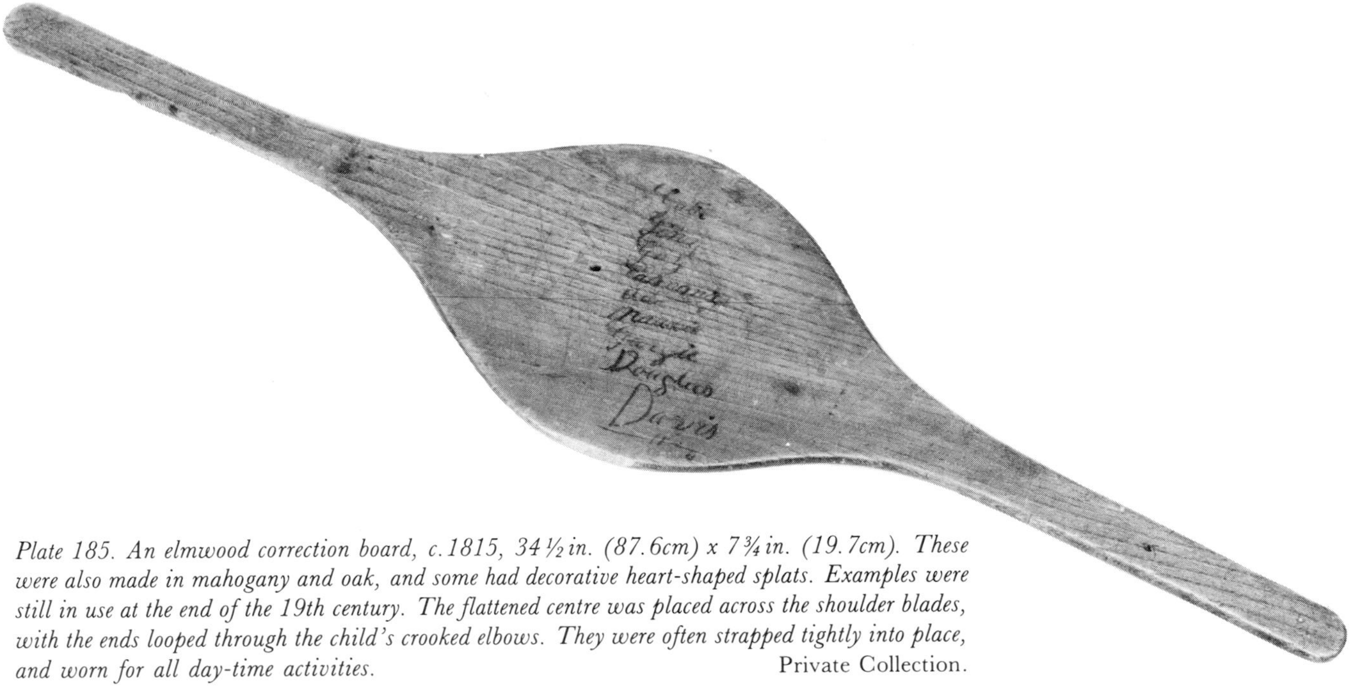

Plate 185. An elmwood correction board, c.1815, 34 ½ in. (87.6cm) x 7 ¾ in. (19.7cm). These were also made in mahogany and oak, and some had decorative heart-shaped splats. Examples were still in use at the end of the 19th century. The flattened centre was placed across the shoulder blades, with the ends looped through the child's crooked elbows. They were often strapped tightly into place, and worn for all day-time activities. Private Collection.

Muskau reported from London in the 1820s that 'those whom nature has mis-shapen are placed within cases of iron until they are transformed into Apollos'. Of course countless children were horribly deformed through rickets, malnutrition, or other diseases, and many, including Charles I and Lord Byron, had to wear corrective boots or other devices. Even King George VI had to wear painful splints in bed at night as a child to correct his knock-knees. However, many other children were forced into merciless contraptions for purely cosmetic reasons. Because of a slight stoop Edith Sitwell recounts that she was 'imprisoned in steel which began under my arms, preventing me from resting them on my sides' and at bedtime her ankles and soles were 'locked in an excruciating contraption'. Even her famous nose was encased in iron in the hope of taming its wayward profile.

Most children of the well-to-do were subject to the indignities of the wooden backboard. Mrs Sherwood described how, from the age of six in the 1780s, she had to wear an iron neck collar and a backboard strapped to her back for the entire day, doing her lessons standing up. Such collars were sometimes cruelly spiked on the inside to prevent the exhausted child from relaxing her erect posture for a moment. In the nineteenth century the future Duchess of Westminster wore a mahogany backboard with a violin string tied tightly round her shoulders, so that it cut into her flesh if she slouched. If the string snapped she had to replace it with her own pocket money. Another kind of deportment board, for correcting curvature of the spine, was devised for lying on full-length and had a hole cut in to fit the head. The board was slightly raised above the floor so that the head was forced well back, keeping the back straight.

Deportment or correction chairs were designed by Sir Astley Cooper (1768-1841) specifically to straighten children's backs, particularly at the dining-table. Sir Astley was surgeon to King George IV. He was created a Baronet and given an epergne costing 500 guineas after successfully operating

Plate 186. A high-backed beechwood posture chair, of simple design, c.1830, painted green, 36in. (91.4cm) x 14in. (35.6cm). The small seat, high legs and straight back forced the child to either sit upright or topple off. Some were made to simulate bamboo or with decorative painting, and seats were usually caned. Such chairs were designed by Sir Astley Cooper (1768-1841) specifically to straighten children's backs.   Private Collection.

Plate 187. A slightly more sophisticated correction chair, with turned legs and rails and typical caned seat.   Strangers Hall Museum, Norwich. Reproduced from
Antique Medical Instruments, by Elisabeth Bennion.

to remove a steatome, or fatty encysted tumour, from the royal scalp. ('I hope it will stay at 'ome and not annoy me any more'.) The chairs, which had high legs, unnaturally small seats and very straight backs, were used well into the nineteenth century in spite of J.C. Loudon's comment in *The Encyclopaedia of Cottage & Villa Architecture and Furniture,* 1833, that 'it is proper to observe that some medical men do not approve of these chairs'.

Medical men were in fact indulging in violent methods of their own to correct curved limbs. The nineteenth century saw the birth of orthopaedic surgery, aimed at correcting the terrible childhood deformities which were so prevalent, thanks to malnutrition and disease, and which had afflicted the humble and the great for centuries. Hugh Owen Thomas invented the Thomas wrench in 1865 to untwist club feet, and also the ominously-named osteoclast. This broke the deformed bones of children so that they could be re-set in corrective splints. It was seen as a great advance on the previous method of sawing through mis-shapen bones and breaking them with mallets and chisels.

Colour Plate 56. A watercolour by Cecil-Elizabeth Drummond, signed C.E.D. and dated April 1st, 1830. It shows a small girl standing before her mother in tears. She has clearly thrown down her detested backboard, which lies on the floor at her feet. Her mother stands stiff and unyielding, her right hand grasping a bunch of birch twigs, no doubt in readiness as a punishment.

Discipline and Punishment

*'Their sinful nature prompts them to rebel
And to delight in paths that lead to Hell'.*
(John Bunyan, 1686.)

'Is it not a fundamental error in Christians to consider children as innocent beings, rather than as beings who bring into the world a corrupt nature and evil disposition which it should be the great aim of education to rectify'.
(Hannah More, *Strictures,* Vol.5, p.44, 1808.)

Among the many punitive devices worn to humiliate children in Victorian Dames' Schools were dunce's hats, placards and finger-stocks. The fingers of the offending child were inserted into the holes with the hands immovably held back to back behind the body, and with the shoulders forced well back. The child was then forced to stand in the corner, or in front of the Dame, to repeat the lessons in which he had failed. Finger-stocks were also used as a prevention and punishment for masturbation, which Ada Ballin, writing in *From Cradle to School, A Book for Mothers,* 1902, warned darkly 'must always be looked for in little children, especially in little girls in the early years of life'. The habit was described with some exaggeration, as 'a danger which is very far-reaching and may lead to ruining the child, body and mind, for life'. She blamed the incidence of this partly on 'wicked nurses' who, when trying to pacify a crying baby in their charge 'have been known to tickle it in this improper way to stop the crying'. Mrs Ballin went on to advise that 'when a habit is discovered it must in young children be put a stop to by such means as tying the hands, strapping the knees together with a pad between them, or some mechanical plan'. The sinister 'mechanical plan' could also have included wrist or arm stocks or polished wooden discs of various sizes placed in pairs between the

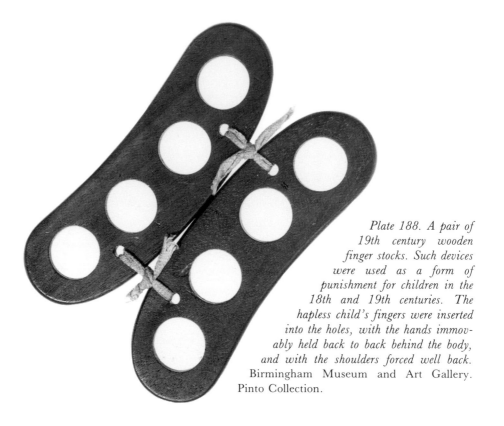

Plate 188. A pair of 19th century wooden finger stocks. Such devices were used as a form of punishment for children in the 18th and 19th centuries. The hapless child's fingers were inserted into the holes, with the hands immovably held back to back behind the body, and with the shoulders forced well back. Birmingham Museum and Art Gallery. Pinto Collection.

knees or calves and the ankles, so that the discs would clatter to the floor if the young offender wriggled. The still widely held belief in original sin allowed children's natural curiosity to be frequently misinterpreted, and even exploited by 'wicked nurses'. Lord Byron's rhythmically-named nurse, May Gray, cajoled her precocious nine year-old charge into bed where she 'played tricks with his person', and then beat him when she was drunk. Perhaps the Byronic 'Mad, Bad and Dangerous to Know' behaviour originated partly from this youthful abuse.

Other Victorian childhood punishments included wooden gags, wrist or arm stocks to prevent thumb-sucking as well as 'self-abuse' bags to go over the head and various types of restraining harness made of straps and wood. Since the punishments were carried out in the firm belief that the child's soul would thus be saved, it was easy to justify such harsh treatment. 'Happiness for the Obedient — Discipline for the Wayward — Knowledge for All' was the philosophy of many schools, while at home the belief that a child was 'never too little to go to Hell' was prevalent. The fearsome Mr Brocklehurst in *Jane Eyre* was no figment of Charlotte Brontë's imagination, and humiliation and pain, meted out in the guise of a Christian education, were the daily lot of most children. Thomas Hood's description of the Irish Schoolmaster was true of many teachers of the time: 'He never spoils the rod and never spares the child.' Even the most conscientious parents erred on the side of cruelty, unaware that a little harmless self-exploration had far less potential for harm than a parental flogging. Early in the eighteenth century John Wesley and his siblings were exhorted to 'bear the rod without loud weeping' because their mother, Susanna, believed that 'when a child is corrected it must be conquered... because this is the only strong and rational foundation of a religious foundation', and Admiral Boscawen's wife noted that 'the rod and I went down to breakfast' after her small son's illness had left him fractious and spoilt by a little more attention than usual. In 1831 Lord Melbourne wrote 'we live in strange times when a girl of thirteen cannot be whipped at a boarding school without its being made a subject of description in the newspapers', and Edward VIII observed ruefully that his father, King George V, 'literally pounded good manners into us'. It comes as something of a relief to read of Sir George Sitwell's reassuring remark to his son, Osbert, who was terrified at the thought of going to Hell. 'My dear boy, if you go to Hell, you'll certainly find all the people you most admire there already — Wellington, Nelson and the Black Prince — and they'll discover a way of getting you out of it soon enough'.

Exercise

'When Charlie has done reading
His book every day,
Then he goes with his hoop in the garden to play,
Or his whip in his hand,
Quickly mounts up across,
And then gallops away
On his fine rocking-horse'.
(Little Rhymes for Little Folks, 1823.)

Miniature wooden horses on wheels, and hobby-horses, have long been part of the fabric of childhood, and during the nineteenth century the nursery of every well-to-do child had a rocking-horse standing in the corner. Although

Plate 189. A 17th century child's rocking-horse, probably of northern European origin. It has a simple box-type seat, probably originally upholstered in leather, mounted on large solid wooden rockers, with a carved wooden horse's head fitted in front. This somewhat rudimentary rocking-horse is of the earlist surviving type, and is very similar to the one used by Charles I as a boy, although that example has a solid body rather than a seat.
Museum of London.

Colour Plate 57. An early 18th century oil portrait of the Dutch School of a small girl riding her rocking-horse, which has a splendid realistically painted head, and is fitted with a bridle. She rides side-saddle as was customary for girls until the beginning of the 20th century.

By Permission of Viscount De Lisle, VC, KG.

toys are beyond the scope of this book, rocking-horses should be mentioned briefly as they served a useful purpose and can almost be regarded as nursery furniture.

In the days before motor cars every child of a certain social status was expected to be able to ride a horse. Not only was he expected to stay on and control the mount efficiently, but he was also expected to have a good 'seat' and look well in the saddle. The rules of deportment, so frequently drummed into upper-class children, were just as important on the back of a horse as in the drawing-room. George III had a 'chamber horse' made to carry four of his children at once. It was a kind of exercise chair, which simulated the motion of riding, and had a mahogany frame with spring seats covered in morocco leather. Four holding-handles and four footboards were provided for the young occupants. However, a rocking-horse was a simpler and more attractive option for most parents.

Colour Plate 58. A large carved wooden rocking-horse from the third quarter of the 19th century, the galloping horse realistically carved, covered in gesso and painted as a traditional dappled-grey, each rocker fitted at the end with a seat for a very small child, and the saddle fitted for 'side saddle' use. 115½ in. (293.4cm.) long. Anonymous.

In use since the end of the sixteenth or beginning of the seventeenth century, early examples have a box seat with a rudimentary wooden horse's head, fitted onto boarded wooden rockers. They were often painted in an attempt to make them more naturalistic, and fitted with a saddlecloth for greater realism. One early example is believed to have been given to King Charles I in 1610, and a similar horse is in the Museum of London. Pieces of the same type, with solid wooden rockers and two-dimensional horses' heads were in use for the first part of the eighteenth century, but as the century progressed the carving of the horses became much more lifelike and ambitious, until by the early nineteenth century very realistic horses with painted bodies and flowing manes and tails, and scaled-down saddles and bridles, were in use. Presented in galloping attitudes, the horses' four outstretched legs were supported on two curved rockers joined by four turned wooden bars.

From the first half of the nineteenth century, fresh air, as well as exercise,

Plate 190. An English School watercolour, showing a small child, born on 27 June, 1830, riding on his wooden rocking-horse. Sotheby's.

was considered essential for the healthy growth and development of children, and rocking-horses were placed in front of open nursery windows when it was too wet to take a walk. Carved wooden horses, their painted decoration covering a thin layer of gesso, later made way for more expensive mounts with expressive faces, flaring nostrils, and real horse-hair manes and tails, their hide bodies stuffed with sawdust and painted to resemble jolly piebald dappled-greys. (Piebald horses were supposed to be lucky, and the breath or hair of a piebald horse was supposed to cure whooping cough.) The scaled-down versions of adult saddles and bridles helped ensure that the child developed his 'seat'.

During the 1880s Dunkley's patented their 'New Safety' rocking-horse with an arrangement of bars or trestles and straps replacing the curved wooden

Plate 191. An oil painting of a boy riding on a rocking-horse, c.1840, circle of George Chinnery. Rocking-horses were definitely educational playthings as well as merely toys. Bonham's.

Plate 192. An unusual child's bouncing horse, probably American, late 19th century. This has a carved wooden horse's head mounted on a leather-upholstered seat. The whole is mounted on a metal spring, the oak case supported on a platform with four wooden wheels, 34in. (86cm) long. Such a toy, although pleasurable, would also have taught a very young child something of the rudiments of riding a horse. Sotheby's.

Plate 193. A 19th century wooden rocking-horse, with saddle and bridle, and horse-hair mane and tail, the wooden body painted dappled-grey and mounted on twin rockers. More expensive models were made of real hide stuffed with sawdust.

Prudential Fine Art
Auctioneers.

Plate 194. A late Victorian rocking-horse, on a trestle base with turned supports, 49⅝ in. (126cm) high x 53½ in. (136cm) long. The trestles gave a more realistic backwards and forwards motion, and gave the horse stability on the floor.
Sotheby's, Sussex.

rockers. These made the beast more stable, and ensured that it remained stationary, rather than moving across the floor as it rocked. The backwards and forwards movement was more life-like, and proved very popular with young riders. Dunkley's were also well-known at the time for a variety of popular children's items, including prams, mailcarts and tricycles, as well as 'steam circuses and roundabouts', which were adorned with the same wild-eyed and jaunty dappled-greys as the rocking-horses.

Chapter 16

LITERACY
AND NUMERACY

Horn Books

'He who ne'er learns his A,B,C,
A Dunce will ever reckon'd be,
But he who his Book doth mind,
Will soon a golden Treasure find'.
(From the *New Royal Primer, or an easy and pleasant Guide to the Art*
of Reading, London, 1765.)

Literacy was embarked upon considerably earlier in the past than we would contemplate today. On 23 July, 1776 Hester Thrale noted that her daughter, Sophie, 'is five years old today. She has read three Epistles and three Gospels. I do not make her get much by heart'. John Ruskin could read and write fluently by the age of four and was by no means exceptional.

One of the earliest aids to literacy was the horn-book, dating from the introduction of printing in the fifteenth century, and from Tudor times toddlers are shown in contemporary portraits with them dangling from their waists. Made from a bat-shaped piece of wood, a printed or manuscript alphabet on paper or parchment was pasted on and enclosed behind a transparent sliver of horn, which protected the letters from the stubbing of sticky little fingers, and gave the objects their name. The name battledore was also used, since the projecting handles allowed the wooden 'bats' to be used to play at battledore and shuttlecock between lessons.

The sheets normally contained the letters of the alphabet, often in upper and lower case, and the numerals one to ten. Sometimes the vowels were set out, or the Lord's Prayer, and the script was usually preceded and terminated by a small cross, signifying that the child should cross himself at the beginning and end of a lesson. This gave the horn-books their third name of 'criss-cross books' — 'And if you know the Christ-cross row, you soon may spell and read'.

The majority of horn-books are made of wood, the horn covering and the pasted-on paper secured by a metal 'frame' of silver or brass, which was nailed on. Others were made of two layers of stiff leather sandwiched together. Some

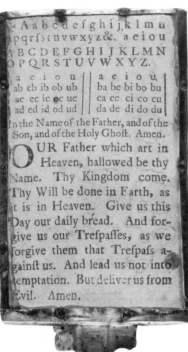

Plate 195. Two examples of horn books. A. A very fine late 17th century silver horn-book, with upper and lower-case alphabets and the Lord's Prayer, the case engraved with a heron amid foliate scrolls, and with the initials of the owners IT and ST, maker's initials WP. Princess Elizabeth (later Queen Elizabeth I), had a horn-book with a frame of filigree silver and a fine leather mount. 4½in. (11.7cm) x 2¼in. (5.9cm).
Sotheby's.

B. A large 18th century horn-book, mounted in silver, containing a printed sheet with upper and lower-case alphabets, vowels and the Lord's Prayer. 6¼in. (15.9cm) x 3in. (7.4cm). Just to the left of the top line of letters can be seen a small cross. This was to remind children to cross themselves at the start of each lesson, and gave rise to the alternative name of 'criss-cross books'. Sometimes the Lord's Prayer was substituted for a religious verse, 'Christe's Cross be my Speede, In all virtue to proceede'.
Sotheby's.

Plate 196. An English School watercolour of two children in a parlour, c.1820, 11½in. (29.2cm) x 9in. (22.9cm). Alongside their toys, a card printed with the letters of the alphabet lies discarded on the floor at their feet. Such folding sheets were known as 'Battledores' after the original printed sheets which were pasted onto bat-shaped tablets of wood.
David Pressland Collection.

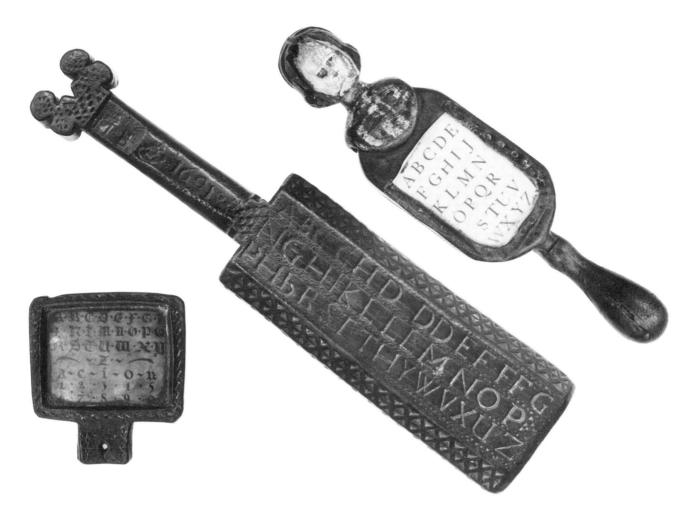

Plate 197. *Left. A small leather horn-book, 17th/18th century.*

Plate 198. *Centre: A rare Welsh variation of a horn-book, shaped as a miniature cricket bat in yew-wood, carved with the letters of the alphabet between decorative borders, the handle with its shaped end is incised with the date 1691. Such a piece would make a very good 'battledore' for playing at shuttlecock between lessons.*

Plate 199. *Right: A rare 18th century horn-book, surmounted by a doll's head which doubles as a rattle. This confirms the early age at which children were expected to learn their letters. A portrait of Miss Campion, aged two in 1661, shows her with a horn-book.*

Birmingham Museum and Art Gallery, Pinto Collection.

Plate 200. *An early horn-book, cast in lead or lead alloy, one side showing the alphabet in upper case, the reverse with a crowned portrait, primitively drawn, and possibly depicting either Charles I or Charles II. This represents one of the earliest alphabets for children, and the mould from which it was cast may also have been used for gingerbread. The letters J and U are typically omitted, I and V being used instead, as was the case with all early alphabets. 1 ⅝ in. (4cm) x 1 ¼ in. (3.2cm).*

Sotheby's.

231

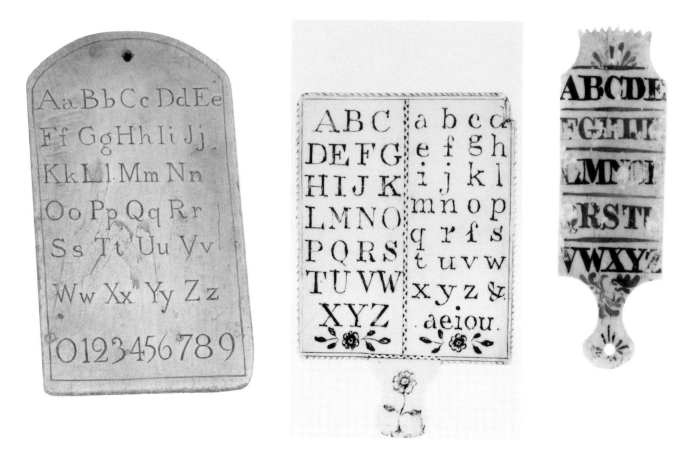

Plate 201. A late 18th or early 19th century sycamore alphabet board, of tombstone shape, inscribed with upper and lower case letters and the numbers 0-9, the arched top with a hole for suspension. 15in. (38cm).

Sotheby's.

Plate 202A and B. A late 18th century horn-book engraved on bone, with 'wriggled' borders similar to contemporary bright-cutting on silver, with the vowels shown and with floral sprigs. The engraved decoration has been painted in black for greater definition. Also shown is another, cruder, example of the same date.

Sotheby's.

rare early examples were made of silver, with finely engraved cases, and Queen Elizabeth I had such a horn-book as a child. Cheaper specimens were made of pewter or lead with cast or moulded letters, and a few fortunate little girls had rattle-dolls combined with their horn-books, confirming the early age at which children were taught their letters.

Horn-books are also found in bone or ivory, with the letters engraved and painted in black or red, and with a flower or some other design on the reverse. As with the more conventional examples, the handles were pierced with holes so that they could be suspended from a ribbon round the child's neck or waist.

The children of liberally-minded parents had horn-books made of gingerbread, pressed into a wooden mould. The letters were sometimes gilded over with gold-leaf, thus allowing the young child to lick 'the gilt off the gingerbread' after a successful recitation of the alphabet. Maria and Richard Edgeworth, *Essays on Practical Education,* 1789, disapproved of such gimmicks, claiming that 'counters, coaxing and gingerbread' were no more effective than 'reiterated pain and terror'. However, hard-pressed governesses were clearly

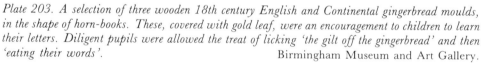

Plate 203. A selection of three wooden 18th century English and Continental gingerbread moulds, in the shape of horn-books. These, covered with gold leaf, were an encouragement to children to learn their letters. Diligent pupils were allowed the treat of licking 'the gilt off the gingerbread' and then 'eating their words'. Birmingham Museum and Art Gallery.

reluctant to relinquish their sticky methods of persuasion, since they were still popular in 1835 when J. Crane wrote:

> 'The bakers to increase their trade,
> Make alphabets of gingerbread,
> That folks might swallow what they read.
> All the letters were digested,
> Hateful ignorance detested.'

Matthew Prior's poem, *Alma,* describes a similar scene.

> 'To Master John the English maid
> A Horn-book gives of gingerbread,
> And that the child may learn the better,
> As he can name, he eats the Letter.'

In this way, the expressions 'eating one's words' and 'swallowing whole' a piece of information, may have found their way into the English language.

Plate 204. *A collection of printed paper battledores, including 'The Child's Battledore', and 'The British Battledore', published by W. Davison, Alnwick, c.1830. These were priced at one penny. When the price of printed books went down at the beginning of the 19th century these sheets, similar to those originally pasted onto the horn-books, were sold. They were still known as horn-books or battledores and continued in a similar form until the last part of the 19th century.* Sotheby's.

Plate 205. *For many girls, working a sampler combined the skills of literacy and embroidery as well as learning an 'improving' text. The earliest age at which girls embarked on samplers appears to have been six, but younger siblings no doubt were helped to learn their letters by their elder sisters' work. This painting from the second half of the 18th century shows Miss Hawkins by George James.* Sotheby's.

As printed books became cheaper and more widespread towards the end of the eighteenth century, horn-books were replaced by folding printed sheets, often with illustrations. Still known as battledores or 'battledoors', these originally sold for one penny each. They remained in use for about one hundred years, although horn-books were still found as late as the 1840s.

Samplers were also used from the seventeenth century to teach girls their letters and numbers, as well as to give them practise in needlework. No sampler is recorded to have been worked by a girl under the age of six years (and that bears the onimous inscription 'This I have done, I thank my God, without correction of the rod'), and so a detailed study of them has not been included in this book.

Other Aids to the Alphabet

Apart from the books which sought to teach children to read, and which are not the subject of this work, the late eighteenth and early nineteenth century saw many aids which could be used to help a small child to learn his letters, and gain some amusement at the same time.

At the most basic level building bricks with pictures, letters and numbers, combined literacy with constructional skills. Wooden bricks were popular in Germany, where many wooden toys were made in the Black Forest area, and

Plate 206. An ivory alphabet, each disc engraved with a letter on one side, the reverse with an illustration and caption. The engraved lines are filled with coloured inks to make them stand out, and the discs are enclosed in the original turned ivory case, 1⅜in. (3.4cm) diameter, late 18th century.   Sotheby's.

Plate 207. A Victorian set of alphabet bricks, the wooden blocks covered with paper printed with letters, numbers and pictures of animals and birds, c.1870. Such bricks are, with certain variations, still in use today, brick-building being one of the earliest skills which a child learns.
Museum of Childhood, Beaumaris, Anglesey.

Plate 208. Another aid to the alphabet. A set of twenty-five lithographed figures in the guise of various trades and occupations. Each one is hand-coloured and has a letter pasted on the wooden stand below, the whole contained in the original card box, 4¾ in. (12cm), c.1840.
Sotheby's.

became widespread in England during the second half of the nineteenth century. They were an integral part of the kindergarten movement introduced into England by Froebel in 1854, and established by the end of the century.

Word-making accessories during the first part of the century included bone or ivory rectangular 'tiles' painted with the letters of the alphabet, and encased in mahogany boxes. A little later devices such as 'Crandall's Building Slabs', patented by H. Jewitt & Co., Leighton Road, London, N.W., in 1867, became popular. These wooden 'bricks' could actually be joined together to make words. Later still, came The Cress Reversible Educational Board, patented in 1912, 1915 and 1916, which had movable wooden letters and numbers which slid intriguingly on grooves around the board. Picture alphabet discs, available from the first part of the nineteenth century, included The Picture Alphabet for a Good Child, whose virtue was rewarded with wooden discs which combined wood engravings for the child to colour, with corresponding letters of the alphabet on the reverse, all contained in a cylindrical sycamore box. These originally cost one shilling.

Guaranteed to curl the lips of even the most hardened governess, were the 'Alphabets Personified', which showed an acrobatic 'Posture Master' contorting his physique into the letters of the alphabet. These date from the end of the eighteenth century, and formed one of the many printed sheets and cards designed to teach children their A.B.C.

Wallis's Revolving Alphabet incorporated a moving alphabet into an engraving of a domestic scene, which was pasted onto wood and then coloured.

Plate 209. 'The Picture Alphabet for a Good Child', comprising thirty-five card discs, with hand-coloured wood-engravings on one side, the appropriate letter of the alphabet on the reverse. In the original turned wooden box, complete with a wood-engraved label coloured by hand, 2in. (5.2cm) diameter, c.1830. For very young children simply colouring the pictures must have constituted a first lesson. Sotheby's.

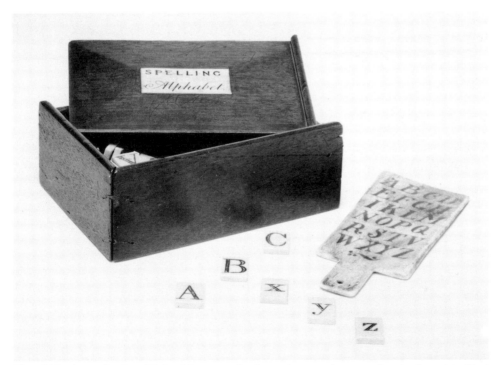

Plate 210. A wooden box filled with rectangular bone pieces, each engraved and coloured in black with a letter of the alphabet in upper or lower case, the bone label on the lid inscribed Spelling Alphabet, c.1880 and an early 19th century horn-book, the upper-case alphabet painted in red on a shaped piece of bone, the handle pierced for suspension, 4¾in. (12.3cm) x 2in. (5.1cm). Sotheby's.

Plate 211. Wallis's 'Revolving Alphabet', c.1830. This consists of an engraved and coloured picture of a fond papa attracting his small child's attention to a letter of the alphabet which appears, as if in a mirror, on the wall. The engraving is pasted onto a shaped piece of wood, with a disc below which is printed with all the letters of the alphabet. As the disc is revolved by means of a wooden pin new letters appear in the 'mirror'. John Wallis was established as a bookseller in Ludgate Street, London by 1777. He moved several times between 1808 and 1811, when he set up the Juvenile Depository in Skinner Street.

Private Collection.

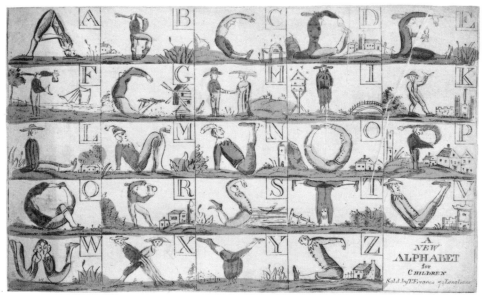

Plate 212. 'A New Alphabet for Children', comprising an engraved sheet with a 'posture master' forming the letters of the alphabet, and coloured by hand, no doubt the work of a young owner. 'Sold by T. Evans, 79 Long Lane', c.1800. There is no J, since this letter was interchangeable with I.

Sotheby's.

Plate 213. 'Improved Moveable Alphabet'. A lithographed card, hand-coloured and showing a family watching as letters appear in an aperture, with a revolving disc behind. This is similar to Wallis's Revolving Alphabet and shows children in an early Victorian parlour, at the feet of their benevolent Papa, c.1840-50. Sotheby's.

One letter appeared at a time through an aperture designed as a picture on the wall of the parlour, eagerly pointed out by a proud papa to the attentive toddler by his side. This worked by a lower disc printed with the letters being revolved. They were made by Edward Wallis, who in 1821 took over John Wallis's Juvenile Depository at 42 Skinner Street, Snow Hill, London. He opened additional premises in Islington in 1827, and continued at both addresses until 1840, by which time he was describing himself as a 'Dissected Map Manufacturer and Publisher'. Wallis's original and amusing idea was imitated by later manufacturers. All these entertaining objects were used to teach children their letters through play and were, of course, used in conjunction with books designed for the same task.

Plate 214. Two dissected puzzles by George Riley, c.1790. 'Riley's Geographical Pastime', comprising forty woodcut hand-coloured illustrations, each showing a figure in his or her national costume, with the name of the appropriate capital city and descriptive text, each cut in two to form a puzzle, in a contemporary labelled wooden box. 15⅝in. (40.3cm) x 21in. (53.1cm); and 'Riley's Biographical and Chronological Tablet of the Old Testament', with thirty-two woodcut portraits of Biblical characters and their lives, each cut into three to make a puzzle, 24¾in. (62.9cm) x 22¼in. (56.6cm).

Sotheby's.

Plate 215. A slate, c.1900, of the type used in schools throughout the 19th century; and an abacus of about the same date.
Cambridge & County Folk Museum.

Slates and Copying-Sticks

Invaluable in the learning of numbers and letters was the slate, used in schoolrooms throughout the nineteenth century. It was the crashing to the floor of Jane Eyre's 'treacherous slate' which elicited Mr Brocklehurst's ominous command 'Let the child who broke her slate come forward'. Sometimes two or more slates were bound together to form a 'book'.

Queen Victoria confessed in later life 'I was not fond of learning as a child — and baffled every attempt to teach me my letters up to five years old — when I consented to learn them by their being written down before me'. Copying-sticks were used during the first half of the nineteenth century to help stubborn cases like Queen Victoria to learn to write their letters. A line of letters, or of hand-writing, on paper, was pasted on to each side of a thin strip of wood. Usually seven or eight inches long and an inch or so wide, the child could hold the stick over his sheet of paper as he slavishly copied the letters before him. No opportunity was lost to instil moral virtues into the small pupil, and a series of improving mottoes was used. These include the questionable 'Faith Dwells with Simplicity', 'Silent waters are seldom shallow', 'Useful employment gives us pleasure', and the more certainly true 'Innumerable inconveniences await us'. During the eighteenth and early nineteenth centuries children were given 'writing sheets' engraved with decorative borders, in order to show off their hand-writing skills as presents to their proud parents.

Colour Plate 59. A miniature of Charles, Thomas and Christina Robertson, by their father Charles Robertson, c.1805. They are shown at their lessons, with quills, pencils and books on the table in front of them.
Private Collection.

Plate 216. Two copying sticks, which were used in the village school at Shepley, near Huddersfield in the 1860s. They are inscribed in copper-plate writing with the immortal words 'Innumerable inconveniences await us' and 'Useful employment gives us pleasure'.
Birmingham Museum & Art Gallery.

Plate 217. A small painted wheelbarrow, c.1860, with a single iron-bound wooden front wheel, 47in. (119.4cm) long. Queen Victoria gardened as a child, and encouraged her children to do the same. At Osborne on the Isle of Wight they were paid for the vegetables they grew. Sotheby's.

Rational Toys

'Ideally everything that children do should be sport and play', wrote John Locke at the end of the seventeenth century, 'learning should be sport to them'. Such words were revolutionary, coming as they did so soon after the Puritan régime when children were seen as embodiments of original sin.

It took almost one hundred years for Locke's words to bear fruit, but by the end of the eighteenth and beginning of the nineteenth century a multitude of educational toys existed for older children. These included jigsaws, or 'dissected puzzles', with a wide variety of subjects covering the natural world, history, geography and religion. Board games played with a teetotum, so as not to instil a love of dice and gaming, card games, cut-out paper dolls and a wide variety of other educational games were used for older children. Sadly, these are beyond the scope of this book.

For practical enjoyment Maria and Richard Edgeworth's *Essays on Practical Education,* 1789, advocated 'rational' toys such as 'sturdy carts, small gardening tools, printing presses, looms and furniture which takes to pieces and reassembles... pencils, scissors, paste, tools and workbenches'. All would be familiar objects to children today.

Gardening was a popular pastime for small children, combining as it did fresh air and exercise with the rudiments of horticulture. When Queen Victoria was a child, Leigh Hunt glimpsed her watering her flowers in Kensington Gardens, followed about by a watchful footman in livery who hovered like a 'gigantic fairy'. Her own children were encouraged to garden at Osborne, on the Isle of Wight, where Prince Albert had himself supervised the planting of the gardens by the use of semaphore from the roof. The royal children had their own wheelbarrows, with their initials painted on, and tools made by Brades, Thornhill and others. They worked on allotments, and were paid for the produce which they grew. The Swiss Cottage, erected in 1853, saw to it that they learnt other practical skills, such as cooking and housekeeping, and had a miniature shop for putting arithmetic into practice.

Plate 218. A wooden counting aid, made with wooden slides which cover the engraved numerals, which could also be used for keeping the scores in games.

Museum of Childhood, Beaumaris, Anglesey.

Aids to Numeracy

One of the earliest aids to numeracy, common since ancient times, was the abacus. It consisted of a wooden frame enclosing parallel wires, through which were threaded coloured wooden beads. The congenial rattling and moving about of the beads attracted even the smallest child, and helped him to learn his numbers and colours by counting the beads. They were often incorporated into Edwardian playpens, as well as high chairs, and later wooden cots.

The last of the Three 'Rs' (reading, writing and 'rithmetic) demanded that the young child should acquire a basic standard of numeracy. Since the last quarter of the eighteenth century 'posture masters' had been used, as with letters, to teach children their numbers in an amusing way. An 'Instructive Puzzle', dated 1789, has ten cards, numbered from nought to nine, pasted onto thin mahogany sheets and hand-coloured, perhaps by their young owner. By the middle of the nineteenth century 'Butter's Tangible Arithmetic and Geometry for Children', published at three shillings, comprised a box of 144 oak cubes and an accompanying book of instructions and diagrams. Butter's also made a range of other educational aids for the older child, which included 'Butter's Dissected Trinomial Cube', 'Butter's Etymological Spelling Book and Exposition', and 'Butter's Graduations in Reading and Spelling'. These were recommended as 'excellent Birthday or Christmas Presents', and must all too often have proved a bitter disappointment to their eager young recipients. More acceptable perhaps would have been a set of Domino-Spel, twenty-eight engraved cards with comical scenes which incorporated domino spots as an aid to numeracy. These were popular during the 1830s.

Chinese Puzzles consisted of pieces of wood in the form of squares, triangles etc., and the older child was required to arrange them into various mathematical figures.

There were also board games of all kinds, played with counters and teetotums, which were designed to teach arithmetic and a host of other subjects ranging from 'Natural Philosophy' to 'Jewish History'. Such games were

Colour Plate 60. A 19th century box of approximately 125 different natural specimens, each one labelled and arranged in the compartments of four trays in the original wooden box. 7in. (17.8cm) x 12in. (30.5cm) x 5in. (12.7cm). They include gum arabic, Fuller's Earth, various ores, and quicksilver, as well as foodstuffs, skins, materials, seeds and insects. Sotheby's.

Plate 219. Butter's 'Tangible Arithmetic and Geometry for Children', 4th Edition, published in 1852 at 3s. 0d. This consisted of a box of 144 oak cubes accompanied by a book of instructions with diagrams, which showed how to use the cubes for addition, subtraction, multiplication and division, as well as fractions, proportions, geometry etc. Birmingham Museum & Art Gallery, Pinto Collection.

Plate 220. 'Domino-Spel'. A set of twenty-eight engraved cards with pictorial scenes incorporating domino spots as an aid to numeracy. It comes contained in an original card box inscribed with the date, 1839.

Sotheby's.

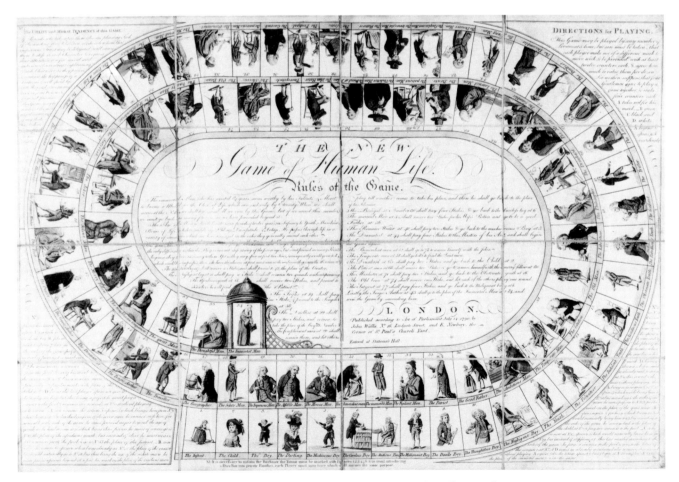

Plate 221. 'The New Game of Human Life'. A folding engraved sheet mounted on linen and coloured by hand, comprising a spiral track composed of eighty-four illustrations with rules at the corners and centre, published 14 July, 1790 by John Wallis, No.16 Ludgate Street and E. Newbery, the corner of St. Paul's Church Yard.

Sotheby's.

245

Plate 222. Wallis' 'Royal Chronological Tables of English History for the Instruction of Youth', the engraved hand-coloured sheet mounted on wood and cut to form a dissected puzzle. In original wooden box. 16⅛ in. (41.1cm) x 23⅜ in. (59.3cm), by John Wallis, 1788. Sotheby's.

Plate 223. Dunnett's 'New Epitome of the English History', the dissected puzzle comprising thirty-two woodcut portraits of the monarchs, coloured by hand. 11¾ in. (29.9cm) x 22¼ in. (56.3cm), William Dunnett, 1830. The label on the interior of the original wooden box is engraved with the following inscription, 'Dunnett's Toy, Dressing Case, Writing Desk, Inkstand and Workbox Repository, 3 Cheapside, London, Bone, Ivory and Wood Chessman, Bagatelle, Backgammon & Chess Boards'. Sotheby's.

Plate 224. An 'Instructive Puzzle', dated 1789. Contained in a mahogany box are ten cards, marked from 0-9, which show the human form contorting itself into the shapes of numbers to amuse and teach small children. The cards are hand-coloured and pasted onto mahogany squares. Cards such as this must often have been as confusing as they were instructive.
Birmingham Museum & Art Gallery, Pinto Collection.

Plate 225. Two mid-19th century bone teetotums, which were used in children's board games instead of dice, which smacked too much of gaming. John Wallis's game, 'A Tour through England and Wales, A New Geographical Pastime', published on 24 December 1794, stipulates that 'the Totum must be marked 1 to 8 on its several faces, with pen and ink'. In Wallis's 'Arithmetical Pastime', published in 1798, the teetotum was used to teach arithmetic. 'To Learn Subtraction: Spin 2 Teetotums, subtract the least number from the greatest'.   Sotheby's.

described as 'Quiet and instructive, as well as amusing. They afford excellent recreation for a winter's evening'. An Arithmetical Pastime, 'Intended to use the Rudiments of Arithmetic under the Idea of Amusement' was made by John Wallis in 1798. Players moved round ninety-nine places on the board in order to reach 100, each resting-place containing an illustration, a number or a direction. The game was played with two teetotums, the numbers on which were to be multiplied, divided, added or subtracted. Arithmetical tables were included in each corner, as well as numbered verses: 'Was all your business

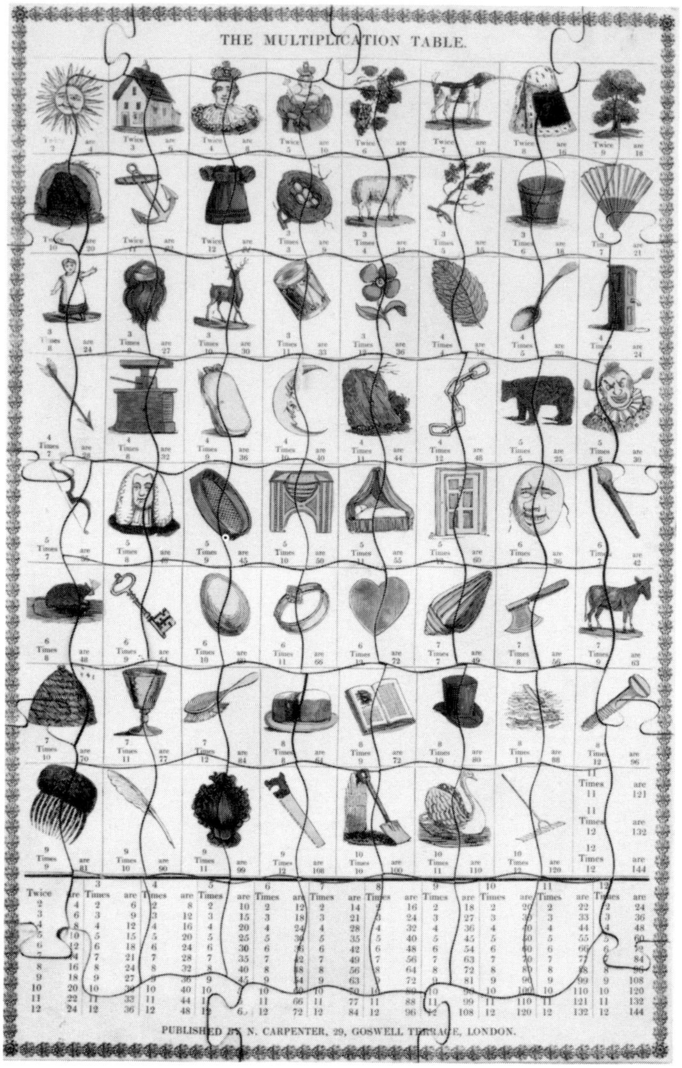

Plate 226. 'The Multiplication Table Neatly Dissected'. A jigsaw puzzle, consisting of a sheet of woodcut illustrations coloured by hand and multiplication tables, mounted on wood and cut out to form a puzzle. It is contained in its original box with sliding lid, 13½ in. (34.3cm) x 8½ in. (21.6cm), published by N. Carpenter, London, c.1830.

By kind permission of Lord and Lady Monson.

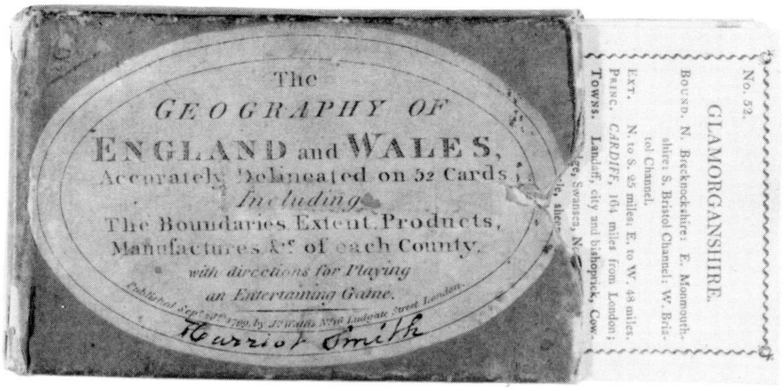

Plate 227. Two educational games for children by J. Wallis. The hand-coloured woodcut historical cards exhibit the History of England in thirty-one cards, probably out of a set of thirty-two, in their original box, c.1800. The Geography of England and Wales contains fifty-two cards, each showing the name of a county, its distinctive features and a short geographical description, in the original box. These were published on 16 September, 1799 by John Wallis 'At his map Warehouse, No.16 Ludgate Street'. The cards are accompanied by 'directions for playing and entertaining the game'.

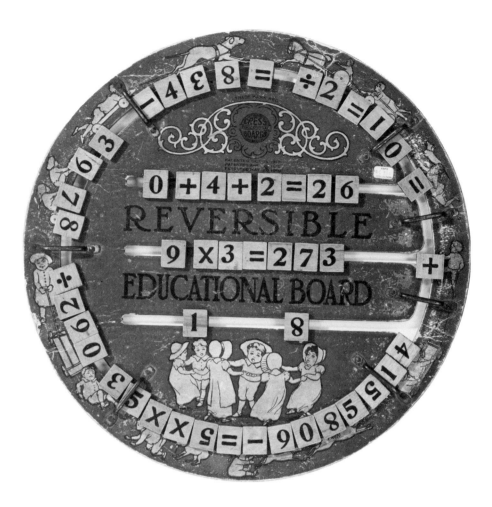

Plate 228. The 'Cress Reversible Educational Board', which was patented in 1912, 1915 and 1916. This was a circular wooden board, 14in. (35.6cm) in diameter, with a groove running around the perimeter, which connects with three horizontal grooves in the centre. Wooden pieces with letters and numbers slide along the grooves to be arranged to form simple words or sums. The decoration clearly shows the influence of Kate Greenaway. Birmingham Museum & Art Gallery, Pinto Collection.

done today, In time, and well, not spoilt by play? Then take your plumb-cake and a spin, If not, stop here a turn, and grin'. Teetotums were small four-sided tops to be spun with the fingers, each facet marked with a number or letter, or group of dots. Because of the association of dice, or 'devil's bones' with gaming, a sinful occupation, the innocent teetotum was considered more suitable for children's games.

The Wallis family were the most prolific makers of children's games and jigsaw or 'dissected' puzzles during the first half of the nineteenth century. These included The New Game of Human Life and The Panorama of Europe.

Clackers

'A deaf, poor, patient widow sits
And awes some thirty infants as she knits.'

Clackers of boxwood, lignum-vitae, beechwood and other woods were used in Dames' Schools to call children to attention and keep order in class. Early examples have a 'trigger' held to the head by a gut loop, while later examples have pivoted spring-loaded 'triggers', a patent for which was taken out in the nineteenth century. Also known as clickets, clappers or snappers, they have their origins in medieval wooden clappers carried by lepers and used to warn of their approach. (The expression 'to run like the clappers' comes from this.) By the nineteenth century they were also used as bird-scarers and burglar alarms, and were used in the Second World War by air raid wardens to warn

Plate 229. A Dame's School clacker, 19th century. These were also known as clackers, clickets, clappers or snappers, and were used for calling unruly children to order. They are usually made of boxwood or lignum-vitae, and operate by means of a 'trigger' which produced a loud click when pressed and then quickly released.
Birmingham Museum & Art Gallery, Pinto Collection.

Plate 230. A painting by William Mulready (1786-1863) entitled The Rattle. *This shows a small child in a cottage interior trying to grasp a wooden rattle, of a type used in Dames' Schools, to call children to order, or to frighten birds. Such things are used nowadays at football matches.*
The Tate Gallery, London.

of a gas attack. Nowadays their main use is by football supporters.

Dames' Schools originated in the seventeenth century, when the demands of Puritanism included a laity literate enough to read the Bible. The 'Dames' were usually local spinsters or housewives willing to take in small children for a nominal fee in order to teach them their letters. Such education was rudimentary, and often included such 'improving employment' as shelling peas. (The School Act which required all children to attend school was not passed until 1870.)

Chapter 17

THE CHRISTENING CEREMONY

Sacrament, Superstition and Tradition

'Array'd a half-angelic sight
In vests of pure baptismal white,
The mother to the font doth bring
The little, helpless nameless thing
With hushes soft and mild caressing
At once to get a name and blessing'.
(Charles Lamb, 1775-1834.)

At a time when superstitions surrounded every aspect of the dicey business of bringing a child into the world, it was considered essential that he should be baptised and received into the Church with all possible speed. Not only was baptism thought to confer protection against illness, kidnapping by evil spirits and other misfortunes, but the fates that awaited children who died unbaptised were too unhappy to contemplate and too many to list. The best that could happen would be that the child's soul would be consigned to limbo, and its body to the northernmost corner of the churchyard reserved for suicides, where anyone foolish or unfortunate enough to tread would be certain to be afflicted with 'grave-scab'. At baptism, too, came the moment when the child's name was uttered for the first time by the priest. Up until then no-one would have called the child by his name for there was an ancient tradition that to do so was unlucky, and could result in the Devil identifying and claiming the child. As late as Victorian and Edwardian times, newborn babies were referred to simply as 'Baby', and Queen Victoria referred resolutely to her first baby, Princess Victoria, as 'the child' until after she had been christened. The 1861 census of Barkway, Hertfordshire, refers to a newborn, and unbaptised, child as 'Babee'.

Thus, baptism was carried out as soon as possible after the birth, usually within the first two or three days, although medieval babies were often baptised on the day of their birth. By the nineteenth century the time had stretched to several weeks, as superstitions and the fear of disease and imminent death faded away.

Because childbirth was, for most women, so traumatic and exhausting, the mother would have a long lying-in period of one month or more, and would be too weak to take part in the christening herself. The baby was, therefore, carried to church in the arms of his godmother. Very often the godmother was one of the women who had attended the mother during her labour, and Mrs Pepys, though herself childless, was pressed into service in this way by Betty Michell in 1668, to whose aid she had gone 'when she began to cry out'. It was customary to name the child after the chief godparent (a woman in the case of a girl, and a man in the case of a boy), but Mrs Pepys' husband, the great Samuel, was disappointed at the baptism of Mrs Browne's son, his new godson, on 26 May, 1661, for whom he had, somewhat reluctantly, bought six spoons and a porringer. So great was our hero's disgust when the boy was named John that he stalked off with his presents, only to return the spoons sheepishly a few weeks later, on 1 August. Later, it became customary for the chief godparent to choose the name, a practice which sometimes lead to undignified wrangling by the font, as in the case of Queen Victoria's christening, when the Prince Regent, later George IV, insisted on changing all the names suggested by her parents.

Once in church, the baby would be unswaddled in a warm corner of the building, perhaps heated for the occasion by a brazier, and carried on a cushion to the font, wrapped in his presenting cloth. Total immersion was carried out until the seventeenth century, when a robe became easier to manage than the time-consuming and fiddly swaddling bands.

After the Church ceremony, during which it was hoped that the child would cry in order to repel the Devil, who could then flee through the open north door of the church, alms would be distributed on the way back to the house where a feast would be waiting. Priest, wet-nurse and midwife would be rewarded by the godparents with gifts of money for their efforts, and the guests would begin their celebrations in earnest. As well as cakes, bread and cheese, meats, biscuits and other *bonnes bouchées* would be set before the company. Much wine was clearly drunk at these affairs. Pepys makes numerous references to rowdy post-baptismal gatherings, and on 14 September 1736, *The Daily Gazetteer* carried a report of a celebration dinner after the baptism of Jacob Houblon's son at Hallingbury in Essex. 'Most of the gentlemen within 15 or 20 miles... were present, and most of the common people within 4 or 5 miles were made so welcome that they lay in heaps round his house dead drunk'. Parson Woodforde, in 1777, records how 'brother John, being at the Christening last night being merry disturbed the whole company so much that they were obliged to break up about 11 o'clock'. Clearly the clergy were particularly vulnerable when it came to offers of hospitality from the exuberant fathers, and were often overwhelmed. The Vicar of Broxbourne confessed to his diary in 1806 'I was at a Christening Dinner at Mr. Cozen's on Tuesday last, — & a very grand and expensive entertainment it was. The guests were so numerous that we were almost *pinioned* during dinner time... My mind seldom recovers its tone for many days afterwards. I am often, particularly after such occasions, almost weary of my life, & wish myself fairly out of it; but I am still more tired of my own weakness and imprudence'. Victorian christenings became far more genteel affairs, since by then they were postponed long enough after the birth for the mother to take part and exert a restraining feminine influence.

For the godparents, christenings were an expensive business, and presents for the child were expected. These were sometimes collected by the midwife in the layette, or christening basket. Early folklore and tradition decreed that a new baby should be presented with three gifts: salt, as a protection against evil, dating from Roman times; an egg as a symbol of fertility; and a coin to ensure future wealth. Indeed, until the beginning of this century boxed sets of silver egg-cups and salt-cellars made popular christening presents, At any rate, to give the child a costly piece of silver or gold plate was considered *de rigueur,* and Thackeray's William Dobbin, when called upon to be a godfather, 'exerted his ingenuity in the purchase of cups, spoons, papboats and corals for this little Christian'. However, not all godparents showed such enthusiasm, and a Victorian commentator somewhat cynically complained that 'the modern idea that has encrusted the ecclesiastical idea is, that the godfather should present a silver mug, or knife, fork, or spoon, or something of that kind, and sponsorship becomes a serious tax on one's benevolence'. Queen Victoria, as always, did exactly what she wanted, and managed to bring her beloved Albert into everything she did. She presented her great-grandson, Prince Albert, the future King George VI, with a marble bust of his dear departed namesake at his christening in 1895.

Christening Fonts

When infant baptism became common, around the third century, it was usual for the basin of the font to be raised off the ground, so that the priest could easily dip the baby in the water. After the seventeenth century, when total immersion for infants died out, and water was poured over the head only, fonts became smaller and smaller.

In royal and aristocratic circles, the importance of the font loomed large as a visible symbol of dynastic aspirations. Prince Arthur, the eldest son of Henry VII and Elizabeth of York, was baptized in 1486 in Winchester Cathedral in a font taken at considerable trouble and expense from Canterbury Cathedral for the occasion. The sum of 6s. 8d. was paid to the bearer, and two pounds to the servant of the Prior of Christ Church, Canterbury.

The baby who was to become Edward VI was baptized by Archbishop Cranmer in 1537 at Hampton Court in a new silver-gilt font, and James, son of the profligate Mary Queen of Scots, was baptized in 1566 in the Chapel Royal at Stirling Castle in a gold font that weighed two stones. Such excess reappeared some hundred years later in 1660, when Mary's great-grandson, Charles II, came to the throne. He somewhat eccentrically commissioned a font to be made at the Treasury's expense, in the expectation of future progeny, as he intended to marry a Spanish princess. In fact, Catherine of

Plate 231. A painting of The Christening by Francis Wheatley (1747-1801). The family cluster round the font to watch the baby, resplendent in lacy cap and robe, being christened.
York City Art Gallery. Reproduced by kind permission of the Dean and Chapter, York Minister.

Braganza, his Portuguese Queen, remained childless. Undeterred by such a detail, he had it used for the baptisms of some of his illegitimate children (who numbered more than thirteen). Queen Victoria was herself baptized in it, but was not amused by the idea of her own offspring sharing a font with 'Old Rowley's' bastards. She commissioned the silver-gilt Lily Font in 1840, for the christening of her first child, Princess Victoria. Made by E.J. and W. Barnard, to designs by Prince Albert, it is still used for royal christenings today.

Sometimes unavoidable accidents occurred to mar the dignity of royal christenings. Ethelred II, who was baptized around 968, 'defiled the sacrament by a natural evacuation', brought on, no doubt, by the blessed unwinding of his swaddling bands and the shock of total immersion in the font. The Bishop thundered 'By God and His mother, this will be a sorry fellow'. Ethelred did, indeed, fulfil his early promise, earning himself the memorable epithet, 'Unready'.

During the Commonwealth, the Puritans did away with much of the ritual associated with baptism. The Book of Common Prayer was not allowed to be used, godparents and the sign of the cross were rejected, and the birthdates of babies, rather than their baptismal dates, were entered into Parish Registers. Although the 'pouring or sprinkling of water' was tolerated, it was not allowed 'in the places where Fonts in the time of Popery were unfitly and superstitiously placed'. Thus, many devout parents arranged for their babies to be quietly and discreetly baptized at home. In 1647, in the midst of Puritan

Plate 232. *A magnificent George III gold christening font by Paul Storr, known as the Portland Font, 1797-98. It is surrounded by the figures of Faith, Hope and Charity, and is in the neo-classical style fashionable at the end of the 18th century. For all its grandeur, the actual bowl measures only 8¼ in. (21.6cm) in diameter.* Christie's.

Plate 233. *The Lily Font, made by E.J. & W. Barnard on the orders of Queen Victoria for the baptism of her first child, Princess Victoria, 'Vicky', in 1840. Made in silver-gilt with the coats-of-arms of Queen Victoria, and the joint arms of Queen Victoria and Prince Albert and the Princess Royal, it is thought that Prince Albert was closely concerned with the design.*
Reproduced by Gracious Permission of Her Majesty the Queen.

suppression, Mary Verney, expecting a child, discussed the christening by letter with her husband, Sir Ralph. 'I will . . . gett a minester in the house that will doe itt in the old way.'

Sickly babies, whose frail health might have suffered from a visit to a cold church (and churches were sometimes very cold; the Rev. Francis Kilvert found chunks of ice floating in his font on St. Valentine's Eve, 1870), were sometimes allowed a home baptism, although they were supposed to bring the child to church for a 'proper' baptism when he was stronger. Thus, parish records often show two baptism dates for the same child within six months of each other. John Evelyn, the diarist, and all his children were baptized at home. In 1768 Parson Woodforde noted in his Diary, 'went over to C. Cary

Plate 234. An oil painting by John Phillip (1817-1867) showing a Scottish Christening. *It is dated 1850, and clearly shows the Minister baptizing the baby, resplendent in lace-edged cap and robe, from a punch bowl on the cottage parlour table.* Aberdeen Art Gallery and Museums.

this night after eleven o'clock and privately baptized a child born this day and very dangerously ill in convulsions'. The next day he sadly wrote 'The poor little infant which I privately baptized last night departed this world this afternoon'. However, he was not always so accommodating if he thought that advantage was being taken. In 1777 he complained that 'Harry Dunnell behaved very impertinent this morning to me because I would not privately name his child for him, he having one child before named privately by me and never had it brought to Church afterwards. He had the impudence to tell me that he would send it to some Meeting House to be named &c — very saucy indeed.'

There were many priests who disapproved of home baptisms, and they could turn into riotous affairs, often at the expense of the poor exhausted mother, in whose bedroom they frequently took place. In 1667 Samuel Pepys 'went by water to Michell's, and there his little house full of his father and mother and the kindred'. Betty, the mother, with whom Pepys carried on a long extra-marital flirtation, looked 'mighty pretty in bed, but her head akeing, not very merry'. However, his sympathy was short-lived and he remarked philosophically, 'But the company mighty merry, and I with them, and so the child was christened'.

Plate 235. *A blue and white English delft punch bowl, made to commemorate the birth of Ann Couch. The bowl is inscribed 'Ann the Daughter of Anthony/Ann Couch, was Born the/20 day of Ianuary, 1755'. The rim is inscribed with the verse 'Ann Couch is my Name/And England is my Nation/St. Ives is my Dwelling Place/and Christ is my Salvation'.*

Colonial Williamsburg Foundation.

Plate 236. *A rare Bristol or Lambeth delft punch bowl made for a christening, inscribed with the initials B.I.M. and the date, 1752. A convivial company is seated round a table, laid with brimming punch bowl and glasses, while a nurse enters from the right carrying the swaddled baby. Sickly infants were often baptized at home in the family punch bowl during the first day or two of life, and then when they were stronger, were taken to the Parish Church to be formally baptized again. Often as much as six months elapsed between the two baptisms, leading to confusion in the parish records which showed two baptisms of the same child within less than one year. Sometimes a new baby was named after a sibling who had died, thus adding to the confusion.* Sotheby's.

Very often such a home baptism would have been carried out, not in a font, but in a punch bowl. Once the baptismal water had been disposed of, the bowl could be filled up with punch to provide refreshment for the guests and alcoholic liquid with which to 'wet the baby's head', an old custom still observed in the last century in country areas. At the christening of the Prince of Wales in 1842, the toasts were drunk from an enormous punch bowl designed by George IV, which contained thirty dozen bottles of mulled claret. As late as 1897 Carola Oman was baptized in the Chapel of All Souls College, Oxford, in the College's largest punch-bowl, there being no font because all Fellows had hitherto been celibate.

Some punch bowls were specially made for the occasion, and some examples in English delftware are known, notably one at Colonial Williamsburg, commemorating the birth of Ann Couch, dated 1755, and another, commemorating Ruth Twiss's birth, in the National Museum of Arts, New York, dated 1705.

Bearing Cloths and Christening Mantles

'Thy scarlet robes, as a child's Bearing cloth, I'll use to carry thee
out of this place'.
(Henry VI, William Shakespeare.)

Baptism was an occasion for everybody to look their best, and when Mrs Pepys attended the Pierce christening in 1660 her husband Samuel remarked with surprise that 'this is the first day that ever I saw my wife wear black patches since we were married'. Lady Shelburne, attending a royal christening in 1768 'was so illuminated with jewels and radiant with gold and silver she must have added splendour even to that magnificent assembly.'

Bearing, or presenting cloths were heavy lengths of sumptuous fabric, and were used during the sixteenth, seventeenth and early eighteenth century to wrap the baby for his christening, as he was carried in the arms of his godmother to the church and back again, when he would be shown off to the assembled guests. Usually made of silk, satin, damask or velvet, in rich tones of crimson, pink or ivory, these cloths were edged in silver or gold lace, silk fringe or, more rarely, embroidery highlighted with spangles. They generally measured around five feet in length, the remaining two sides being slightly shorter, and they were lined in silk or taffeta. Once in church, the bearing cloth

Plate 237. A pink satin bearing, or presenting, cloth, edged with a wide border of silver lace, English, c.1660-70. Such things were normally about 5ft. (152.4cm) long, and slightly smaller in width. Embroidered motifs included flowers, initials and occasionally emblems or texts.

David Knight.

Plate 238. A christening mantle of magenta wool, with a deep border of quilted cream silk, c.1860. Trimmings of fur, swansdown or silk fringe were common with these opulent little garments, and the handsome outfit was often completed by a feather-trimmed hat.
Museum of London.

would be removed, along with the swaddling bands and under-garments, and the baby would be briefly immersed in the font.

They have been known at least since Tudor times. The infant Queen Elizabeth I's bearing cloth was of purple velvet, and she was carried by her senior godmother, the Dowager Duchess of Norfolk. They are mentioned by Shakespeare, and also in a contemporary account of an unfortunate effort to cure James I of his melancholia, when a pig was dressed up as a baby 'in a rich Mantle' for a mock christening. Lord William Howard's Accounts for 1623 mention 'For 5 yard of damaske to make a bearing cloth £3 6s. 6d. For taffetie to lyne it 32s. For lace, eleven onceis to it 57s.' The material was often so stiff and heavy that it needed more than one lady to hold it up, and Pepys notes in his *Diary* for 1663 that Lady Jemimah Crewe was 'one of the four ladies that hold up the mantle at the christening this afternoon of the Duke's child'.

As swaddling became less and less widespread during the second half of the eighteenth century, and christening robes became fashionable now that total immersion was no longer practised, so the bearing cloth was replaced by a cape or mantle, worn over a robe, much smaller in size and more manageable to

Plate 239. A 19th century christening veil, with a border of trailing flowers in white embroidery, reminiscent of Ayrshire whitework. The translucency of the very fine muslin allowed the baby's face to show through, while protecting the newborn child from the hazards of germs and chills on his first visit out-of-doors. Richard Hamilton was christened in October 1900 wearing 'a long cloak of corded silk... and a bonnet with a tiny plume on it, and over his face a lace veil'. The origin of christening veils was probably the chrisom cloth put in early times over the child's head to preserve the chrism oil with which the infant's forehead would have been anointed.
Museum of London.

wrap a tiny baby up against the cold. Poorer families in the eighteenth century used either a knitted woollen shawl or, during the nineteenth century, a Paisley shawl.

More affluent mothers would have preferred an ostentatious cape, of satin or velvet, known as a mantle. These splendid garments were generally trimmed with fur, braid or silk fringe, and later, swansdown, and were often quilted against the cold, and embroidered with flowers and other motifs. In 1698 Mary Thresher, née East, listed among her first child's layette '1 blew and whit flowered Sattain Mantle lind with blew Sarsnett and lacet with old silver plate lace', and, nearly two hundred years later, in 1879, the *Daily Chronicle* carried the advertisement 'Quilters Wanted for infants' cloaks'. George III's daughter, christened in 1770, wore a white satin mantle lined with pink and edged in ermine, set with £1,000 worth of jewels, the cost of the whole garment being estimated at an amazing £2,800. Lesser mortals could still put on a good show, and Susan Sibbald recalled the christening of her sister in 1792, when the baby wore 'a most beautiful blue and white satin mantle; blue

Colour Plate 61. A small section of a bearing or presenting cloth of crimson velvet applied with a border of gold lace, embroidered with spangles or sequins. 17th century, 62in. (157.5cm) x 38in. (96.5cm).
Christie's South Kensington.

Colour Plate 62 A portrait of the Cholmondeley Sisters, British School, c.1600-10. This famous painting commemorates the fact that the twin sisters, born on the same day, were also married on the same day and 'brought to Bed' the same day with their babies. The wide-awake babies, their eyes cast upwards in apprehension, are both clearly swaddled under their fine crimson damask presenting cloths, which are edged in gold lace. As with all mothers at this date, the Cholmondeley Sisters would have been forced to stay in bed, no doubt utterly exhausted, for some weeks, and were not allowed to mingle with society until they had been 'churched' in a ritual service of symbolic cleansing and thanksgiving conducted by their parish priest. The Tate Gallery, London.

hat and feathers, presents from Lady Paine, one of her godmothers'. Dickens' Baby Kitterbell from *Sketches by Boz,* 1836, was less ceremoniously 'packed up in a blue mantle trimmed with white fur' for his christening.

Mary Clive, writing in the same year, commits to paper, in a steam of purple prose, her feelings on the subject of mantles. These reveal much about the importance of visible splendour in Victorian Society, and about the often unrealistic and ambivalent way in which that Society regarded children. 'I cannot overcome the wish to have Georgey christened in a mantle although I have persuaded myself not to have a seven guinea one. But I mean to have a white satin one covered with India muslin and I should be very much obliged to you to get me five yards of *faultless* white satin. It must be a most luscious article, soft as down and white as snow, with a *soupçon* of a pink blush upon it... all these virtues they say can be got for six or seven shillings a yard. It must be a French satin as the best English have a degree of wiriness always. In short it must be a satin that you could not help loving. It must be trimmed either with silk fringe or with swansdown. Swansdown seems to be a beau ideal... Bunting would look so *very* pretty in satin and swansdown'.

Such garments had their pitfalls, and a potential mishap was deftly avoided by the Duchess of Buccleuch at the christening of the Prince of Wales by the Archbishop of Canterbury in 1842, when she 'neatly picked His Royal Highness, mantle and lace and all, out of the voluminous folds of the Primate's lawn sleeves and the dangers of his wig'.

In addition to all this finery, the baby would have worn a veil over his face to protect him from the damp and chill of the church, and from any germs which might be circulating. The translucency of the fine 'India' muslin would have allowed the baby's small face to show through, and formed a link with the past when a chrisom cloth was placed over the baby's face to preserve the chrisom oil, with which his forehead had been anointed. Richard Hamilton, christened in October 1900, wore 'a long cloak of corded silk... and a bonnet with a tiny plume on it, and over his face a lace veil'.

Christening Sets

'And thus, without the Needle we may see
We should without our Bibs and Biggins bee,
No shirts or smockes, our nakedness to hide,
No garments gay to make us magnified'.
(*The Prayse of the Needle,* by John Taylor, early seventeenth century.)

Since the swaddling bands which seventeenth century babies wore beneath their presenting cloths made no allowance for show and display in the way that later christening robes did, all the needlewoman's skill was lavished on the presenting cloth itself, and on the sets of tiny garments which were a traditional christening present to a baby, to be worn for his baptism.

These included bibs of varying length, to protect the other clothes from 'slobber', collars, cuffs or sleeves (since the baby's arms were left free of

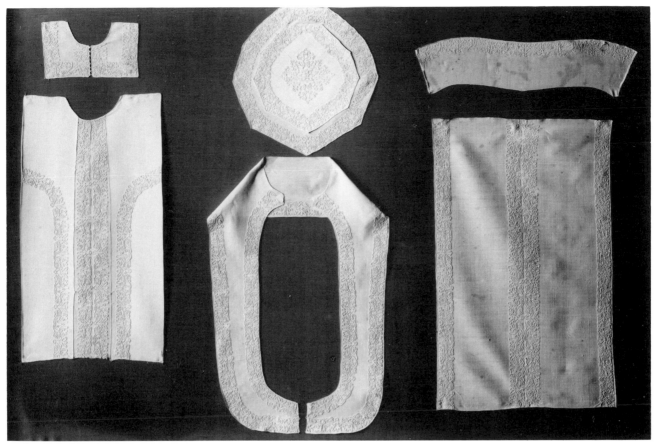

Plate 240. *Some items from a 17th century baby's christening set. They are made of linen decorated with cord applied in a vermicular pattern, and are typical of the restrained garments worn by babies in 17th century England. The set comprises (from left to right) a bib collar, a two-layered piece, possibly used as a pin-cushion cover, a headpiece to be fastened underneath the chin below a cap, a long bib, a 'Stayband', with upturned collar worn over the head, the long ends pinned down over the long bib, and a large piece to be tied over the lower half of the body. Such sets also usually included a pair of detachable sleeves, a pair of mittens, a shirt to be worn beneath the swaddling bands and at least one cap to be worn over the headpiece.* Castle Museum, Nottingham.

Plate 241. *A pair of baby's mittens of fine linen, covered and cuffed in Mechlin lace, English or Flemish, c.1730. Such mittens generally formed part of a christening set in the 17th and early 18th century.* David Knight.

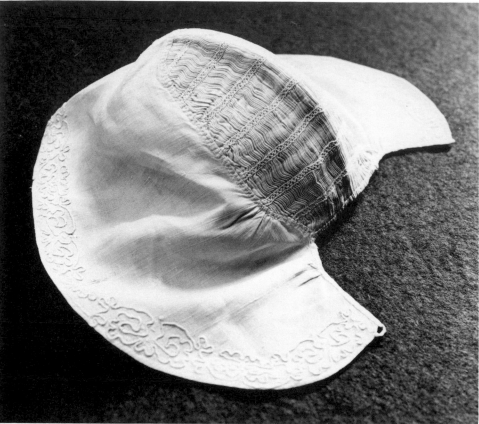

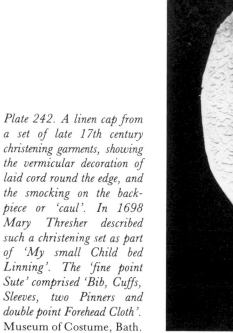

Plate 242. A linen cap from a set of late 17th century christening garments, showing the vermicular decoration of laid cord round the edge, and the smocking on the backpiece or 'caul'. In 1698 Mary Thresher described such a christening set as part of 'My small Child bed Linning'. The 'fine point Sute' comprised 'Bib, Cuffs, Sleeves, two Pinners and double point Forehead Cloth'. Museum of Costume, Bath.

Plate 243A and B. A linen baby's cap with a central insertion of Holliepoint decoration, the detail of which is seen left. The insertion, which is decorated with birds and flowering plants, is inscribed with the name 'Sufanna Porter' and the date March 26 1748. Such a piece would almost certainly have been made for a christening. Holliepoint panels were often inserted into small garments such as the shoulder seams of baby's shirts, bibs and caps. A very fine version of needle-lace peculiar to England, the design appears as pinpricks on a white ground. As well as providing decoration, the tiny holes also allowed for ventilation. Colonial Williamsburg Foundation.

Colour Plate 63. A Portrait of the Saltonstall Family, c.1636-37, by David des Granges. This is an allegorical portrait showing, in bed, the dead first wife and mother of the elder children, while the second wife carries the child of the second marriage. The babe, who is tightly swaddled under his magnificent crimson presenting cloth, also wears a special christening set of baby linen, which includes a clearly visible long bib, cap and forehead cloth. The Tate Gallery, London.

swaddling), and at least two caps or 'biggins' with a separate headpiece fastened underneath the chin, mittens, a shirt to be worn underneath the swaddling bands, and a 'stayband' with turned-up collar to be worn over the head with the long ends pinned down over the bib. The caps replaced the earlier chrism or chrisom cloth, which was placed over the child's head to prevent the chrism oil, with which he had been anointed, from being rubbed off.

Various contemporary references can be found to most of these garments. A charming dialogue created in the 1560s by Claudius Hollyband and Peter Erondell, two Huguenot refugees, described a mother instructing her nurse on the washing of her child, and gives us a glimpse of the arcane sequence of a sixteenth century baby's garments. 'How now, how doth the childe?... Unswaddle him, undoe his swadling bands... wash him before me... Pull off

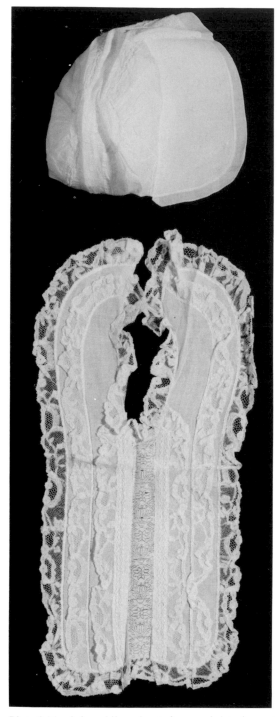

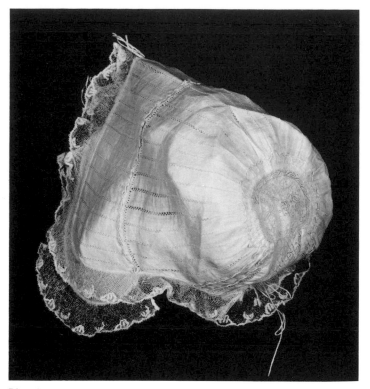

Plate 245. Another linen baby's cap with drawn thread work and a circular Holliepoint insertion in the crown, featuring two birds amid flowering sprigs. The hem is edged in a double row of lace, mid-18th century. Colonial Williamsburg Foundation.

Plate 244. A long bib and cap from a christening set of the second half of the 18th century. Made of fine linen lawn, with Brussels lace trim, both pieces have insertions of Holliepoint lace, showing the geometric patterns typical of the end of the 18th century. Although very intricately worked, the designs have a primitive quality, with some of the motifs reminiscent of folk patterns found on Fair Isle knitting patterns, or Turkish rugs. Sometimes initials or dates are incorporated into the designs. Phillips.

Plate 246. Ivory satin embroidered christening bonnet, worn by Prince Arthur of Connaught at his christening in 1850. Sotheby's.

his shirt, thou art pretty and fat my little darling... Now swaddle him again. But first put on his biggin (cap) and his little band with an edge (stayband, worn with the collar turned up over the head and the long ends pinned down over the bib). Where is his white petticote? Give him his coat of changeable (shot) taffeta and his sattin sleeves; Where is his bibbe? Let him have his gathered aprone with stringes and hang a muckinder (handkerchief) to it.'

The list of Child Bed Linning compiled by Mary East in 1698 includes an entry for a possible christening set: '1 fine point (lace) Sute of Bib, Cuffs, gloves, two pinners (caps) and double point forehead Cloth'.

Seventeenth century christening sets were of fine linen, generally with a simple white vermicular pattern in laid linen cord, while eighteenth century sets displayed insertions of Holliepoint lace in the shoulder seams of the shirts, or on the crown of the cap, or down the front of the bib. When swaddling was abandoned during the eighteenth century, robes came into fashion and the need for these tiny, beautifully finished garments died away.

Christening Robes

*'Take this white vesture for a token of the innocencie, which by God's grace in this holy
sacramente of Baptisme, is given unto thee.'*
(Prayer Book of Edward VI, 1549.)

*'Its eyes are blue and bright,
Its cheeks like rose;
Its simple robes unite
Whitest of calicoes
With lawn, and satin bows.'*
(The Christening, Thomas Hardy (1840-1928).)

The white robe which a baby traditionally wears for his baptism represents the new life, free from sin, into which he has been spiritually reborn. This finds its origin in the chrisom cloth, a white robe put on the baby in earlier times, between immersion and anointing, which was supposed to be worn for three or four weeks until the child's mother came to be churched. The chrisom cloth was then given to the priest and used in the ritual ablutions after the Eucharist. If the child died during this time, he was buried in his chrisom cloth, and such infant deaths are recorded as 'chrisoms' in the Bills of Mortality.

Around the end of the seventeenth century, when swaddling began in some cases to be cautiously abandoned, the christening sets of small garments which were worn with the swaddling bands, and the magnificent bearing cloths in which the child was carried to church, were replaced by white satin robes, which were worn over a petticoat. They were open down the front, or sometimes the back, and fastened with satin ribbon ties. They were invariably high waisted, with small vertical pin-tucks on the bodice, and a stiff A-line skirt of moderate length, which was richly decorated with lace or self-coloured embroidery, and edged with silk braid or looped fringes of metallic thread. The

straight elbow-length sleeves were bordered by deep turned-back cuffs, and the whole design was formal and stately. Mary Thresher, née East, lists among the many garments of 'My small Child bed Linning' in 1698 '1 Rich white Sattain Mantle lind with Sasnet (thin silk fabric) with Cape and Sleeves of ye same.' (At this date the word mantle could also refer to a robe.) Poorer families made do with linen robes, sometimes printed in indigo, and two such robes are in the Museum of Costume, Bath.

In the third quarter of the eighteenth century muslin began to be imported into Europe from India, and was much in favour for filmy ladies' dresses, which were embroidered with white tambour-work embroidery. Around 1800 a flax-growing and linen-weaving industry was started in Lancashire and in Scotland. Workers from the Continent settled first in Glasgow and Paisley, where a remarkably successful industry in woven shawls with oriental patterns developed, and a little later the textile industry spread to Ayrshire. Almost at

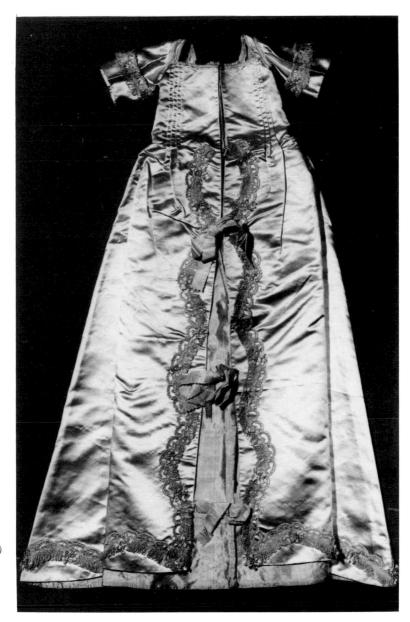

Plate 248. A cream satin christening robe, c.1760-80, trimmed with looped cream silk braid, and lined in thin cream silk. As with most late 17th and 18th century robes it opens down the front, and fastens with three pairs of cream silk ties. The short sleeves have typical turn-back cuffs. 34in. (86.4cm) long. Manchester City Art Galleries.

once the heavy, stiff satin christening robes of the eighteenth century fell from fashion, to be replaced by light, gauzy wisps of 'sewed' muslin in Empire style which allowed admirable freedom from restrictions of movement, in a revolutionary and freedom-loving age. These had the highest of waists and were embroidered with restrained leafy sprigs and borders of white trailing flowers. Embroidery done with the tambour hook was supplanted by the fine form of needlepoint lace, which came to be known as Ayrshire whitework, although it was carried on in other centres besides Ayrshire, notably in Ireland. Worked, as the name suggests, in white thread on muslin of almost transparent appearance, Ayrshire work comprised raised satin stitch and French knots, a special and distinctive feature being cut-work holes which were infilled with minutely detailed needlepoint fillings.

At first, during the 1820s and 1830s, patterns were rather a higgledy-piggledy affair, passed on by ladies to one another in manuscript form and

Plate 249. A late 17th century ivory silk christening robe, the bodice and side panels of the skirt embroidered with bold scrolling leaves and flowers, in a style reminiscent of crewel embroidery, and trimmed with fringed braid and chenille. This robe is reputed to have been worn by Richard Goodhugh, later High Sheriff of Kent, in 1697. Phillips.

270

Plate 250. A christening robe of fine white muslin, embroidered in the manner of Aryshire white-work, mid-19th century. The V-shaped bodice is typical of the period, and the intricacy of the detailed needlepoint lace fillings can be seen in the centres of the flowers. Museum of London.

pasted into albums. However, by the 1830s patterns were appearing in domestic journals, and were being sold by retailers, lithographed onto thin cartridge paper, ready to be traced with blue powder and pin pricks onto the muslin. Soon dedicated amateur needlewomen were joined by an army of out-workers largely organised by Mrs Jamieson. The wives and daughters of local miners, cotton mill workers and iron-workers soon formed a prolific work-force. As the cottage craft mushroomed into a huge industry, workers were subdivided into what amounted to a production line, with each woman

responsible for a different pattern or stitch, those responsible for the minutely-worked needlepoint 'fillings' being paid the most. The printed patterns were supplied to the women in their cottages by agents, and the finished work was taken back to the factories to be made up. Baby clothes, and particularly christening robes, in 'sewed muslin' were all the rage, and during the 1850s the annual turnover in whitework was estimated to be more than £750,000,

Plate 253. The royal christening robe, made for the baptism of Princess Victoria, Queen Victoria's eldest child, on 10 February 1841. It was also worn by the infant Prince of Wales, later King Edward VII, at his christening, and was subsequently given by Queen Victoria to the Duchess of York (later Queen Mary), all of whose children were baptized in it. It has been continuously used by the Royal Family ever since, and is kept in a special airtight container at Buckingham Palace. Royal christenings were glamorous affairs. Princess Vicky, the Princess Royal, had a christening cake surmounted by a sugar figure of Britannia, who held a miniature pink sugar representation of the royal infant in a basket. Even more lavish was the christening cake of the Prince of Wales a year later. It measured eight feet in diameter and was cut at a reception in the Waterloo Chamber of Windsor Castle after the service in St. George's Chapel, Windsor.

Reproduced by Gracious Permission of Her Majesty the Queen.

Plate 254. A detail of the skirt of a mid-19th century christening robe. The central panel, with its insertions of amazingly fine and detailed needlepoint lace, shows in its design the influence of contemporary Paisley shawls, which in turn were influenced by Indian and Persian designs. The simple hem is trimmed with a narrow layer of Valenciennes lace, a feature pointing to an origin away from Ayrshire.

The Embroiderers' Guild Collection.

with the United States taking one-third of this each year. One Glasgow firm employed some twenty to thirty thousand embroiderers, and workers were well paid, skilled women earning as much as ten shillings a week, the average wage of men at that time. The long, painstaking work in candlelit cottages ruined the sight of many women, and some were forced to rub whisky into their eyes in a painful and pitiful effort to temporarily improve their vision so that they could meet an agent's deadline. Many were helped by glass lace-makers' lamps which shed a beam of light onto the work. In Ireland, where a rival industry sprang up, and where women were desperate for work owing to the potato famine, beginners were offered only sixpence a week.

By the 1840s, christening robes had lower waists, with a fashionable V-shape outlined by the tucks and rows of lace on the bodice, which reflected women's dresses of the period. The lavish whitework embroidery was concentrated on the bodice and the triangular front panel of the long skirt. Typical of the patterns used in Ayrshire whitework were the intricately worked trailing leaves, ferns and sprays of bellflowers, rococo cartouche-shaped holes filled with minute panels of trellis and other diaper patterns in needlepoint, and flower sprays in padded satin and buttonhole stitches, with the centres showing

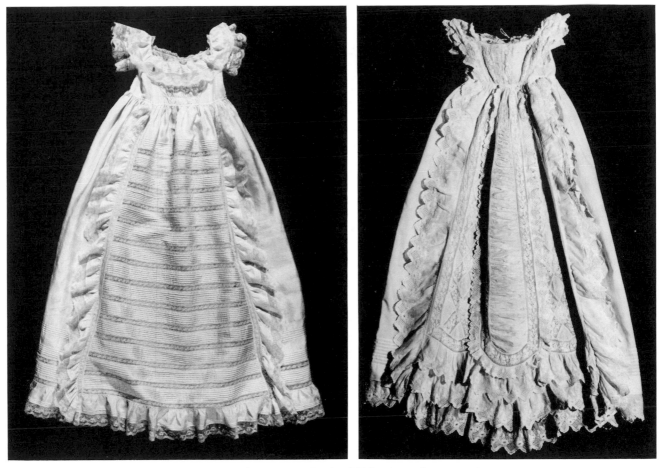

Plate 255. *A cream silk christening robe with pin-tucks and bands of Valenciennes lace, worn by Sir Winston Churchill at his baptism on 27 December 1874 in the Chapel at Blenheim, 41½ in. (106cm).* Private Collection.

Plate 256. *A white cotton christening robe in full-blown Victorian style, with ruched skirt panels and lace inserts, and edged with pin-tucks and lavish broderie anglaise flounces, used in 1877. Such a dress would have created a fairytale impression far removed from the recent traumas of the baby's birth and first perilous few days of life. Perhaps too, there was a conscious effort on the part of many women to put behind them the ugliness and pain of childbirth.* Manchester City Art Gallery.

the same needlepoint infillings. Also characteristic are motifs of a vaguely oriental flavour, reminiscent of those seen on the woven shawls made at nearby Paisley, and drawing their influence in turn from the woven fabrics of Kashmir and other Indian and Persian textiles. Lace tended not to be used on hems and borders, but scalloped or dentate edges were preferred.

In order to accommodate all this virtuoso embroidery, the skirts of christening robes became longer and longer, and forty-five inches was not an unusual length for a christening robe in the middle of the nineteenth century. In 1903 Alice Morse Earle commented that '25 years ago the christening robe was so long that when the child was held on the arm of its standing nurse or mother, the edge of the robe barely escaped touching the ground.' This fashion for long baby's robes was largely phased out by the introduction of the perambulator, although a model in which a tiny baby could lie down was not developed until the 1870s, when the attention of fashion was focused on the face, and bonnets became all the rage. However, competitive mothers were prepared to go to any lengths to ensure that their baby did them justice on his christening day, the flames of their maternal ambition fanned by journals such as *Enquire Within Upon Everything,* 1886, which stated that for his christening 'the infant should be robed in the choicest manner that the circumstances will allow'. Cecilia Ridley was clearly susceptible to this kind of advice, and determined not to be constrained by 'circumstances'. In 1844 she wrote, 'Baby re-entered his long clothes for the day in order to wear the beautiful robe that is kept for the occasion and which he has almost outgrown now. It is a foolish thing, a vast of money, but very pretty of its kind. Little darling, he really looks so pretty'. Sometimes the embroidery on these long robes stopped short of the waist, allowing the skirt to be shortened and used again.

The huge American imports of whitework embroidery ceased with the outbreak of the Civil War and the consequent cotton shortage, and the development of automatic machine embroidery in the 1850s helped to ensure the end of the Ayrshire industry by around 1870. Broderie anglaise on cotton was much quicker and easier to work than the minutely-detailed Ayrshire work, with borders of large holes arranged to make daisy and flowerhead patterns, which were simply edged in buttonhole stitch. By the 1860s, machine-cut borders ready-holed with geometric patterns for amateurs to work were popular, and by-passed the laborious marking of the pattern with a pricking wheel, and the cutting with scissors or piercing with a stiletto of the small holes. By the 1870s the Swiss could reproduce the whole process cheaply and quickly by machine, as well as turning out vast quantities of strips of machine-made edging lace.

Towards the end of the century rows of tiny pin-tucks were used for decorative detailing on popular Princess line christening robes, and were alternated with insertions of lace. Hems and sleeves were also edged with narrow rows of Valenciennes lace. Mary Hamilton's son, Richard, was christened in 1900 in a robe 'of the finest lawn, very long, with a bodice composed of minute rows of Valenciennes lace; and to wear under it, a slip ornamented with lace and tucks done with tiny feather-stitching'. Her third child was baptized in a robe (possibly the same) 'of lawn and Valenciennes lace all finely tucked, a filmy garment of which Mrs Powersfort remarked "It might have been blown together".'

If anything, christening robes became more, rather than less elaborate as the twentieth century dawned, with the widespread use of commercial and domestic sewing machines, and with stores such as Harrods and the Army and Navy pandering to the fantasies of mothers like Mary Hamilton who, no doubt, longed to submerge themselves and their babies beneath knots of ribbons, puffed sleeves and Vandyke flounces, after the recent rigorous realities of childbirth.

Chapter 18

CHRISTENING GIFTS

Pin-Cushions

'Angels guard thee lovely blossom,
Hover round and shield from ill,
Crown thy parents largest wishes,
And their fondest hopes fulfil.'
(From a pin-cushion dated 1838.)

The blessed advent of the safety pin did not occur until 1878, and until that time the endless small garments in a baby's layette were fastened with tapes, ribbons, buttons or ordinary pins.

Terrible accidents must have happened all too regularly. Richard Steele described the helpless sufferings of a baby in *The Tatler*, 1709. 'The girl was very proud of the womanly employment of a nurse and took upon her to strip and dress me anew because I made a noise, to see what ailed me; she did so and stuck a pin in every joint about me. I still cried, upon which she lays me on my face in her lap; and to quiet me, fell a-nailing in all the pins, by clapping me on the back.' Charles Dickens' Kitterbell, some century and a half later, relates 'we have just discovered the cause of little Frederick's restlessness. It is not fever, as I apprehended, but a small pin which nurse accidentally stuck in his leg yesterday evening. We have taken it out, and he appears more composed, though he still sobs a good deal'.

Pins were a very expensive commodity, usually made of brass, and with the coiled wire heads being added separately. As many as twenty different people could be involved in the complete process of making a pin, and so the idea of a woman having to earn her 'pin-money' was often a harsh reality. Solid pins were not made until 1797, but from 1840 the process was speeded up, and the cost fell. A cushion stuck with pins for the new baby would clearly, therefore, be a most useful and handsome present to a new mother, often from the baby's aunt or elder sister. Kind donors would take great care, however, not to give their present until after the baby had been born, probably at the time of the christening a few days later, since an old tradition linked pain in childbirth with pins. A saying warned 'More pins, more pain' and no self-respecting midwife would allow pins anywhere near a woman in labour. Indeed, in country areas up until the eighteenth century, it was common for a midwife

Plate 257a). A cream cotton pin-cushion, with a lace border, inscribed in pins
GOD BLESS THE BABE
AND MAY IT LIVE
AND A DEAL OF COMFORT
MAY IT GIVE.
MARY LUCAS. HERS.
the reverse with a basket of flowers within a lozenge border and the date January 22. 1787.
b) A velvet pin-cushion, with a border of painted flowers, inscribed in pins 'Angels guard thee lovely blossom, Hover round and shield from ill, Crown thy parents' largest wishes, and their fondest hopes fulfil', 1838.
c) A pink silk pin-cushion with fringe border, and with the inscription 'Bless the Babe and Save the Mother 1862'. Bethnal Green Museum of Childhood.

to unfasten all the pins and untie all the knots in a mother's clothing, and to open all the windows and locks in the birthing room. This was thought to help the easy entry of the child into the world. However, the notorious midwife and monthly nurse, Sarah Gamp, in Dickens' *Martin Chuzzlewit,* upbraided Mr Wilks, who came to inform her of the onset of his wife's labour, with the words, 'Don't say it's you, Mr. Wilks, and that poor creatur Mrs. Wilks with not even a pin cushion ready'.

Such cushions date from at least the middle of the seventeenth century, with most surviving examples coming from the late eighteenth or nineteenth century. They are generally of cream-coloured or pink satin (the tradition of pink for a girl and blue for a boy was yet to come), although velvet and cotton examples are also known. An inscription, together with decorative motifs such as hearts and flowers, was drawn out in pins sunk into the cushion. Often the name and date of birth of the child is found, along with jubilant, thankful or downright anxious mottoes concerning the baby's birth. Popular inscriptions include:-

> God preserve them both from Danger.
>
> May He whose cradle was a manger
> Bless and keep the little stranger.
>
> Boy or Girl I care not whether,
> May happiness attend the Mother.
>
> Long Live the Babe
>
> Welcome Sweet Babe
>
> Welcome Little Stranger
>
> May Health protect the smiling Babe,
> And happiness the Mother.
>
> Bless the Babe and Save the Mother.
>
> Kind Heaven the tender blossom spare,
> And make it thy peculiar care.
>
> Hail to this teeming stage of strife,
> Hail lovely miniature of life.

Sometimes the cushions were edged with a border of Ayrshire whitework embroidery, or loops of small threaded beads, with a silk or metal fringe, or

Colour Plate 64. A beadwork layette basket, second half of the 17th century. Such shallow rectangular baskets, with their bold primitive designs of pastoral scenes, insects, animals, birds and flowers, were entirely worked in tiny glass beads and were made to contain the smaller items of a baby's layette, or to receive gifts of money and jewellery, or small pieces of silver, at a christening.
Christie's South Kensington.

even more pins. They were often filled with sand to keep the pins sharp and clean, and iron pins were sometimes added for good luck, echoing the legend of St. Dunstan.

Such pin-cushions were still being given and received as late as the 1920s, in spite of the petulant 'Surgeon's Advice to Mothers' contained in *The Englishwoman's Domestic Magazine,* 1859. 'We shall never be satisfied till the abominable use of the pin is avoided in toto in an infant's dressing, and a texture made for all the undergarments of a child of a cool and elastic material'.

Layette or Christening Baskets

Elaborate 'baskets' exist from the seventeenth century, and are known as layette baskets. However, from the nature of their decoration it seems likely

Colour Plate 65. A Dutch silver baby linen, or layette basket, made by Hans Coenradt Brechtel, The Hague, 1652. Such silver examples are very rare, and layette baskets are more commonly found in Dutch delftware, and occasionally English delftware. Two English examples in the possession of the Colonial Williamsburg Foundation, and the City Museum, Liverpool, are dated 1679 and 1681 respectively.

By Gracious Permission of
Her Royal Highness Princess Juliana of The Netherlands.

that they were also used to contain all the small gifts, such as money, jewellery, spoons or other small items of silver, which were given at a christening.

The most common seventeenth century examples are made of beadwork, with examples dating from the 1660s. Popular motifs include those seen on contemporary embroideries — flowers, insects, animals, birds, and Biblical or bucolic scenes. The baskets are of shallow rectangular or oval shape, with outward-sloping wired sides, and some have three-dimensional flowers and leaves on the handles or corners, worked in beads on a wire frame.

Rare 'baskets' of this shape are also known in English or Dutch delftware and in silver.

By the middle of the eighteenth century, canework baskets of rectangular or oval shape are found, often lined in quilted satin or cotton. By the nineteenth century lace, satin ribbons and embroidered muslin had combined to disguise the baskets in a froth of pale blue or pink and white, and the contents included tiny hairbrushes, powder-boxes and other small items necessary for the baby's 'toilette', as well as a clean set of clothes.

By the middle of the nineteenth century, two-tiered baskets on legs were in fashion, lavishly trimmed with large floppy bows and lacy frills. The interior was invariably quilted, with pockets for small items, and attached pads for

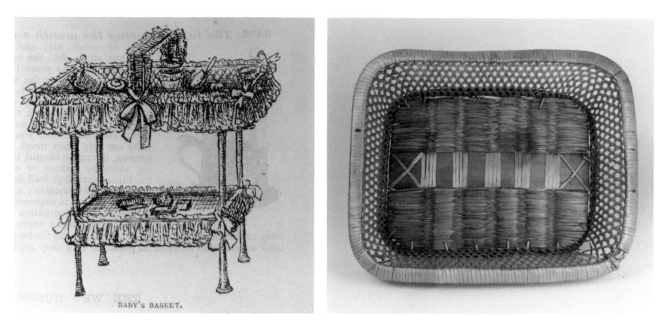

Plate 259. *A Victorian baby's basket, reproduced from Mrs Beeton's* The Book of Household Management, *first published in 1861. Before the baby was born the monthly nurse was to ensure that 'All the things which will be required to dress the baby the first time should be laid in the basket in readiness, in the order in which they are to be put on; as well as scissors, thread, a few pieces of soft linen rag and two or three flannel squares'.*

Plate 260. *A wickerwork layette basket from the Fens, first half of the 19th century. Woven into the design of the central band are two crosses at either end, as a protection against witchcraft. It is thought that these baskets were also used to hold the small presents which might be given at a christening.* Cambridge and County Folk Museum.

holding pins. Mrs Beeton, *The Book of Household Management*, stipulates that 'all the things which will be required to dress the baby the first time should be laid in the basket in readiness, in the order in which they are to be put on; as well as scissors, thread, a few pieces of soft linen rag and two or three flannel squares'. (The thread may have been for sewing up the sleeves of the baby's gowns to prevent thumb-sucking.)

Poor women simply made do with a shallow, handle-less basket, and in the Fens there was a tradition of weaving a cross into the corners of the basket in order to keep witches and evil spirits away from the new-born baby.

Less Expensive Christening Gifts

Among other inexpensive presents made to commemorate a baby's birth and given to him or his parents at the christening, were the small Staffordshire pottery cradles made from the end of the seventeenth century. Decorated in cream slip trailed on a dark brown ground, or dark brown slip on a cream or terracotta-coloured ground, sometimes with a baby's initials and date of birth, these were also given as wedding presents, to wish the couple happiness and the gift of children, and as such must be seen in the light of latter-day fertility symbols. They were thought to have been placed or hung beside the new

Plate 261. *Small pottery cradles, such as this slipware example dated 1672, and with the initials RB, were given at weddings to the newly-married couple as a symbol of hopes for future fertility. They were also given as presents at the time of a birth.* Sotheby's.

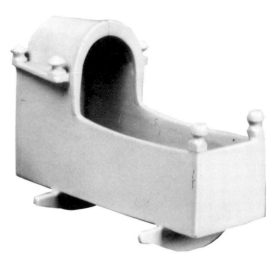

Plate 262. *A Staffordshire salt-glaze miniature cradle, mid-18th century.* Christie's.

Plate 263. *A Prattware model of a sleeping baby in a wicker cradle, late 18th/early 19th century.* Christie's.

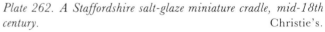

Plate 264. *An interesting earthenware cradle, probably by Ralph Wood of Burslem, c.1785. It is covered in apparently randomly-placed applied motifs, which include a figure, possibly a child, flowerheads, draped swags, urns, gardeners and with the flagship Villa de Paris (sic.), all covered in green, blue and manganese translucent glazes. There is a tradition that this was possibly associated with Lord Rodney's daughter.* Christie's.

Colour Plate 66. A Lowestoft birth tablet inscribed with the name Henriette Gall, and the date of her birth, April 18 1796, in dark manganese. It is uncertain how these were used. They are too large to hang round the neck of the child (and would anyhow be too fragile), although they may have hung from or above the cradle. The decoration includes simple chinoiserie scenes, ships, flowers, figures and birds and animals.

Plate 265. A tyg, or four-handled loving cup, in Wiltshire brownware, incised with the inscription 'HERE IS THE GEST OF THE BARLY KORNE/GLAD HAM I THE CILD IS BORN/RK SK/1692. Such a splendidly primitive piece of brown-glazed peasant pottery demonstrates all the spontaneous joy which was felt at the safe birth of a child.
Salisbury and South Wiltshire Museum.

Plate 266. A very rare Lambeth delft birth tablet, painted in blue with the inscription Alexander/Tillet; Born/Ian^y ^e_y 22^d/ 1747. The shaped and painted border shows the influence of Chinese porcelain in the diaper border, and traces of the baroque in the four scallop shells. It is pierced at the top for suspension, 7⅞ in. (20cm). Alexander Tillet lived his entire life in Lambeth as a cooper and saltpetre refiner. He is recorded in 1831, at the then very great age of eighty four, as a subscriber to the Topographical Dictionary, and still living in Lambeth.   Sotheby's.

Plate 267. A pair of Bristol pearlware spirit barrels, painted by William Fifield, with scenes entitled 'Jane in Misery' and 'Jane in Comfort', with the initials A.M.W. and the date 1834. The undersides bear the inscription 'A small memento of/regard, towards a much/Lov'd Daughter, This is/Painted for her Nurse/by her affectionate/Father, W. Fifield/May 26th 1834'. William Fifield was the leading painter at the Bristol Pottery, and signed pieces by him are dated between 1808 and 1849. Christie's.

baby's cradle, as receptacles for the small gifts or money brought by well-wishers to a christening. Other earthenware examples, in the manner of Ralph Wood or Thomas Whieldon, were covered with translucent coloured lead glazes, or decorated in Prattware colours of ochre, green, yellow, brown and blue.

Earthenware tygs or loving cups are also found with inscriptions commemorating a child's birth, and these were no doubt passed round during the festivities after the service in church.

Sometimes commemorative tablets in earthenware or porcelain were made to celebrate a birth. English delftware examples from the middle years of the eighteenth century are very rare. More common, though still rare, are the small circular porcelain birth tablets, which were unique to the Lowestoft factory. Only seven coloured examples appear to be recorded out of a total of some thirty-three or so made at this small East Anglian factory, the remaining pieces having decoration in underglaze-blue. They date from 1765 to 1799 and several were made for the children of workers at the factory. The pierced suspension holes indicate that they were made to be hung, and possibly they were hung from the cradle once the child had been named at the baptism service to show that he was no longer so vulnerable to the forces of evil. The decoration included simple chinoiserie scenes, ships, flowers, figures, birds and animals. One such tablet, in the Castle Museum, Norwich, records the birth of Martha Liffin on August 17th 1794, and sadly, on the reverse, the death of her mother Mary on 4th May 1795. Only nine months after the birth of Martha, it is possible that Mary perished from another birth, following so close on the heels of the first.

Christening Cups and Mugs

One of the most popular christening presents of all time is the silver christening cup. The gift of a mug or cup to a new-born baby anticipated the time when he would be weaned and able to drink for himself, an important stage in any child's life, but made even more so at a time when the weaning process was so fraught with danger and difficulty. These mugs were sometimes known as 'tooth mugs', since they coincided with the cutting of teeth, and silver was a favourite choice as it was thought to prevent the spreading of infection. In fact, silver is now known to have anti-bacterial properties, and so the old habit of mounting drinking vessels in silver was a sensible precaution.

Tudor magnificence was formidably expressed in the christening cups which were lavished on its dynastic heirs. After her christening at the Chapel of the Observant Franciscans at Greenwich in 1533, the infant Queen Elizabeth I was presented with a gold standing cup by Archbishop Cranmer, and another 'fretted with pearl' was given by the Duchess of Norfolk. Four years later Mary Tudor, Henry VIII's eldest daughter, gave her baby half-brother, the future King Edward VI, a gold cup on the occasion of his baptism in 1537.

Unfortunately some of these glittering symbols of status and wealth were destined for an ignominious end. Dr John Dee of Mortlake in Surrey, a friend of Queen Elizabeth I, was forced to pawn his daughter's silver christening cup in order to pay his mounting debts. In 1594 Sir James Melville, Mary Queen of Scots' envoy to the Court of Elizabeth, described the gifts at the christening of Mary's grandson, Henry. They included 'great cups of massy gold, two especially which were enough for me to lift and set them down upon the... table'. He then added ruefully, 'But, I say, these which were of gold, which should have been kept in store to posterity, were soon melted and spent'. However, lesser cups continued to be given and were enjoyed by the recipients into old age, before being handed down to future generations. In 1638 Joyce Jeffries of Herefordshire paid £5 5s. 6d. for a silver tankard for her god-daughter Joyce Walsh who was, according to the custom of the time, named after her, and in 1836 Charles Dickens described in *Sketches by Boz* a very typical contemporary christening present. It was 'a handsome silver mug for the infant Kitterbell, upon which he (Dumps) ordered the initials F.C.W.K., with the customary untrained grape-vine-looking flourishes, and a large full stop, to be engraved forthwith.'

Early mugs are rare nowadays. Some simple late seventeenth century examples engraved with chinoiserie figures and birds in a deft, economical style, still exist, as do some plain mugs simply engraved with dates and initials. Baluster-shaped mugs were raised up by hammering a sheet of silver over a wooden stake, and were popular during the eighteenth century, with an applied rim often being added for extra strength. Engraved coats-of-arms were often added to these, and to the practical tankard-shaped mugs with flared stepped bases and strap handles. Barrel-shaped mugs first appeared around the 1760s, and remained in fashion until the first quarter of the nineteenth

Plate 268. An Elizabethan silver-gilt wine cup of 1587, engraved with roses, thistles, bunches of fruit and ornamental swags. Inside the bowl is a faintly pricked inscription, which reads 'MARIA CORBETT R.N. BAPTIZATUS FUIT ULTIMO JANIARII A 1587' (Maria Corbett to be baptized on the last day of January in the year 1587). Cups of gold or silver-gilt were usual as christening presents for high-born Tudor babies.
The Worshipful Company of Goldsmiths.

Plate 269. A Charles II silver christening mug, maker's mark 'IC' with a mullet below, 1680, 3in. (7.6cm) high. Christie's.

Plate 270. A plain James II silver christening mug, by Thomas Havers, Norwich, 1688, inscribed with the initials 'L.W.' and the date 1688, 2¼ in. (5.7cm) high. Such a plain and simple piece, with flat, untapered base, would have been eminently sensible for a small child to use. Christie's.

Plate 271. A James II mug, maker's mark 'IS', 1688, 3½ in. (8.9cm) high, with typical lively engraving of an oriental bird in flight, between two rows of horizontal ribbing, Chinoiserie figures are also sometimes found at this date. The bands of ribbing were revived at the end of the 18th century. Christie's.

Plate 272. A William and Mary child's mug, with typical bulbous body, reeded cylindrical neck and scroll handle, by Thomas Havers, Norwich, 1689. Christie's.

Plate 273. A George I christening mug, possibly by Matthew Lofthouse, London, 1726, 3½ in. (8.9cm) high. The front has been engraved with a crest, below the rim which has been applied for extra strength. The hallmark, which can clearly be seen to the right of the handle, is more usually found on the base in early 18th century silver. Sotheby's.

Plate 274. A Queen Anne christening mug of thistle or bell shape, the bottom applied with a band of strapwork in high relief below a moulded central border, and with the initials WG/IE just visible below the rim, by Thomas Cleghorne, Edinburgh, 1703, 3in. (7.6cm) high. This kind of applied strapwork and 'cut-card' work is typical of Queen Anne silver, and was much in vogue again during the last part of the 19th century and the first years of the 20th, when double-handled 'pap bowls' or 'porringers' and mugs in the Queen Anne revival style were much in evidence in the catalogues of large stores, such as the Army & Navy and Harrods, as well as goldsmiths and jewellers such as Mappin & Webb or Garrard. Sotheby's.

Plate 275. A George II christening mug, with wide strap handle, by Richard Bayley, London, 1744, 3½ in. (8.9cm) high. Sotheby's.

Plate 276. A George III christening mug, of baluster shape on a circular foot, with typical scroll handle with kick terminal, by Walter Brind, London, 1767, 2¾ in. (7cm) high. This is a very typical mid-Georgian shape, raised up from a sheet of silver by hammering over a wooden stake. It would appear that no rim band has been applied for extra strength, and as a result the top edge can be seen to have split. Bonhams.

Plate 277. A George IV christening mug. Though of simple cup shape, the surface is covered with a riot of chased ivy leaves and berries spiralling upwards over the surface, on a matted ground, the handle in the form of a vine branch. By Philip Rundell, 1820, 3in. (7.6cm) high. Christie's.

Plate 278. A charmingly simple little silver lustre mug, decorated in resist technique with sprig borders flanking the monogram WMP and the date 1812, 3¾in. (9.5cm) high, probably Staffordshire. No doubt this was given to a poor child, whose godparents could not afford a real silver mug.   Sotheby's.

Plate 279. A Victorian silver christening mug, of basic Georgian shape, but with the typical plethora of embossing and engraving so beloved of the Victorians. The front with an applied figure of a jockey on horseback. Birmingham, 1876, 5⅛in. (13cm) high.   Bonhams.

century. A tube of rolled sheet metal was joined with a soldered seam, which was often concealed by the handle. Engraved hoops and staves, or chased bands of reeding were often added to decorate the basic barrel or cylindrical-shaped body. Until the 1770s most mugs were hallmarked underneath the base, but later Georgian mugs were generally marked in a horizontal line below the rim, usually to the right of the handle. Late eighteenth century mugs feature bands of bright-cutting so typical of silver flatware and tea and coffee pots of the same period, while Regency silver mugs show the exuberance and superb quality of the early nineteenth century. Neo-classical mugs of campana or thistle shape, have handles formed of twisted serpents, and are embossed with borders of scales or fruiting vine, showing a degree of worldly sophistication quite unsuited to the nursery.

The same classical, and even bacchanalian, scenes are shown in mid-Victorian mugs, and a little later pieces showing Gothic influence appear, along with somewhat hackneyed revivals of George II florally-embossed rococo, or George III bright-cut, examples. By the 1870s and 1880s the Aesthetic Movement was beginning to inspire silversmiths, and the resulting 'Japonaiseries' of engraved herons and bulrushes and bamboo-shaped handles started to appear on nursery tea-tables. Fashionable mothers, such as Ellen Terry, were at the time ransacking Liberty's for kimonos for their children,

Plate 280. A selection of silver christening mugs.
Top Left: *A low mug by William Bateman, London, 1827.* Top Right: *A mug by C.E., London, 1894.* Below Left: *By T.S., London, 1872.* Below Centre: *By Messrs. Barnard, London, 1859.* Below Right: *By William Hutton & Sons, London, 1859.*

Stephen Halliwell, Christie's South Kensington.

Plate 281. A selection of christening mugs, illustrating various styles of the 19th century.
Top: *A George III barrel-shaped mug by William Bateman, London, 1813.*
Centre Left: *A William IV mug by John Williams Barnard, 1835. This shows all the superb workmanship and exuberant decoration of the late Regency style.*
Centre Right: *A Victorian mug by W. Spurrier & Co., Birmingham in the Japanese style made popular by the Aesthetic Movement.*
Below Left: *A George III mug by Rebecca Emes and Edward Barnard, London, 1809.*
Below Right: *A George IV mug by John Angell, London, 1823.*

J. Mavec & Company Ltd., New York.

Plate 282. *A Victorian silver-gilt christening cup by Mortimer and Hunt, London, 1839, encrusted with a typical Victorian* mélange *of fruiting vine, winged cherub's heads and wheat-sheaves. The inscription reads 'The Lady Victoria Alexandra Hare from her Godmother Victoria R, May 23, 1840'. This cup is in no way designed for use by the infant Victoria Alexandra. In shape it resembles a chalice more than a child's cup, and was merely a vehicle for the silversmith's art, to be displayed proudly when the child had grown up.* Sotheby's.

Plate 283. A silver christening beaker designed by C.R. Ashbee in Arts and Crafts style. Made by Ashbee's Guild of Handicraft in Chipping Campden, it bears a London hallmark for (?) 1905. Charles Ashbee founded his Guild of Handicraft in 1888 in response to the teachings of William Morris and John Ruskin. It was run on idealistically Socialist principles, inspired by the idea of a medieval guild, and employed East End boys and amateurs, working in a co-operative with Ashbee, who nonetheless paternalistically dominated most of the designs. This simple beaker displays much of the spirit of Arts and Crafts silver, with the marks of the hammering still clearly visible in protest at the sterility of machine-made pieces, and the clear uncluttered calligraphy so typical of Eric Gill and others. The beaker was made for Felicity, one of the four daughters of Ashbee's marriage, which he enjoyed alongside 'Grecian friendships'.
Cheltenham Art Gallery and Museums.

Plate 284. An unusual Arts and Crafts two-handled sugar bowl and cover, designed by C.R. Ashbee and made by his Guild of Handicraft in Chipping Campden. It bears a London hallmark for 1912. The base is set with semi-precious stones reminiscent of medieval metalwork, in tune with Ashbee's pre-Raphaelite sympathies. The domed cover is surmounted by a knop in the form of two children, supposed to represent Felicity Ashbee, for whom this cup was made as a gift from her godfather, and her elder sister, Mary. One or two-handled bowls were a favourite subject of Ashbee's.
Cheltenham Art Gallery & Museums.

and hanging the walls of their nurseries with Japanese prints. Kate Greenaway and other illustrators of children's books also inspired scenes of children at play and fictional characters, so that at last silverware was designed to appeal directly to children.

Around the turn of the century the work of C.R. Ashbee and other members of the Arts and Crafts Movement showed a preference for simple shapes in silverware, with the marks of the hammering still visible on the surface. This was a reaction against the increasing mass-production and mechanisation elsewhere in the design world. For decoration they relied on simple calligraphy in a manner reminiscent of the work of Eric Gill and other artist craftsmen, and the use of semi-precious stones which harked back to Gothic metalwork.

Needless to say, the revivals in 'Charles II' or 'Queen Anne' styles filled the

Plate 285. A page from Mappin & Webb's 1903 Catalogue, *showing a variety of boxed presentation christening sets, including mugs, napkin rings, egg-cups, spoons and 'Porridge Bowls' or porringers. The example at bottom left is in the fashionable Queen Anne revival style, in reality a copy of a late 17th century style.*
Mappin & Webb Ltd.

catalogues of the large emporia, such as Harrods or the Army & Navy Stores, and specialist high-class jewellers such as Mappin & Webb, or Garrard, ensuring that the children of the affluent, but less imaginative, middle-classes maintained the mealtime tastes and traditions of their forebears. Indeed this was a continuing trend, and the Army & Navy Stores *Catalogue* for 1935-36 showed only two 'modern' designs out of a total of twelve.

From about the middle of the seventeenth century a particular type of cup was made for christenings in the Channel Islands. These cups were wide and shallow, with double scroll handles, and were often engraved with the initials of the child, which were rather curiously split up into syllables, so that the name Mary Godfrey would be inscribed with the initials M.G.F. Often a pidgin French is included in the inscription, as in a Guernsey example dated

Plate 286. An 18th century silver Channel Islands christening cup, of typical shallow shape, with double cast foliate scroll handles, with the initials P.VP, by Pierre Amiraux. The engraving is generally somewhat crude, and the Guernsey examples are a little deeper than their Jersey counterparts with an everted rim and a foot rim. The three initials are a common feature. Sotheby's.

Plate 287. An American silver mug by Black, Starr & Frost, c.1890, 3½ in. (8.9cm) high. During the 18th century Samuel Minott and Joseph Loring were making mugs in Boston and Charles Farley was making mugs at Portland, Maine, c.1815. Tiffany of New York made many christening items around the turn of the century.

Stephen Halliwell, Christie's South Kensington.

1779. 'A MBDPQ DON DE IMR SON PAREIN ET DE BRG SA MAREINE'. Jersey pieces have no footrim, while Guernsey examples often do have this feature.

Some American christening mugs are known, with a number of eighteenth century Boston makers, including Samuel Minott and Joseph Loring. Charles Farley was known to have made christening mugs at Portland, Maine, c.1815, and the New York firm of Tiffany & Co. produced some fine and imaginative designs.

For godparents who could not afford a silver christening mug, and there were many, an amusing alternative would have been a small child's earthenware mug decorated in silver lustre. From the 1830s and 1840s cylindrical Staffordshire bone china mugs proliferate, with stepped bases and scrolled handles. They are simply decorated with sprays of coloured garden flowers flanking the date and name or initials of the child in gilding.

Spoons

After christening cups, the most enduringly popular present to a godchild was a set of spoons, and many a privileged child has been 'born with a silver spoon in his mouth'.

Early records of nursery silver make mention of christening spoons, and these were often of the type known as 'Apostle spoons'. The child of a rich godparent would receive a set of thirteen such spoons, depicting Christ and his twelve Apostles, while less fortunate children would receive just one, often

Plate 288. A selection of Apostle and seal-top spoons:
Left to Right: *Charles I seal-top, by Robert Robinson of Hull, c.1630; James I seal-top, by Daniel Cary, London, 1609; Commonwealth seal-top, by James Birkby, Hull, c.1650; Apostle spoon by Edward Mangy, Hull, c.1660; Commonwealth seal-top by William Cary, London, 1655, with the initials SR and the inscription 'Borne good friday the 13th April 1655 Baptised the 24th of the same mounth 1655'; Commonwealth seal-top spoon by Stephen Venables, London, 1649; Charles I seal-top, by Robert Robinson, Hull, c.1630.* Sotheby's.

Plate 289. *A Victorian silver-gilt set of a child's knife, fork and spoon, of the type given frequently as a christening present, by George Adams, London, 1869.*

Stephen Halliwell, Christie's South Kensington.

Plate 290. *A very fine Victorian silver-gilt christening set, London, 1850. The knife, fork and spoon chased with fruiting vine, by G.W. Adams for Chawner & Co. The dish, by E.J. & W. Barnard & Sons, is engraved with a small girl feeding a turkey and a baby boy playing with a lamb, possibly by Donalds & Son, who were employed by Barnard & Sons at this date. Donalds 'engraved and designed' a tea tray at the Great Exhibition in 1851, for the manufacturing silver-smith George Angell, and William Donalds, an engraver, of 29 Artillery Place, West, was a beneficiary in 1850 in the Will of George Angell's father, John.* Sotheby's.

Plate 291. An Edwardian set of knife, fork and spoon, incorporating a napkin ring, in a velvet-lined case. The knife has a mother-of-pearl handle, and the all-over engraving of scrolls and trailing leaves is typical of the turn of the century. Napkin rings often left a space for the recipient's initials to be engraved. A very similar set was included in Mappin & Webb's 1888 Catalogue, described as 'Richly Engraved', and costing £3 15s. 0d. It appeared again in their 1903 Catalogue at the cheaper price of £2 12s. 6d.

Stephen Halliwell, Christie's South Kensington.

Plate 292. A Victorian silver-gilt christening set, the gift of Queen Victoria to her godson, Victor Cavendish. The beaker is chased with a band of infant bacchanalians romping round the border, while the dish has a vine-leaf border in relief. The knife, fork and spoon are similarly decorated with vines. The beaker and dish bear the maker's marks of George Angell, London, and the date 1863. The knife and fork are inscribed 'To Victor Christian William Cavendish from his Godmother Victoria R' and dated 'June 25th 1868'.

The Devonshire Collection, Chatsworth. Reproduced by kind permission of the Chatsworth Settlement Trustees.

depicting the saint whose name he bore. In 1558, 'a spoyne, the gyft of Master Fletcher, all gylt wyth the pychure of Saynte Matthewe' was presented to young Matthewe Quayle 'at hys chrisome', but plainer seal-top spoons were given too, in pewter rather than silver, to the sons of the poor.

On 16 May 1661, Samuel Pepys reluctantly accepted to stand godfather to Mrs Browne's son, John, 'which, however, did trouble me very much to be at charge to no purpose, so that I could not sleep hardly at night, but in the morning I bethought myself, and I think it is very well I should do it'. Two days later he went shopping in Cheapside, and on 19 May 'rose early, and having made myself fine, and put 6 spoons and a porringer of silver in my pocket to give away today, Sir W. Pen and I took coach'. A seventeenth century silver spoon recorded by Eric Delieb (Investing in Silver, 1970) is inscribed 'Rich. Elnor. Joane/At Ye Font Stone/Their word did give/How you shouldst live', and is clearly the gift of conscientious, if not rich, godparents.

In Jersey it was customary for boys to be presented with a soup spoon, and for girls to receive a set of six teaspoons, made by local silversmiths.

By Victorian times, when material values had firmly asserted themselves,

Plate 293. A page from Mappin & Webb's 1903 Catalogue, showing a variety of christening mugs, the majority of styles inspired by earlier examples. Most were available in sterling silver or electroplate. Although at first sight an unsuitable material for children's mugs, silver was valued for its anti-bacterial properties, the rims of ceramic drinking vessels having been mounted in silver since Tudor times. Mappin & Webb Ltd.

Plate 294. A late Victorian christening set by Martin Hall & Co., Sheffield, 1898, 5in. (12.7cm). This comprises an eggcup, spoon and napkin ring enclosed in a velvet-lined morocco presentation case. A slightly more elaborate set, with engraved leaves and ferns, is featured in Mappin & Webb's Catalogue for 1903 at two guineas. Curiously, a very similar set in the 1888 Catalogue retailed at three guineas. Stephen Halliwell, Christie's South Kensington.

Plate 295. (Left). Centre, front: A child's silver napkin ring, designed as a wishbone, with a small figure of a hare perched on the top, Birmingham, 1913, highly impractical as the napkin falls out, and the wishbone is liable to snap between small, clumsy fingers.

Back: A more modern child's napkin ring, sentimentally engraved with anthropomorphic woodland animals and toadstools in the style of Molly Brett and other children's illustrators of the time, London, 1945.

Left and right: An Edwardian spoon and pusher, the spoon, Birmingham, 1904, embossed with the nursery rhyme This Little Pig went to Market, *and the handle of the pusher, Birmingham, 1911, with a design of flowers and scrollwork in diluted Art Nouveau style.*

Private Collection.

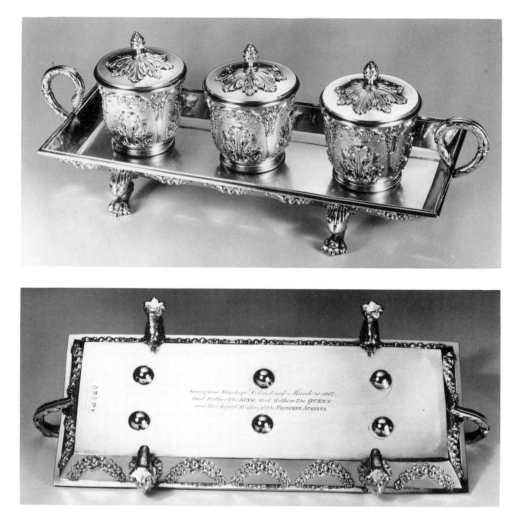

The Worshipful Company
of Goldsmiths.

the single spoon had been joined by a small knife and fork to form a set, and this was invariably contained in a morocco-leather case lined in satin. The pieces were often gilded and decorated with the initials of the recipient, or, in the case of well-bred babies, with the family crest. The handles of these were often superbly chased with fruiting vine or bacchanalian *putti,* a curious choice for a child in a century which later saw the rise of the Temperance Movement.

After the development of die-stamping in Birmingham and Sheffield, new designs emerged, often heavily embossed with shells and scrolls. Although at first sight splendid in appearance, and opulently gilded, these later pieces, with their tubular handles, were often of poor quality. They appeared in profusion in the catalogues of the great shops of the day, those Meccas of the middle-classes, as well as in the catalogues of silversmiths such as Garrard and Mappin & Webb. Particularly fine sets were accompanied by a small plate, sometimes engraved with a scene of children at play, within an elaborately chased border. Other knife, fork and spoon sets were accompanied by an engraved or engine-turned napkin ring, the height of gentility, or by an egg-cup, a last vestige of the ancient superstition of presenting new-born babies with an egg as a symbol of future fertility. The old custom of giving salt to a baby to repel evil was also, perhaps subconsciously, resurrected by the Victorians and Edwardians in the boxed sets of salt-cellars which fashionable emporia sold as suitable for christening gifts. Towards the end of the nineteenth century, sets of spoons and

Plate 297. Two silver porringers of the type sometimes given as christening presents. On the left a William III single-handled porringer by Timothy Ley, London, 1698. This style was copied in pewter and delftware for the poor. On the right, a Commonwealth double-handled porringer, engraved with a border of acanthus leaves and fruiting vine, maker's mark C.S., a sword in between, London, 1658. This shape, with certain modifications, was popular well into the 18th century, and such pieces were revived by the late Victorians and Edwardians, when the Queen Anne style was once more fashionable. Called 'Pap Bowls' or 'Porridge Bowls', they appear in Mappin & Webb's 1903 Catalogue, and were sold with a spoon for five pounds.
Sotheby's.

Plate 298. A child's silver christening porringer and plate made specifically with children in mind, Birmingham, 1906-7. Round the edge of the bowl and plate a frieze of Noah's ark animals march in pairs. In the centre of the plate is the monogram of the recipient, and the inside of the bowl is gilt to keep it clean, as was the case with so many Victorian and Edwardian pieces.
Private Collection.

Plate 299. A silver christening bowl, Sheffield, 1932, the surface still showing the marks of hammering, and with a frieze in low relief of a girl feeding rabbits, another girl chasing a dog, and a boy watching the dog confronting a rabbit. Such narrative pieces, designed specifically to appeal to children, are typical of some of the best in 20th century christening silver, their design reflecting the illustration in contemporary children's books.
Private Collection.

pushers became popular for children. The rake-like action of the pusher propelled the food towards the wide-bowled spoons. With their short, looped handles they were easy for little fingers to manipulate, and made a useful transition between spoons and more adult knives and forks.

Bowls and Porringers

In 1642 Joyce Jeffries of Herefordshire paid a Hereford goldsmith 'for a silver christening bowle to little Joyce Lawrence at 5 shillings and 8 pence an ounze, 48 shillings 10 pence.' Twenty-one years later, in 1663, Sir Ralph Verney gave his godson '1 silver sugar box and coddel (caudle) cup'.

Bowls and boxes for sugar, as well as porringers in silver and pewter, made popular seventeenth century christening presents, and porringers, a sugar box and spoons, and a cup are listed in the 1688 inventory of the nursery silver of the Prince of Wales. Double-handled bowls (or porringers as they were called) had bellied sides, engraved with stiff leaves or fruiting vine, or gadrooning, while smaller porringers, similar to, and often confused with, bleeding bowls, had small cup-shaped bowls and pierced flat handles.

In the middle of the eighteenth century the double-handled bowls assumed a classical vase or urn shape, and at the turn of the nineteenth and twentieth centuries, porringers or 'porridge bowls' in 'Queen Anne style' enjoyed a revival, with 'cut card' and strapwork decoration, and 'spot hammering' much in evidence. William Thackeray's historical novel, *Henry Esmond*, subtitled *A Colonel in the Service of Her Majesty Queen Anne*, helped to make the style popular once again. The Queen Anne Revival style became immensely fashionable architecturally for private houses and public buildings, and it was said that 'cheap builders are possessed by the idea that red brick, a blue pot and fat sunflower in the window are all that is needed to be fashionably aesthetic and Queen Anne.' Needless to say, the style, which extended to all branches of the decorative arts, was satirized by Gilbert and Sullivan in their opera, *Patience*. 'Be eloquent in praise of the very dull old days which have long since passed away, And convince 'em if you can, that the reign of good Queen Anne was culture's palmiest day'. At any rate, the jewellers shops of the late nineteenth and first part of the twentieth century needed no convincing, and their catalogues teemed with porridge bowls in the 'antique' or 'Queen Anne' style.

Hairbrushes and Powder-Boxes

'It is not to tease you and hurt you, my Sweet,
But only for kindness and care,
That I wash you, and dress you, and make you look neat,
And comb out your tanglesome hair.'
(Anon.)

'A bit of talcum
Is always walcum'.
(Ogden Nash (1902-1971), Reflection on Babies.)

By the end of the nineteenth century a popular christening present was a small silver hairbrush, perhaps accompanied by a silver-mounted cut-glass bowl for talcum powder. Ivory-backed brushes were also fashionable by the end of the nineteenth century, and the doll, 'Princess Daisy', had an ivory powder box and hairbrush among the extensive items of her layette. Sometimes the word 'Baby' or the child's initials in silver were added as a finishing touch, even on the 'Ivorene' and celluloid brushes which replaced expensive ivory examples during the first part of the twentieth century.

Much attention was paid to the hair of Victorian and Edwardian girls, which assumed almost Rapunzel-like length, a considerable milestone being reached

Plate 300. An Edwardian baby's christening gift set, comprising a cut-glass powder bowl with silver lid and a silver hairbrush. These pieces are hallmarked for Birmingham, 1909 and enclosed in their original pink satin-lined morocco case.   Private Collection.

Plate 301. A baby's hairbrush made in celluloid to simulate ivory, with the word 'Baby' in silver on the top, c.1900. Celluloid was patented in America in 1869 and by the turn of the century plastics were providing a cheap substitute for ivory.   Cambridge and County Folk Museum.

when the tresses were long enough to be sat upon. To keep the hair in fine condition, one hundred strokes of the hairbrush was a daily, or even twice-daily, ritual, and girls were not released from these rigours until the advent of the shingle haircut in the 1920s.

Jewellery

Jewellery was a popular present for small girls, along with the string of coral beads which had been *de rigueur* for centuries. The layette of the famous late Victorian doll, 'Princess Daisy', included as christening presents: '1 gold bracelet, and 1 gold brooch', as well as '1 Necklace in real pearls with diamond clasp'. Since at least the seventeenth century well-born girls wore strings of pearls, tied with a ribbon, and such necklaces are seen in paintings of the royal children by Van Dyck. Poorer children were often presented with a silver brooch, either with their name, or with the word 'Baby', since to name a child before the christening was considered unlucky. Many such brooches were made from the 1880s until the outbreak of the First World War. They proliferated during the trade depression of the 1880s-90s, when silver jewellery was a cheap alternative to gold, and were mainly made in Birmingham and Chester. They were die-stamped, with the letters added by hand. Finishing touches, such as trailing ivy leaves, were added by an engraver.

Rattles

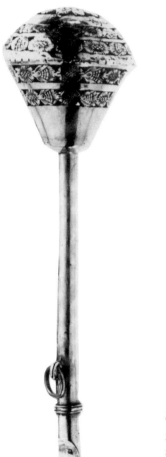

'Go pretty child, and bear this flower
Unto thy little Saviour;
And tell Him, by that bud now blown,
He is the Rose of Sharon known:
When thou has said so, stick it there
Upon his bib, or stomacher:
And tell Him (for good handsel too)
That thou has brought a whistle new,
Made of a clean straight oaten reed
To charm His cries (at time of need):
Tell Him, for coral, thou hast none;
But if thou hadst, He should have one;
But poor thou art, and known to be
Even as moneyless as He.'
(A Child's Present *by Robert Herrick, 1591-1674.*)

'Behold the child, by Nature's kindly law,
Pleased with a rattle, tickled with a straw'.
(Essay on Man, *Alexander Pope, 1734.*)

'I threw away my rattle before I was two months old, and would not make use of
my coral until they had taken the bells away from it.'
(The Spectator, *Joseph Addison, 1672-1719.*)

Plate 302. A rare early silver pear-shaped rattle, pierced and engraved with flower-heads and fan motifs, the whistle initialled MC/HL above a date, and with a ring for suspension below a ribbed collar, maker's mark PA, c.1620, 6½in. (16.5cm) long. Very few rattles are known prior to 1700, and this is clearly an echo of the type carried by Edward VI in Holbein's painting (Plate 303). Sotheby's.

Since earliest times makeshift rattles, of dried peas or stones contained in gourds or terracotta vessels, have been known, but it is likely that the first silver examples were medieval. William Horman's *Vulgaria,* 1519, includes the quotation 'I will bye a rattell to styll my baby for cryenge', and a portrait of Prince Edward, later King Edward VI, painted by Holbein in 1538, shows him splendidly dressed in brocade and velvet, and clutching a silver rattle in the shape of a pierced sphere on the end of a stick. In 1654 Hans Eworth painted the infant Francis Thynne holding a piece of coral mounted in silver with three silver bells suspended from the handle, the whole hanging from his waist by a double silver chain, and it is this design which was to remain in fashion for more than three hundred years, incorporating as it did the dual benefits of noisy plaything, and coral amulet and teething stick.

The Puritans, violently opposed to any practice which smacked of ritual or superstition, tried to put a stop to the giving of corals at a christening, but the custom never died out. The Earl of Bristol on 'Mar. 14th 1690. Paid Abraham Chambers for a corrail sett in gold £1 10s. 0d.', while in 1706 the Countess of Lauderdale purchased from an Edinburgh jeweller 'a silver gumstick with bells and a piece of fine coral' at £1 8s. 0d. Rattles were also exported to America, and John Leacock and William Young advertised in the *Pennsylvania Gazette,* 1761, 'wissels and bells imported from London', as well as 'spare pieces of coral for whistles and bells'. Similar items were advertised in the *Boston Gazette* in the same year.

Plate 303. A portrait of Edward VI as a child by Hans Holbein the Younger. Edward was born on 12 October 1537, and this portrait was probably painted within his first year of life. He holds a silver rattle pierced with decoratively arranged holes.

The National Gallery of Art, Washington, Andrew W. Mellon Collection.

Plate 304. Left to Right:
A George IV silver-gilt rattle, with bands of engraved scalework between deeply chased floral borders, six bells, ring, whistle and coral, by John Reily, London, 1821. A George III silver-gilt rattle chased with roses and other flowers which heralds the florid style of Victorian rattles, two tiers of six bells, by Charles Rawlings, London, 1819. A George III silver-gilt rattle with twelve bells, bright-cut and wriggle-worked with formal stiff leaves and flowers. An elegant and unpretentious piece in the neo-classical taste, by John Hutson, London, 1797. Another George III silver-gilt rattle by John Hutson, with similar bright-cut and wriggle-worked decoration in spiral wreaths, ten bells and mother-of-pearl teether, London, 1796. Sotheby's.

Plate 305. An early 18th century gold and coral baby's rattle of typically restrained knopped and facetted shape, the haft engraved later with a crest and with six bells attached to leafy brackets, the coral inserted into a characteristically plain stiff leaf mount, with a loop for suspension, 6½ in. (16.5cm) long, first quarter of the 18th century. Sotheby's.

Few rattles exist prior to the middle of the eighteenth century, and the early ones which remain show the formal simplicity and restraint of Queen Anne or early Georgian silver, often with octagonal hafts with plain ribbed decoration, and pleasing scalloped or foliate mounts. The bells are usually plain also, but for central ribbing to give them strength, and a simple loop attached for suspension. Sometimes a crest, or the owner's initials, are engraved on the haft, but these can be later additions. The hafts frequently incorporated a whistle, another traditional and suitably noisy plaything guaranteed to delight any baby in its unsubtle efforts to attract parental attention. Such rattles are to be found in silver, silver-gilt and, occasionally, gold, and although the basic

301

Plate 306. *A silver rattle by Samuel Pemberton, 1802, and a Victorian silver rattle, c.1874. These clearly show the difference in style between the simple Georgian example with its restrained row of bright-cut engraving, and the florid Victorian piece with its heavy chasing and embossing.*
I. Freeman & Son,
Simon Kaye Ltd.

Plate 307. *A 19th century cane rattle, of the type used by poor children whose parents could not afford silver.*
Cambridge and County
Folk Museum.

design changed little, the surface decoration became ever more elaborate as the eighteenth century progressed, the rococo style being successfully expressed in *repoussé* shells, flowers and scrolls. Even the tiny bells had chased mounts, and the stiff leaf mounts which held the coral teething stick in place were engraved with naturalistic veining. Jean-Jacques Rousseau abhorred such luxurious playthings for children, and advocated the use of natural branches as gum-sticks.

During the last quarter of the eighteenth century neo-classical taste predominated under the influence of the Adam Brothers, and this was reflected in the bright-cut and wriggle-worked decoration on the hafts and mouthpieces of rattles. This took the form of delicate swags and spirals of flowers, paterae and simple geometric borders, which echoed the designs of contemporary teaspoons and other small pieces of silver. A gold rattle at Leith Hall, Aberdeenshire, was 'invoiced by Patrick Robertson of Edinburgh in 1785 at £9 8s. 6d., including 8/6d. duty and 3/6d. for engraving'.

During the nineteenth century, the thin, light silver of Georgian rattles gave way to much heavier, more elaborate pieces which reflected the solid enjoyment of material objects so typical of the Victorian age. Cecilia Ridley's bosom swells with maternal pride in a letter to her mother dated 1842, 'Lady Ridley has sent Baby a beautiful coral set in engraved gold and with two little gold bells and the crest engraved on it. It is really a beautiful thing and Baby

has it hung around his waist and plays with it'. This was not always the case, as some Victorian rattles were too heavy for the hapless infant to hold in his small hands, and they remained suspended from the mother's châtelaine, only to be played with at proscribed moments of organised fun.

Late eighteenth and early nineteenth century rattles should bear a full set of hallmarks (though earlier pieces were often unmarked). These usually appear on the foliate or dentil mount which holds the 'gumstick', and the maker's initials are generally found on the whistle terminal. Often the bells and mounts are dented and battered, evidence of having been gnawed upon voraciously during a bout of teething, or hurled from the cradle in a frenzy of rage or frustration.

During the second half of the nineteenth century, teething rings came into fashion, and at the same time the superstitious beliefs in the protective magical qualities of coral subsided, as more scientific evidence emerged about the transmission of infectious diseases. While coral rattles with bells were still made in the traditional style, a host of mass-produced hollow rattles appeared, which incorporated teething sticks or rings in mother-of-pearl, ivory or bone. The forms these silver rattles took included jesters, children inspired by the drawings of Kate Greenaway, Mr Punch, and later on teddy bears, elephants, policemen and Peter Rabbit. Marks on twentieth century examples are often divided and appear on the main body of the piece rather than the mount. The whistle seems to have become a thing of the past, too much no doubt for the nerves of 'modern' mothers and nannies. The small bells also gradually disappeared in the more safety conscious climate of the twentieth century, to be replaced by bells inside the hollow body of the rattle. However, silver rattles with corals of eighteenth century design remained popular. They were still sold

Plate 309. A silver rattle of Mr Punch, Birmingham, 1908. Unfortunately the original teething stick is missing, and has been replaced with a later wooden stick. Christie's.

Plate 310. Two 20th century hollow rattles, the one on the left showing Humpty-Dumpty, by D. & N., Chester, 1922, 4½in. (11.5cm); the right-hand example showing a small girl in the style of Kate Greenaway, by C.S. and F.S., Birmingham, 1931.

Stephen Halliwell, Christie's South Kensington.

Plate 311. A silver rattle in the form of Peter Rabbit, Birmingham, 1936-37, 4½in. (11.5cm) high. This example is incomplete, and has sadly lost its teething ring. Sotheby's.

by Mappin & Webb in 1903 at £1 each, and in the 1950s 'Miss Read' notes the date of Malcolm Annett's christening in her *Village Diary*, and mentions that she is 'looking forward to a trip into Caxley to find a really attractive silver rattle and coral, worthy of such a fine boy'. By this time a number of synthetic materials had come into use, including celluloid, which could quite successfully imitate ivory, and other plastics. Poor children, of course, had always had alternatives to silver and gold, and these included wicker, ivory, bone, 'Mauchline-ware', wood and tin.

Some of the better known makers of silver rattles include:

Hester Bateman and other members of the Bateman family, 1760s, 1770s and 1780s.
William Bayley, 1759.
Margaret Bentley, or Binley, London, 1765.
Francis Clark, Birmingham, 1826.
Henry Croswell, 1804.
John Fray, 1748.
H.T., Birmingham, 1852.
John Hutson.
Edward Jay, 1757.
Samuel Meriton, 1739.
E. Morley, 1786.
P.A., 1620.
Samuel Pemberton, Birmingham, 1802.

Charles Rawlings, London 1820 and 1823.
John Reily.
George Ridout, emigrated to the United States, eighteenth century.
Patrick Robertson, Edinburgh, 1785.
Nicholas Roosevelt, New York, eighteenth century.
Sandilands Drinkwater.
S.B., c.1785.
John Stoyle, Dublin, c.1790.
Joseph Taylor, Birmingham, 1912.
George Unite, 1886 and 1888.
Duncan Urquhart.
Thomas Wallace, 1802.
Joseph Willmore, Birmingham, 1805 and 1827.

Chapter 19

DEATH

'Look upward; that's towards her, whose happy state
We now lament not, but congratulate'.
(*The Second Anniversarie*, John Donne, 1612.)

'Bye O my Baby,
When I was a lady,
O then my baby didn't cry;
But my baby is weeping
For want of good keeping
O I fear my poor baby will die.'
(*Gammer Gurton's Garland*, or *The Nursery Parnassus*, 1794.)

Death was a rampant spectre which haunted every loving mother's subconscious, and the statistics of infant mortality make salutory reading.

Forty per cent of *all* deaths in the seventeenth century occurred in children under the age of two years. 'Twice five times suffered she the childbed pains, yet of her children only five remains', lamented the inscription on the tomb of the Laird of Enterkin's wife in 1676. According to the London Bills of Mortality, between 1730 and 1779 526,973 deaths out of a total of 1,178,346 were of children under the age of five, many under one year old. John Wesley, born in 1703, was one of nineteen children, of whom a bare six reached maturity, and of Queen Anne's seventeen pregnancies in sixteen years, ten ended in miscarriage and only one child survived infancy. Of every thousand children born in England and Wales in 1851, only 522 reached the age of five, and in his 'Drooping Buds', published in *Household Words* in 1852, Charles Dickens campaigned for the newly-opened Great Ormond Street Hospital for Sick Children, the first of its kind in England, in the following, deliberately emotive words: 'Our children perish out of our homes; not because there is in them an inherent dangerous sickness... but because there is... a want of sanitary discipline and a want of medical knowledge. What should we say of a rose tree in which one bud of every three dropped to the soil dead?... Of all the coffins that are made in London, more than one in every three is made for a little child; a child that has not yet two figures to its age.' Even the twentieth century began badly. As late as 1911, 32,000 babies of under one year died of 'summer diarrhoea', and an Edwardian father who lost two daughters in one year wrote to his brother, in a state of shock, 'God bless you

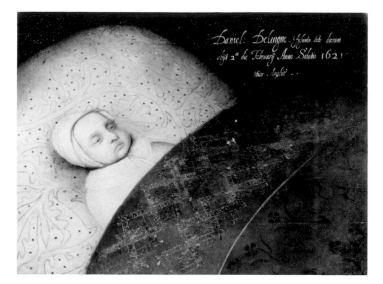

Plate 312. A portrait of Daniel Delingne on his deathbed, aged eight days, inscribed and dated 1621, English School. Such portraits are rare, although dead children were commemorated in various ways. Skulls strategically placed at the foot of a broken column in a 17th century portrait, or putti floating on clouds, symbolically ascending into Heaven, represent the pessimistic and the optimistic points of view.   Sotheby's.

Plates 313A and B. A 17th century stone 'weeper', or tomb figure, showing a small child. Clearly shown are his lace-edge coif, cuffs and falling bands, or deep collar, so typical of the middle of the 17th century. At his shoulders can clearly be seen the hanging sleeves, which were also used as leading strings and became narrower as the century progressed.

Touchwood Antiques, Stow-on-the-Wold.

and your children, but do not love them'. How much greater was the well-known loss of the Dean of Carlisle who, fifty-five years earlier, in 1856, lost five small daughters from scarlet fever in as many weeks.

Plate 314. A 17th century portrait in white salt-glazed stoneware of Lydia Dwight on her deathbed, by her father, the Fulham potter, John Dwight. She was baptized at Wigan on 24 July 1667, and died at Fulham six years later. It is inscribed 'Lydia Dwight dyed March 3, 1673', and shows the young child, still wearing her lace-edged head band, her hands folded over a posy of spring flowers symbolising her youth. A father's anguish is expressed in the tenderness of the portrait mingled with the starkly realistic portrayal of death.

The statistics are harrowing, and can only be compared nowadays to the plight of many parents in the Third World. The reasons were largely the same. Lack of contraception, inadequate ante-natal care and ignorance of childbirth techniques; poor housing conditions and contaminated water supplies, leading to virulent epidemics of disease unchecked by inoculation or antibiotics; and a gross lack of hygiene, particularly relating to feeding. Sadly, cruelty and neglect were also salient factors.

For parents, deprived of any contraceptives except luck and superstition, there was safety in numbers. In the seventeenth century Sir John Verney remarked with stoical realism when two of his fifteen children died that he was yet left with a baker's dozen, and Dr Johnson offered cold comfort to his friend, James Boswell, on the death of his young son: 'you must remember that to keep 3 out of 4 is more than your share. Mrs Thrale has but 4 out of 11'.

Separated by centuries, we can comfortably believe that our forebears were in some way different to us, accustomed, and therefore inured, to grief. In fact, Hester Thrale was devastated by the deaths of her children. Laid low by exhaustion and depression, she wrote on the fifth birthday of her daughter, Sophia, on 23 July 1776, 'I have listened to Babies learning till I am half stupefied — and all my pains have answered so poorly — I have not heart to battle with Sophy. I will not make her life miserable as I suppose it will be short — not for want of Health indeed, for no girl can have better, but Harry and Lucy are dead, and why should Sophy live? The instructions I labor'd to give them — what did they end in? The Grave — and every recollection brings only new Regret... At present I can not begin battling with Babies — I have already spent my whole youth at it and lost my Reward at last'. There were legions like her, and their stories make distressing reading. In 1800 Mrs Douglas wrote from King's Ferry on the Hudson river to her brother-in-law

Plate 315. Two views of the mourning locket ordered from London by Mrs Douglas after the death of her husband and daughter, within ten minutes of each other, from yellow fever in 1800, a few days after the birth of another daughter. The figures were painted by 'An Artist of Merit', with the faces done by Samuel Shelley, 'the first Miniature Painter in London'. The 'platt' of hair is that of Mr Douglas and Betsey.
Private Collection.

in London, 'How shall I find words to express myself on a subject which so deeply afflicts and wounds my almost broken heart?' She was describing the deaths of her daughter, Betsey, and her husband within ten minutes of each other from yellow fever, while she was feeding her new baby of a few days old in another room. Her husband, on the road to recovery she believed, had suffered a relapse 'Intirely owing to his being witness to the trying scene of his darling child in her Last moments'.

Feelings such as these could only be endured in an acceptance of God's perceived will, and the beliefs that a dead child was 'too good for this life' or that 'those whom God loves die young' were prevalent. The conviction of Sir William Brownlow, whose wife bore him nineteen children between 1626 and 1648, that 'though my children die, the Lord liveth and they exchange but a temporal life for an eternal one', was a common one and offered much consolation.

Consolation was also to be gained from tangible expressions of grief. Small children kneel in prayer on memorials in churches, or ascend to heaven as *putti* in family portraits. Some were even painted on their deathbeds, their small faces framed with embroidery and lace. Mourning jewellery was worn by sorrowing mothers, and often contained a lock of the dead child's hair as a keepsake or talisman. The American Mrs Douglas, whose heart was broken in 1800, was eventually consoled in some part by ordering from London 'A locket pretty large, the size Emblematick of my own and children's situation, as handsome as mourning will admit. There must be 6 figures, myself and children, around a tomb with the spirit rising from it, expressive of the Loss of two friends'. She was later asked to send 'as soon as possible some of the Hair you wish introduced into the Locket as the artists of Tast here assure us nothing Elligant and Proper can be made without it. Everything of that kind is done intirely with Hair, instead of Painting or drawing'. The locket was eventually completed with painting *and* hair, and was despatched to Mrs Douglas in 1801. The figures were painted by an 'Artist of Merit', but with the faces touched in by 'the first Miniature Painter in London, Mr Shelly' (Samuel Shelley, ?1750-1808). The hair forming the plinth of the monument was from Mrs Douglas's mother, while the 'Platt' surrounding it was of her husband's and Betsey's hair. 'The Willow shadowing the Urn is composed of the three united'. Deciding on the details of such a commission must have been a cathartic process, and many other mothers were helped in just such a way.

SELECT
BIBLIOGRAPHY

General Reading

Anon   *The Queen's Closet,* London, 1664.

Aslin, Elizabeth   *The Aesthetic Movement,* Ferndale Editions, London, 1981.

Barrie, J.M.   *Peter Pan and Wendy,* 1911.

Beeton, S.   *The Englishwoman's Domestic Magazine,* 1859.

Briggs, Asa   *Victorian Things,* B.T. Batsford Ltd., London, 1988.

Davidson, Angus   *Miss Douglas of New York,* Sidgwick & Jackson, 1952.

Edgeworth, Maria and Richard   *Essays on Practical Education,* 1789.

Fildes, Valerie   *Breasts, Bottles and Babies,* Edinburgh University, 1986. *Wet Nursing,* Basil Blackwell, 1988.

Fraser, Antonia   *The Weaker Vessel,* Weidenfeld & Nicolson, London, 1984.

Fulford, Roger (ed.)   *Dearest Child: Letters between Queen Victoria and the Princess Royal, 1858-1861,* Evans, London, 1964.

Garland, Madge   *The Changing Face of Childhood,* Hutchinson & Co., London, 1963.

Gathorne-Hardy, Jonathan   *The Rise and Fall of the British Nanny,* Hodder & Stoughton Ltd., London, 1972.

Girouard, Mark   *A Country House Companion,* Century Hutchinson, 1987.

Hanway, Jonas   *An Earnest Appeal for Mercy to the Children of the Poor,* 1766.

Hayter, Alethea   *Opium and the Romantic Imagination,* Faber & Faber, London, 1968.

Hughes-Hallett, Penelope (ed.)   *Childhood,* Collins, 1988.

Kidd, Charles and Montague-Smith, Patrick   *Debrett's Book of Royal Children,* Macmillan, London, 1982.

Kosky, Jules   *Mutual Friends,* Weidenfeld and Nicolson, London, 1989.

Lasdun, Susan   *Making Victorians,* Victor Gollancz Ltd., London, 1983.

Locke, John   *Some Thoughts Concerning Education,* 1693.

Longford, Elizabeth   *Victoria R.I.,* Weidenfeld & Nicolson, London, 1964.

McClure, Ruth K.   *Coram's Children,* Yale University Press, 1981.

Murray, Janet Horowitz   *Strong-Minded Women,* Penguin, 1985.

O'Hara, Georgina   *The World of the Baby,* Michael Joseph, London, 1989.

Opie, Iona and Peter (ed.)   *The Oxford Book of Nursery Rhymes,* Oxford University Press, 1951.

Opie, Iona and Tatem, Moira (ed.)   *A Dictionary of Superstitions,* Oxford University Press, 1989.

Pinchbeck, I. and Hewitt, M.   *Children in English Society, Vol.1,* Routledge & Kegan Paul, London, 1969.

Pullar, Philippa   *Consuming Passions,* Hamish Hamilton, London, 1977.

Rousseau, Jean Jacques   *Emile,* Paris, 1762.

Sitwell, Osbert   *The Scarlet Tree,* Macmillan, London, 1946.

Tomalin, Claire (comp.) *Parents and Children,* Oxford University Press, 1981.
Wallace, Ann and *Royal Mothers,* Piatkus, London, 1987.
  Taylor, Gabrielle
Warner, Marina *Queen Victoria's Sketchbook,* Macmillan, London, 1979.

Diaries and Contemporary Sources
(in addition to those specifically mentioned in the text)

Army & Navy Catalogue, 1898-1913.
Mrs. Beeton's Book of Household Management, Ward Lock, London, 1861-1960.
Clive, Mary (ed.) *From the Diary and Family Papers of Mrs. Archer Clive,* (1801-73), The Bodley Head, London, 1949.
Dickens, Charles, *Sketches by Boz,* 1836-37; *Oliver Twist,* 1837-38; *Dombey & Son,* 1847-48.
Enquire Within Upon Everything, Hodder & Sons, London, 1886.
Evelyn, John, *Diary,* ed. E.S. de Beer, Oxford University Press, 1959.
Harrods Catalogue, 1895. (Repr. *Victorian Shopping,* David & Charles, Newton Abbott, 1972.)
Kilvert, Revd. Francis, *Diary,* ed. William Plomer, Jonathan Cape, London, 1938-40.
Loudon, J.C., *Encyclopaedia of Cottage, Farm and Villa Architecture and Furniture,* 1833 and subsequent editions. Reprinted Christopher Gilbert, *Loudon's Furniture Designs,* S.R. Publishers Ltd., 1970.
Lyttelton, Lady Sarah, *Correspondence,* ed. Mrs. Hugh Wyndham, John Murray, London, 1912.
Pepys, Samuel, *Diary,* ed. Henry B. Wheatley, G. Bell, London, 1938.
Thackeray, William, *Vanity Fair,* 1847-48.
Verney, Sir Harry, ed., *The Verneys of Claydon,* Pergamon Press, Oxford, 1968.
Woodforde, James, *The Diary of a Country Parson, 1758-1781,* ed. John Beresford, Oxford University Press, 1924.

Exhibition Catalogues

Children's Furniture Towneley Hall, Burnley, Lancashire.
Royal Children The Queen's Gallery, Buckingham Palace, 1963.
The Age of Innocence The Holburne Institute, Holburne Museum, Bath, 1969-70.
Childhood in 17th Century by Rosalind K. Marshall, Scottish National Portrait Gallery, Edinburgh, 1976.
Children and Food Preston Manor, Brighton, January-April 1977.
Childhood Sotheby's in aid of the Save the Children Fund, London, January, 1988.
The Age of Innocence Museum Services of Blackburn, Burnley & Lancashire County, 1989.
Walter Crane The Whitworth Art Gallery, Manchester, 1989.

Treen

Pinto, Edward H. *Treen and Other Wooden Bygones,* Bell & Hyman, London, 1968.

Nurseries

Aslet, Clive *The Osborne Nurseries, Country Life,* 3 December, 1988.
White, Colin *The World of the Nursery,* E.P. Dutton Inc., New York, 1984.

History of Childcare

Dick, Diana — *Yesterday's Babies,* The Bodley Head, London, 1987.
Hardyment, Christina — *Dream Babies,* Jonathan Cape, 1983.
Stone, Lawrence — *The Family, Sex and Marriage in England 1500-1800,* Weidenfeld and Nicolson, London, 1977.

Childbirth

Bennion, Elisabeth — *Antique Medical Instruments,* Sotheby's Publications, London, 1979.

Breastfeeding and Bottle-Feeding

Fildes, Valerie — *Breasts, Bottles and Babies,* Edinburgh University Press, 1986.
Haskell, Arnold and Lewis, Min — *Infantilia, The Archaeology of the Nursery,* Dennis Dobson, London, 1971.

Ceramics

Flick, Pauline — *Children's China,* Medallion Collectors' Series, Constable, 1983.
Godden, Geoffrey — *Illustrated Guide to Lowestoft Porcelain,* Barrie & Jenkins, London.
Irvine, Louise — *Royal Doulton Series Ware,* vol.3, Richard Dennis, 1986.
Riley, Noël — *Gifts for Good Children,* A History of Children's China, Part I, 1790-1890, Richard Dennis Publications, to be published December 1991.

Furniture

Chinnery, Victor — *Oak Furniture,* Antique Collectors' Club, Woodbridge, 1979.
Edwards, Ralph — *Shorter Dictionary of English Furniture,* Country Life, 1964.
Gelles, Edward — *Nursery Furniture,* Constable, Medallion Collectors' Series, 1982.

Costume and Christening Robes

Clabburn, Pamela — *'My small Child Bed Linning',* Costume 13, 1979.
Cunnington, Phillis and Buck, Anne — *Children's Costume in England,* Adam and Charles Black, London, 1965.
Ewing, Elizabeth — *History of Children's Costume,* B.T. Batsford Ltd., London, 1977.
Hughes, Therle — *English Domestic Needlework,* Abbey Fine Arts, London, 1961.
Synge, Lanto (ed.) — *Royal School of Needlework Book of Embroidery,* Collins, 1987.

Prams

Hampshire, Jack — *Prams, Mail Carts & Bassinets,* Midas Collectors' Library, 1980.

Christening

Walkley, Christina — *Welcome Sweet Babe,* Peter Owen, London, 1987.

Silver

Halliwell, Stephen — *Collecting Small Silverware,* Phaidon, Christie's, London, 1988.

Places to visit

Museums to Visit

American Museum in Britain, Bath.
The Baby Carriage Collection, Biddenden, Kent.
Birmingham Museum & Art Gallery.
Bowes Museum, Barnard Castle, Co. Durham.
Brighton Museum and Art Gallery.
Cambridge Folk Museum.
Castle Museum, Nottingham.
Castle Museum, York.
Christchurch Mansion, Ipswich.
Gallery of English Costume, Platt Hall, Manchester.
Geffrye Museum, London, E.2.
Judge's Lodgings, Manchester.
Museum of Childhood, Beaumaris, Anglesey.
Museum of Childhood, Sudbury, Derbyshire.
Museum of Childhood, Edinburgh.
Museum of Childhood, Bethnal Green, London.
Museum of Costume, Bath.

Museum of London.
National Portrait Gallery, London.
Science Museum, London.
Strangers' Hall, Norwich.
Tate Gallery, London.
Victoria and Albert Museum, London.
Whitworth Art Gallery, Manchester.

Houses to Visit

Arlington Court, Warwickshire.
Calke Abbey, Derbyshire.
Cardiff Castle, Wales.
Chatsworth House, Derbyshire.
Erdigg, Clwyd.
Kensington Palace, London.
Osborne House, Isle of Wight.
Shakespeare Birthplace Trust, Stratford-upon-Avon.
Snowshill, Gloucestershire.
Wallington Hall, Northumberland.

The Antique Collectors' Club

The Antique Collectors' Club was formed in 1966 and now has a five figure membership spread throughout the world. It publishes the only independently run monthly antiques magazine, *Antique Collecting,* which caters for those collectors who are interested in widening their knowledge of antiques, both by greater awareness of quality and by discussion of the factors which influence the price that is likely to be asked. The Antique Collectors' Club pioneered the provision of information on prices for collectors and the magazine still leads in the provision of detailed articles on a variety of subjects.

It was in response to the enormous demand for information on 'what to pay' that the price guide series was introduced in 1968 with the first edition of *The Price Guide to Antique Furniture* (completely revised 1978 and 1989), a book which broke new ground by illustrating the more common types of antique furniture, the sort that collectors could buy in shops and at auctions rather than the rare museum pieces which had previously been used (and still to a large extent are used) to make up the limited amount of illustrations in books published by commercial publishers. Many other price guides have followed, all copiously illustrated, and greatly appreciated by collectors for the valuable information they contain, quite apart from prices. The Antique Collectors' Club also publishes other books on antiques, including horology and art reference works, and a full book list is available.

Club membership, which is open to all collectors, costs £17.50 per annum. Members receive free of charge *Antique Collecting,* the Club's magazine (published ten times a year), which contains well-illustrated articles dealing with the practical aspects of collecting not normally dealt with by magazines. Prices, features of value, investment potential, fakes and forgeries are all given prominence in the magazine.

Among other facilities available to members are private buying and selling facilities, the longest list of "For Sales" of any antiques magazine, an annual ceramics conference and the opportunity to meet other collectors at their local antique collectors' clubs. There are over eighty in Britain and more than a dozen overseas. Members may also buy the Club's publications at special pre-publication prices.

As its motto implies, the Club is an amateur organisation designed to help collectors get the most out of their hobby: it is informal and friendly and gives enormous enjoyment to all concerned.

For Collectors — By Collectors — About Collecting

The Antique Collectors' Club, 5 Church Street, Woodbridge, Suffolk

INDEX